W9-CIG-410

16063 79

Courting Change

Courting Change

Queer Parents, Judges, and the Transformation of American Family Law

Kimberly D. Richman

NEW YORK UNIVERSITY PRESS

New York and London

NEW YORK UNIVERSITY PRESS
New York and London
www.nyupress.org

© 2009 by New York University
All rights reserved

Library of Congress Cataloging-in-Publication Data
Richman, Kimberly D.
Courting change : queer parents, judges, and the transformation of American family law /
Kimberly D. Richman.
p. cm.
Includes bibliographical references and index.
ISBN-13: 978-0-8147-7595-0 (cl : alk. paper)
ISBN-10: 0-8147-7595-0 (cl : alk. paper)
1. Gay parents—Legal status, laws, etc.—United States. I. Title.
KF540.R53   2008
346.7301'7—dc22   2008025479

New York University Press books are printed on acid-free paper, and
their binding materials are chosen for strength and durability. We strive
to use environmentally responsible suppliers and materials to the greatest
extent possible in publishing our books.

Manufactured in the United States of America

10 9 8 7 6 5 4 3 2 1

In loving memory of my grandparents,
Rose Seifert Treiber and Louis Treiber

and

Dedicated to all of the courageous mothers
and fathers whose children have been taken from
them because of who they are and who they love.

Contents

Acknowledgments

I began this project at the University of California–Irvine's Department of Criminology, Law and Society. I benefited enormously from the excellent faculty and intellectual community of graduate students there, and particularly from Valerie Jenness, Kitty Calavita, and John Dombrink, as well as Ryken Grattet of UC-Davis. I am especially thankful to Kitty Calavita, whose intelligence and keen analytical eye enriched this project from the beginning, and to Valerie Jenness, my mentor and friend, whose contributions not only to this project but to my development as a scholar are too numerous to count. Even after graduate school, Val has continued to be a trusted source of advice and support.

Many other scholars contributed valuable feedback, insight, and ideas at various stages of the development of this book, or in particular chapters. These include Jonathan Goldberg-Hiller, Richard Leo, Bill Maurer, Peter Nardi, Laura Beth Nielsen, Dan Pinello, Joe Rollins, Cliff Rosky, Austin Sarat, Julie Shapiro, Jonathan Simon, Susan Sterett, George Thomas, Bill Thompson, Martha Umphrey, Valerie Zukin, and participants in the 2000 and 2001 LSA Graduate Student Workshops in Miami and Budapest, as well as the 2003 LSA Summer Institute at UC Berkeley. I am grateful to the editors and anonymous reviewers at *Law & Society Review*, *Law & Social Inquiry*, and *Law & Sexuality*, who provided valuable feedback on articles that served as precursors to some of the chapters in this book. I also thank Elizabeth Knoll, Josh Gamson, and anonymous reviewers at NYU Press for their valuable feedback on my book proposal and early conceptions of the book. Thanks finally to Bill Benemann at the Bancroft Library at UC Berkeley for coordinating access to case materials.

Crucial financial support was provided by a grant from the National Science Foundation (Grant #SES-0004287), as well as from the American Sociological Association, the University of California, and the University of San Francisco. I am deeply indebted to Dean Jennifer Turpin and the University of San Francisco for granting the sabbatical leave that allowed me to complete the book. I am also grateful for the writing retreats and welcoming work environment provided by the University of San Francisco, and especially my colleagues in the Department of Sociology—I am thankful every day to be surrounded by such amazing people, and for the opportunity to work with colleagues who are truly friends. Thanks in particular to Stephanie Sears and Josh Gamson for their support, emotional and otherwise, during the book-writing process. I am also appreciative of the hard work of Shona Doyle and Amy Joseph, who have made my work life infinitely easier with their professionalism and warmth, and the diligent research assistance of Courtney Krametbauer, Sarah Takahama, Erin Vuksich, and Eric Asmar.

Thanks to NYU Press, Gabrielle Begue, Despina Papazoglou Gimbel, and particularly Deborah Gershenowitz for their dedication to this book from the start. Deborah has been nothing but supportive and encouraging as an editor and has advocated consistently for me, even while dealing with her own important life events. Her excitement is infectious and has helped motivate me to write, even when my energy flagged.

Books don't get written without the often intangible but invaluable support of family and friends. I thank my family for their love and encouragement and for understanding when I was incommunicado for weeks on end. My parents, Judith Treiber and Peter Richman, and stepparents, Danny Esquibel and Susan Richman, and my sisters, Stacey Richman-Arnold and Jessica Richman, have never wavered in their confidence in me or their support for this enterprise. My close friends (too numerous to list—you know who you are) have selflessly listened as I griped about writer's block and offered valuable and much-appreciated encouragement. I am grateful to the members of the San Quentin TRUST for the Development of Incarcerated Men, who allowed me a seven-month leave of absence as their Executive Advisor while I completed this book and were unquestioningly supportive. I also thank the staff at Samovar Tea Lounge in San Francisco for their hospitality and sustenance during the writing process.

Most important, I owe a deep debt of gratitude to all the attorneys, judges, activists, and parents who generously provided legal materials and referrals or agreed to be interviewed for this project. These include Roberta Achtenberg, Michael Adams, Robin Berkovitz, Beverly Collins, Kate Coyne, Kathy Crandall, Beatrice Dohrn, Steve Drizin, Julie Eldridge,

Paula Ettelbrick, Donna Hitchens, Kate Kendell, Marla Liston, Pat Logue, William Monroe, Mary Morgan, Tam Nomoto-Schumann, Alice Philipson, Nancy Polikoff, Abby R. Rubenfeld, Sandra Russo, Robin Young, and the staff at Lambda and NCLR, as well as several anonymous judges and parents in San Francisco, Orange County, Los Angeles County, San Mateo County, and San Diego County (California) and in Illinois, Ohio, and Tennessee who generously made time in their very busy schedules to be interviewed. I cannot help but be in awe of the tremendous dedication and intelligence of the attorneys and activists at Lambda, NCLR, and elsewhere, who have dedicated a significant portion of their lives to protecting and defending the basic civil rights of LGBT parents and families. I am particularly thankful to the parents who agreed to be interviewed, providing honest, heartfelt, and often tearful accounts of their battles to retain custody of their children. Their courage, openness, and love for their children never ceased to amaze me, and I thank them for allowing me to tell their story. This book is for them, and for the hundreds of other gay and lesbian parents whose stories are told here, or have yet to be told.

Last but certainly not least, I want to thank Richard Leo, my husband, for his limitless encouragement, love, and support. From the simplest pep talk to the grandest gestures, from reading my drafts to washing my breakfast dishes, Richard has never once hesitated to do whatever it took to help me realize my goal of publishing this work. For ten years he has supported me intellectually, emotionally, even physically, in everything I've done, and this book is certainly no exception. Thank you for the dinners, our life together, and everything else.

1

A Double-Edged Sword?

Indeterminacy and Family Law

The strength and genius of common law lies in its ability to
adapt to the changing needs of the society it governs.
—*In re Parentage of A.B.*[1]

In 1999, an Indiana social worker petitioned to adopt three
children, siblings, all of whom had severe disabilities and had been in
foster care for most of their lives. The adoption was near completion
when the children's foster parents petitioned to stop the adoption of one
of the children. They called their local pastor, rallied the community, and
put pressure on the adoption board to disallow the adoption of the little
girl by the social worker—and they were successful. The two boys were
adopted by the social worker and were cared for by him according to
their special needs, while their sister remained in the home of her foster
parents. A year later, law enforcement made a terrible discovery: the girl,
whom the foster parents had insisted on keeping, had been molested and
sexually abused repeatedly by her foster father. Now her foster father
is in prison, and the little girl is left in a broken foster home while her
brothers miss her and ask their adoptive father why she couldn't come
and live with them. He doesn't have the heart to tell them, it's because
he is gay.

What is it that makes an adoption board, community, or judge balk at
the thought of allowing a gay man to adopt a little girl, instead leaving
her in foster care and separating her from her brothers? How is it that
in Florida, where a movement auspiciously called "Save the Children"
made it illegal for gay men and lesbians to adopt children, a father who

I

was convicted for the murder of his first wife can gain sole custody of the children from his second marriage, on the grounds that their mother is a lesbian? Although these questions yield no easy or simple answer, they highlight the complexity and contradictions of an area of gay rights litigation overlooked by many in the early years of the gay rights movement: family law.

Consider the striking irony that the tragic Indiana case described above occurred at the close of a decade often dubbed the "gayby boom" by family law and gay rights communities, for its explosion of publicly visible gay- and lesbian-headed families—made possible by a combination of reproductive technology, growing tolerance, and legal innovation. While countries around the world reconsider the family form and begin to formally recognize same-sex relationships, case law in the United States presents a very eclectic picture. On the one hand, all but two states' courts have struck down laws prohibiting gay men and lesbians from adopting, and progressively more courts have begun to recognize the validity of same-sex second-parent or stepparent adoptions in twenty-five states. Yet in 2002, the same year that a Pennsylvania Court of Appeals unanimously affirmed the validity of such adoptions for gay and lesbian couples, the Supreme Court of Alabama denied custody to a lesbian mother, calling her sexuality "abhorrent, immoral, detestable, a crime against nature, and a violation of the laws of nature."[2] More recently, the U.S. Supreme Court, on the heels of its landmark 2003 decision striking down sodomy laws in *Lawrence v Texas*, refused to hear the latest challenge to Florida's restrictive adoption law, effectively sanctioning its ban on gay adoptions.[3] What is the parent, the scholar, or the average citizen to make of this seemingly incoherent literature of law?

In this book, I argue that this incoherency is neither accidental nor inexplicable but is in fact a necessary feature—within certain bounds—of an area of law whose continued relevance and function rely on its ability to adapt to changes in the social organization of family and sexuality. This is certainly not to say that there is anything necessary, or even acceptable, about a judge feeling free to call a lesbian mother "detestable" and blocking her from seeing her child—or about an adoption board or judge having the power to block an adoption desired by both parent and child solely on the basis of a person's sexual orientation. Rather, I argue, in an era when it is increasingly apparent that laws regarding family were not drawn up with same-sex couples or gay- and lesbian-headed families in mind, a degree of flexibility is in fact a virtue that allows parents, attorneys, and eventually judges to construct more inclusive and contextually sensitive frameworks and arguments. At the same time, because unbounded discretion can easily become bias, it is important to acknowledge and understand the double-edged sword that is judicial indeterminacy.

Family law, among legal professionals and those familiar with the field, is notorious as one of the most indeterminate and discretionary areas of American law. While criminal sentencing, for instance, has become increasingly fixed in statutory guidelines (and therefore largely taken out of the hands of judges), child custody decision-making remains governed by one—and only one—overarching rule: the decision must be in "the best interest of the child." This standard is seen as less discriminatory than past gender-specific guidelines, and may seem like a common-sense rule of thumb to most parents and others, but start asking different people to define exactly what the "best interest of the child" is in any given case, and one begins to realize the problem: no two people have the same definition. As one attorney specializing in this area noted in an interview, "These kinds of decisions really strike at the core of people's opinions about how to raise their children. And there is really no consensus in this country about the best way to raise children. . . . they're Solomonic decisions in a lot of ways."[4]

One example illustrates this point particularly well: On October 20, 1995, judges in the Michigan case of *McGuffin v Overton* denied custody to Carol Porter, the surviving co-parent of two boys and the partner of their biological mother, Leigh McGuffin, who died that January. Both boys carried Porter's last name, and McGuffin had stipulated in her will and power of attorney that she wished Porter to have custody of the children. Instead, however, the court opted to give custody to the children's estranged biological father, who had never played a role in their life. The rationale was that Porter was not actually their parent, because she was not a blood relation. *Four days later*, however, an almost identical fact situation presented itself in a different court in the case of *Matter of Guardianship of Astonn H.*, and the judge in that case came to the exact opposite finding: that despite the lack of blood relation, the child had come to rely on the woman as a "psychological parent," and therefore she should be awarded custody.[5] Clearly, these judges differed in their opinion of what was in these children's best interest after their mothers' deaths, and of what role biology should play in that determination. In this sense, the legal standard for child custody is both an index of variation in Americans' attitudes about family, parenthood, and child welfare, and it is a marker of the oft-critiqued and well-documented indeterminacy of law.

In the field of law and society, the indeterminacy (or open-endedness) of law is a theme of longstanding significance.[6] As early as the 1920s and '30s, progressive legal scholars and judges, such as Jerome Frank and Karl Llewellyn, noted that any given case could just as likely be decided according to "what the judge had for breakfast" as according to what the facts were or what the prior legal precedent said. This may be a slight exaggeration, but its main thesis was duly noted and revived later by Critical Legal Studies (CLS) scholars toward the end of the twentieth century: the law is not as predictable and rational as it may seem. Moreover, social mores and institutions can and do have an influence on law, and vice versa. Because historically most judges have come from a relatively affluent straight white male demographic, their standpoint as citizens in a position of privilege necessarily has affected their ability (or desire) to mete justice in a way that is equitable and sensitive to the needs of marginalized populations.[7] While some people—particularly minorities who have struggled for legal recognition of their civil rights over the course of the twentieth century—may not find this surprising, for many judges, legal professionals, and even members of the mainstream public, such a claim is near heresy. If we cannot depend on the law to be neutral, predictable, and rational, how can anyone have confidence in the system and support it?

The Legal Realists of the 1920s and '30s launched the empirical critique of the indeterminacy of law, contrasting the early-twentieth-century Supreme Court decisions of *Lochner v New York* and *Muller v Oregon* as cases in point.[8] Whereas *Lochner* found in 1905 that workers' hours could not legally be restricted in the name of the workers' well-being and rights (or for any other reasons) because it violated their freedom of contract, *Muller*—decided three years later—came to the exact opposite determination. The difference? In *Muller*, the workers in question were women. The implication for critics was twofold: first, that the courts were not, as they claimed, bound by *stare decisis* (the concept of following past precedents) to come to the same decision when faced with the same set of legal principles and similar facts; and second, that this discretion would presumably follow the contours of the judges' biases and social conceptions of race, class, and gender (and later, sexual orientation). In the cases of *Muller* and *Lochner*, this meant adopting a paternalistic rationale for "protecting" women's reproductive function by abridging their purported freedom of contract—which would otherwise rationalize a limitless work day.

Yet it is not without a touch of irony that in this famous example of indeterminacy, the sexist bias of the judges' rationale ultimately resulted in a gain for workers' rights (at least for some workers). This twist underscores several important points about the indeterminacy of law. First, rather than focusing only on case outcomes and the inability to predict them, it is important to look at the entire judicial narrative— that is, not just the final decision of each case but also the reasoning by which the judges arrive there. These rationales, particularly when recorded for posterity in a precedent-setting appellate case, are just as important and even more revealing of how judges' discretion operates. One would not necessarily read gender bias into the *Muller* decision's *outcome*—after all, saving women from a twelve- or sixteen-hour work day would by and large be considered a good result—until one realizes that this decision was premised on sexist and paternalistic beliefs about women's fragility and primary function as child bearers. Thus, it is safe to assume that if the ultimate findings of the judges belie any expectation of predictability, so do the paths of reasoning by which they arrive at these results.

Second, the indeterminacy thesis, as originally conceived and as later interpreted, is both an empirical *and*, implicitly, a normative critique of law and what sociologist Max Weber called "formal rationality," that is, consistency and immunity to social and political influences. Not only is law indeterminate, but this indeterminacy is necessarily undesirable, since it affords room for bias in judicial decision-making. In fact, the troubling implications of the indeterminacy thesis are part and parcel of its resonance as a critique. Indeed, scores of studies, ranging from criminal law to civil litigation to family law, have found that indeterminate legal principles and judicial discretion can and have resulted in bias based on race, class, or gender. A study by Landsman and Rakos found that judges in civil cases were just as likely as jurors to allow biasing materials, which were ruled inadmissible after they were presented, to affect their ultimate decisions in differential ways.[9] Ards, Darity, and Myers found that alimony and child-support awards in the District of Columbia varied greatly according to race, even when other economic factors were held constant.[10] Beginning in the 1980s, Critical Legal scholars carried the empirical critique to the extreme, arguing that every instance of judicial decision-making, and every rule, was inherently unpredictable—a so-called radical indeterminacy that recognizes the constancy of *no* legal principle. Soon after, postmodernists extended the *normative* critique as well, but they turned it on its head to make the argument that there are, and should be, no "right answers" in *any* case—since any concept of "rightness" was inherently subjective.

These critiques suggest the importance of the final point raised by analysis of the *Muller* and *Lochner* cases, which is crucial to the application of the indeterminacy thesis to gay, lesbian, bisexual, and transgender (LGBT) parents' custody and adoption: legal indeterminacy, as both an empirical and a normative critique, is best thought of not as a black-and-white dichotomous evaluation but in shades of gray. The fact that the *Muller* case broke with precedent and relied on sexist assumptions but ultimately had an arguably positive humanitarian result in its support for reasonable work hours suggests as much. Orienting to indeterminacy as absolute, or as all good or bad, ultimately misses the mark and obscures the utility of an "openness" in law that can facilitate positive social change, even if it also accommodates bias in some situations. After all, had *Muller* applied the same logic and come to the same conclusion as the earlier *Lochner* case, the result would have been that the women who were subject to the decision would have been forced to work over ten hours a day. That *Muller* is remembered as a sexist decision is ironic in this sense, but also useful in that it teaches us to look below the surface and beyond any particular result, whether positive or negative, to expose ideological currents that reify marginalized statuses and may be applied to more harmful ends in a different situation—if this indeterminacy is not effectively "managed" by those who aim to protect the marginalized. At the same time, certain overarching principles are necessary to keep us from devolving into a legal nihilism that ultimately protects no one and renders moot the law's utility as a tool of social change.

In this sense, the critique of indeterminacy, as traditionally conceived, can usefully be looked at through the lens of feminist jurisprudence. Feminist legal scholars such as Frances Olsen and Katherine Bartlett argue that the law is overly concerned with predictability and "objectivity"— in the form of supposedly value-free precedent-based decision-making— ultimately a masculine interpretation of justice.[11] A feminist interpretation of law would be more contextually sensitive, serving an informal and open, rather than formal and closed, notion of justice—but justice nonetheless. As Bartlett explains,

Feminist practical reasoning challenges the legitimacy of the norms of those who claim to speak, through rules, for the community. . . . [It] differs from other forms of [legal] reasoning . . . in the strength of its commitment to the notion that there is not one, but many overlapping communities to which one might look for "reason."[12]

Arguing that different communities might conceptualize justice and reason in different ways, and that this diversity of interpretation is a good thing, is another way of saying that judicial narratives may differ in their results and their rationales—and that that is okay. Thus, a feminist approach to legal indeterminacy might be to consider it with cautious optimism—wary of the potential for abuse by biased judges but strategically and ideologically welcoming of the space afforded by this indeterminacy to respond to diversity and change in meaningful ways. This, of course, requires that litigants and attorneys actively "work" the indeterminacy of law in ways that will serve the progressive purpose of expanding rather than contracting possibilities for new (or newly recognized) communities and social institutions.

Both the gendered nature and the dynamic social structure of family make these points especially à propos to analyses of custody and adoption law. A particularly salient manifestation of the indeterminate nature of law is the "best interest of the child" standard—a standard invoked almost universally in family law. While the phrasing of this legal standard is fixed, its meaning and interpretation are anything but static. Family law scholar Stephen Parker discusses the cultural and temporal relativity of the best-interest standard as an ideal illustration of law's indeterminacy. He gives concrete examples of differing interpretations of the best-interest standard in custody determinations, concluding that "[t]he difference between the two decision-*makers* is in their assumptions as to what are normal conditions for the operation of the best interest principle."[13] Although it is true that some jurisdictions have specified guidelines for determining the best interest of the child, which are discussed in more detail in chapter 2, these standards are certainly not uniform. Moreover, many of the criteria contained in the guidelines are themselves vague and subject to interpretation. Kathryn Mercer notes that "[t]he history of child custody law has been seen as a struggle between rules and discretion."[14] Whereas the pull of rules may be present in the evolution of the overarching principles of child custody, from traditional paternal or maternal presumptions to the more modern "best interest of the child" standard, discretion has been a constant feature—if anything, enhanced by the purportedly gender-neutral "best interest" framework. Although this notoriously vague standard has without doubt provided cover for infringement on gay and lesbian parents' rights in the past, it also offers a malleability that was not available in earlier gender-specific standards or other more determinate rules—and that is increasingly necessary in an era of rapid change in the structure of family.

As perhaps the most hotly contested of alternative family forms, gay- and lesbian-headed families are particularly vulnerable to the instability that can be caused by this wide discretion. It is increasingly apparent that the homosexuality of one or more parents in a custody dispute— whether between a same-sex couple or a man and woman—introduces an added element of contestation.[15] The fact that judges are given great discretion in deciding these cases means that there is room for discrimination, or at least biased assumptions about the place of gay men and lesbians in society. Indeed, the history of gay and lesbian parents' treatment in custody cases, particularly those arising from the divorce of a lesbian, gay, bisexual, or transgender (hereafter LGBT) parent from his or her former heterosexual spouse, is not surprisingly rife with examples of homophobia. As with *Muller*, there are even examples of seemingly favorable resolutions based on ideologically discriminatory or pejorative grounds—such as allowing a gay father to retain custody of his child, but only because the judges have determined that he is not "flamboyant" (as they assume most gay men would be), is relatively closeted, and does not wish his child to become gay.[16] It would not be difficult, therefore, to take a perfunctory look at family law decisions in the twentieth century and come to the conclusion that the indeterminacy of family law has been a vehicle for homophobic bias, in either the rationales or the outcomes, or in both. Witness the dozens of appellate cases in which the mere presence of a homosexual parent was considered by judges to be a threat *per se* to children's well-being.[17]

And yet both the feminist concern for context and a more nuanced application of the indeterminacy thesis tell us to look beyond the black-and-white, cut-and-dried assumption that indeterminacy is *always* bad for gay and lesbian parents. If there were ever an area of law that *required* adaptability to changes in social structure and circumstances, it is family law. As legal scholar Herman Pritchett noted, "A legal system cannot be static in a dynamic world."[18] Indeed, analysts of common law have noted, and appropriately so, its historically contingent nature.

James Tully, for instance, has compared common law to an old city, with its maze of winding, nonlinear streets and awkward intersections.[19] The disorderly layout of the city is counterintuitive and confusing to the modern viewer, but it makes sense if it is viewed with a historical lens on the different time periods in which the streets were laid. So too, areas of common law that are open to discretion, such as family law, are best understood as constantly evolving and therefore resistant to any fixed or totalitarian tendencies. That the growing presence of gay and lesbian parents and families represents a profound shift in modern definitions of family speaks to the utility of such a malleability and ability to adapt in different eras of social life.

Indeed, given the relatively new social realities of the gayby boom and the expanding public and legal acceptance of alternative sexualities, courts are increasingly being forced to deal with the intersection of sexuality and family law in a way that compels them to question—or at least temporarily suspend—their standard operating assumptions of the past. In the 1980s and '90s, open LGBT parents began to emerge from the closet and into the courtroom in far greater numbers—either forcing increased acceptance in court or entering the legal arena because of increasing acceptance (or both). The presence of these nontraditional families in the courtroom disrupts the standard categories on which family law and its understandings of sexuality and parenthood are based. By challenging the boundaries of legal definitions of family and parental fitness—to the extent that these things are defined in any coherent way— these litigants also challenge social understandings of these terms.

Although this observation begs the perennial "chicken and egg" question of whether legal change spurs social change or vice versa, more recent sociolegal theorizing in the "constitutive" tradition would argue that this question misses the point—in other words, that legal and social understandings of family, parenthood, and sexuality mutually constitute one another in a reciprocal process of cultural diffusion. This happens not just through the direct effects of any particular legal development or judicial decision, but through the "radiating effects of litigation"—that is, through the circulation of new ideas and cultural understandings of legal rights and identities—and the injection of these ideas into public discourse and social life.[20] As constitutive scholar Michael McCann asserts, "Although judicial victories often do not translate automatically into desired social change, they can help to redefine the terms of both immediate and long-term struggles among social groups."[21] It is all the more important, then, that legal reasoning not be closed to the possibility of shifts in recognition of new and emerging family forms and conceptions of sexuality and that it allow this mutual construction and diffusion of meaning to happen.

This begins to answer the question, in theoretical terms at least, of why gay or lesbian parents, or we as a society, should care about the indeterminacy of law and its application to family law. In practical terms, we should care for the reason at the heart of the normative critique of indeterminacy discussed earlier—because in the past this indeterminacy, in the form of judicial discretion, has manifested itself as discrimination—and it is not hard to see how this could (or even does) happen today. Yet, with the insights of Critical Race Theory and feminist theory, it is not hard to see how discrimination persists even in the *absence* of complete indeterminacy. A case in point is criminal sentencing, where a growing trend toward determinate sentencing policies and mandatory minimum sentences for specified types of crime has done nothing to curb the widely disproportionate sentencing and incarceration of African Americans. If anything, these determinate sentencing policies lend a guise of legitimacy and impartiality to the trend toward overincarceration of minorities. This legitimating function of law is, along with indeterminacy itself, a core component of the CLS critique—and yet it persists even in the absence of explicit indeterminacy. Thus, a more nuanced approach must look deeper than the assumption that eradicating indeterminacy will eradicate discrimination; instead, understanding the contours of indeterminacy expands the possibilities for exploiting the space it affords for progressive social and legal change.

In a related concern, critical analysis of the indeterminacy of law and how it can be harnessed to aid LGBT families helps to reconcile concerns about legal legitimacy and the "gap" between the legal elite and average citizens. CLS scholar Mark Tushnet notes that evaluations of the indeterminacy thesis, and the sense of legitimacy tied to a determinate (or predictable) legal system, expose the difference between how elite legal actors—lawyers, scholars, and judges—think and how ordinary citizens think of law and legitimacy. Whereas those in the know are able to reconcile a degree of indeterminacy and fidelity to a democratic legal system because of their broader knowledge of how common law and legal reasoning work, "Ordinary citizens . . . believe that the law's claims on them have force only because the law is, as they believe, determinate."[22] Rather than forcing the law to hide behind a veil of rigid determinacy in order to retain legitimacy in the eyes of the average citizen—or, on the other hand, rejecting legal means altogether out of a lack of confidence in an unpredictable legal system—showing how indeterminacy can be harnessed to helpfully advance new rights and legal identities for LGBT parents resolves this crisis of legitimacy without asserting a false sense of predictability and rationality in law.

Moreover, in a time fraught with public concern over "activist judges" and the courts' role in progressive politics, it is important to dispel, or at least complicate, the perception of legal indeterminacy and judicial discretion as absolute, or as uniformly inappropriate or harmful. Although the stories of gay and lesbian parents in this book are by no means uniformly happy—and in fact many are quite tragic—it is important not to lose sight of the larger picture. A long tradition of literature on law and society has shown that many laws and legal strategies have unanticipated latent effects, sometimes good and sometimes bad, and the indeterminacy of family law and judicial discretion is no different. As one prominent activist and attorney interviewed for this book commented, "judges write decisions that help define our cultural sense of where the law should be. . . . So when they're thoughtful and good, they can be very influential; when they're not thoughtful and bad, they can also be very influential."[23] By examining the variable potential of judicial indeterminacy, and its crucial role in a democratic common-law system aimed at recognizing and responding meaningfully to social change, we can enrich the public discourse with a more nuanced and therefore more realistic assessment of "judicial activism" and its consequences.[24]

Finally, in an age rife with conflict over legal recognition of gay family relationships, when same-sex couples in many states have seen their rights rolled back as part of a backlash against the growing movement toward same-sex marriage, many observers have become cynical about the ability of the courts to facilitate a move beyond outdated and unyielding legal concepts of family and sexuality. A somewhat counterintuitive focus on the *creative potential* of legal indeterminacy in engendering an openness to new forms of family and new assessments of sexuality brings a refreshing optimism. At the same time, it highlights avenues where concerted efforts by activists and attorneys for gay and lesbian parents might be most effective by *working* the indeterminacy of family law to this end. Despite some conservatives' commentaries to the contrary, it is increasingly apparent that the universal expectation of the heterosexual nuclear family is neither empirically correct nor sound from a policy perspective. A legal framework that affords space for reinterpretation and

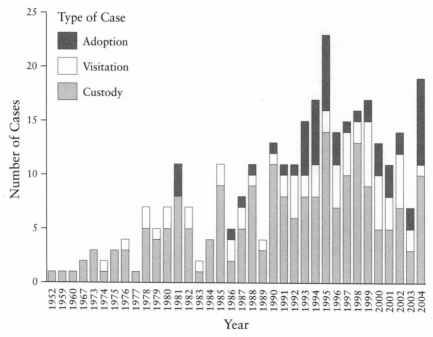

Summary of Cases by Year and Type
(years not represented on chart had no cases)

active efforts to reframe definitions of family and parenthood over time to accommodate this growing reality is not only possible but prudent.

Description of the Study

The findings and arguments presented in this book are based on archival and interview data gathered between 1999 and 2004. The archival analysis includes every published appeals court judicial decision in a child custody, visitation, or adoption case involving one or more known gay, bisexual, lesbian, or transgender parent in the United States between 1952 and 2004—316 in all.[25]

These decisions were gathered using both LEXIS and Westlaw search engines, as well as citations in the literature and information provided by gay and lesbian legal-advocacy organizations such as Lambda Legal Defense and Education Fund (Lambda) and the National Center for Lesbian Rights (NCLR). Additional archival information included briefs, trial transcripts, expert reports, and other case materials provided by these organizations, attorneys, and litigants in specific cases. The cases include three general categories of claims: divorce cases involving a heterosexual marriage in which one party subsequently comes out as gay or lesbian and a custody or visitation dispute ensues; adoption cases in which either a single gay man or lesbian, or a same-sex couple, wishes to adopt a child or in which the nonbiological parent in a same-sex couple wishes to formally adopt the child whom he or she planned with his or her partner (known as a "second-parent adoption"); and cases involving the breakup of a same-sex couple, in which the nonbiological parent (or more often in male couples, the nonadoptive parent) seeks custody or visitation rights.[26] There were also a handful of cases in which a third party, such as a grandparent or aunt, challenged a LGBT parent for custody.

These judicial decisions were supplemented with interviews conducted between December 2001 and June 2002 with key players in the legal

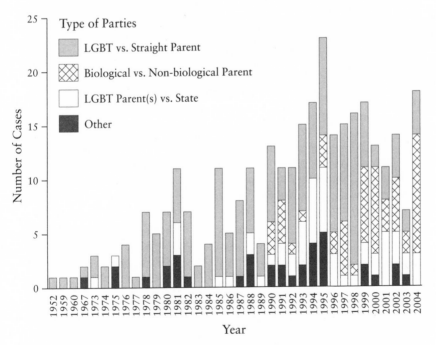

Cases by Year and Type of Parties

process—including several of the attorneys who tried the cases in the archival dataset, the litigant parents in some of these cases, and present family court judges. The interview participants—thirty-six in all—came from several jurisdictions in California, New York, Illinois, Ohio, Tennessee, and Washington, D.C. These participants were recruited through a combination of purposive and snowball sampling. The attorneys who were interviewed were chosen specifically because of their experience with the cases included in the book. I sought out those attorneys—most of them affiliated with major gay rights organizations such as Lambda and NCLR—who had tried the most cases in the dataset and who at the time were widely considered to be the preeminent attorneys in this area of law.[27] The attorneys were also instrumental in gaining access to litigants, a handful of whom agreed to be interviewed.[28]

The judges were the largest group of interviewees (twenty interviews) and were the only group not recruited through their involvement in the actual appellate cases in the dataset. There were two reasons for this: first, most of the judges involved in the original cases had either retired or moved on to a different area of law, and therefore I was not able to locate them; and second, appellate justices are not assigned solely to family law panels and therefore are not as focused on family law specifically. Therefore, I sought interviews with present trial-level family court judges in the jurisdictions from which cases in the archival data had come, relying mostly on personal contacts and snowball sampling. I did, however, make purposeful attempts to interview the supervising and presiding judges on each of the family law panels from which I recruited, as well as those judges with the most experience in family law.

The interviews generally lasted between forty minutes and two hours, averaging slightly over one hour. All but four were tape-recorded and transcribed, with the permission of the interviewees.[29] The interviews not only provided additional information and documentation about the cases and the actors involved in them but also complemented the case analysis with additional information about how judges make decisions about custody, adoption, and visitation. The interviews also shed light on the particularities of judicial discourse by providing their own, often similar but sometimes different, voice on many of the same topics discussed by the judges in the written decisions. In other words, they allowed for more of an understanding of the judges' interpretation by both complementing the archival narratives and providing a competing interpretation to be contrasted in some cases. For instance, many of the interviewed judges admitted freely that family law is notoriously discretionary and can be subject to the particular judge's own beliefs and interpretations. Such an explicit narrative regarding the indeterminacy of law, however, was conspicuously absent from most of the case decisions. Finally, the attorneys and litigants who were interviewed also provided me with additional case materials, including legal briefs, *amicus curiae* (or "friend of the court") briefs, trial transcripts, and other documents related to the judicial decisions included in the study.

Such a study spanning over fifty years and combining longitudinal and cross-sectional data offers both temporal and topical diversity, illustrating broad trends in the types of cases likely to be heard in the courts over time, the types of legal arguments developed, and their relative success. However, the cases are arranged and discussed here thematically rather than chronologically, with a focus on the practical and analytical manifestations and effects of the indeterminacy of family law. As has been noted previously, narrative research analyzes "discourse [that] may or may not be linear in time and place."[30] Likewise, although the cases span across forty-seven states and the District of Columbia, because family law is so general and decentralized, they are not grouped by state.[31] This organization is intentional, in that the contention of this book is that changes in treatment and recognition of gay and lesbian parents is due not just to locale or the mere passage of time but to specific features of family law and its indeterminacy—as well as to parents and attorneys who have learned to navigate this indeterminacy.

To be fair, because this book looks at cases from jurisdictions all over the United States, one might argue that the indeterminacy seen in family law cases is simply the product of different political cultures in different states—surely one would expect case decisions regarding any area of gay rights to be different in New York, for instance, than they are in the South. The corollary argument might be presented, then, that attitudes and definitions of family and sexuality are not likely to change in each locale, as long as New York remains New York and the South remains the South. But take for instance the following example: in the same year—1996—the majority in *In re R.E.W.* decided that Georgia's antisodomy law at that time could *not* be considered as a justification for restricting a gay parent's visitation, while in the nearby state of Virginia, the majority in *Bottoms v Bottoms* ruled that such a sodomy law *could* be used as justification in revoking custody of her child from lesbian mother Sharon Bottoms.[32] The data are replete with similar examples and comparisons, all lending credence to the proposition that the law in this area is clearly unsettled and highly indeterminate in both its rationales and its outcomes.

A Look at Things to Come

In the chapters that follow, I examine various aspects of the judicial narratives in gay and lesbian parents' custody and adoption cases that illustrate the functions and implications of *measured* indeterminacy, as well as its dysfunctions. Before looking at the data in depth, however, it is important to set the stage. To that end, chapter 2 provides an overview of gay and lesbian rights, family law, and the historical and social constructions of sexuality and family. The chapter situates the book's focus on LGBT custody and adoption in its social, historical, and legal context, bringing the reader up-to-date and providing a framework within which to understand the position of gay- and lesbian-headed families in the United States and the intersection of family, sexuality, and law more broadly. First, it briefly describes the significance of family in the gay community. For example, long before the gayby boom of the 1980s and '90s, when gay and lesbian parents began appearing in the courts in large numbers, families were being built in gay and lesbian communities. These "families of choice" helped to challenge the traditional notion of family and the concept that people have to be linked genetically in order to be considered a family. Next, the chapter gives a brief history of the right to privacy, the development of a general gay rights legal doctrine, and other developments relevant to the legal treatment of LGBT parents and families, noting some of the major milestones and hurdles faced by these parents in family law. These include many assumptions about gay and lesbian parents' fitness (or supposed lack thereof), including moral and developmental concerns as well as assumptions about the incompatibility of homosexuality and family. The well-documented answers to these concerns from the field of child psychology are briefly summarized in the chapter, as is a broad discussion of the construction and misconstruction of sexuality in American society and law. After detailing the family law process and basic legal structure of custody and adoption, the chapter concludes with a snapshot of gay/lesbian parenthood in America, including a summary of the legal landscape, the gay/lesbian-headed family's myriad forms, and the types of cases documented in appellate decisions over the past fifty years.

The next three chapters present the analysis of indeterminacy and how it functions and affects the treatment of LGBT parents and families over time in family law. Chapter 3 analyzes the constructions of sexual and parental identity in judicial decisions. It looks at how the court uses and responds to the labels of "parent," "legal stranger," "deviant," and "homosexual," the historical assumption of incompatibility between the identities of "homosexual" and "parent," and how this perception changed over time. In many cases, the courts and the families with whom they deal are in stark disagreement as to the appropriate construction of these identities and how they come together. This gap between how a judge may see a litigant and how a litigant identifies him- or herself (or how a child identifies him or her) can have severe consequences, including the termination of an adoption in progress or of any contact between parent and child. Yet because of the fluidity of family law, parents and courts are able to create "in-between" spaces and compromises by which new parental and sexual identities can be forged.

Chapter 4 examines the deployment, successes, and failures of rights discourses in the context of gay and lesbian parents' custody and adoption. Taking the well-documented abstraction and ambiguity of "rights" in general as a starting point, I examine the paradoxical and problematic position of rights discourses in this family law context, which fundamentally sits at the intersection of the individual (i.e., privacy rights) and the collective (i.e., family). Most people assume that in the United States after the civil rights movement, the constitutional rights to equal protection, privacy, and freedom of association are ubiquitous. In chapter 4, however, I show that this is not necessarily the case when it comes to gay/lesbian family rights. In fact, in many instances, parents are chastised for advancing such rights arguments during a custody case, because it is seen as selfish or inappropriate. In the chapter I show how indeterminate constitutional and other rights really are—and that in fact there is a "right" way and a "wrong" way to invoke one's rights, so to speak. Precisely because of the indeterminacy of rights and their application to family law, a more nuanced understanding and new forms of rights claims, which bridge the individual and the collective, emerges—making them more protective and supportive of newer family forms and types of relationships.

Chapter 5 looks at the role of dissenting opinions—often overlooked in studies of judicial decision-making and social change—in paving the way for change over time. Over one-quarter of all the custody and adoption cases involving gay and lesbian parents in the United States have included a dissent—a document written by those judges who disagree with the decision of the majority in the case, to express why they thought the case was decided incorrectly. As a form of "back talk" to prevailing opinions, these dissents are in some ways preconditioned by the indeterminacy of the judicial opinions to which they are responding and reacting, but they are also emblematic of the indeterminacy and the "settling" process in law. By offering a contradictory interpretation, dissents show the law as an unsettled and dynamic process. It could be argued that the existence of dissents adds to the perceived legitimacy of judge-made law by maintaining an appearance of diligence in decision-making and evincing an openness to alternative ideas. Yet, at the same time, dissents allow opposing opinions to be marked for posterity, exercising what one judge has called the "never say die option."[33] In this way, I argue, dissent is a built-in mechanism that helps to catalyze the process of legal change over time, crucial to recognition of alternative family forms and the rights of gay/lesbian parents.

Each of these analytical themes—identity, rights, and dissent—taken separately, illustrate the workings, contours, and consequences of the indeterminacy of law. The common thread, woven throughout, is that the interpretive space afforded by family law's notorious vagueness, though often yielding confounding or undesirable results, goes hand in hand with judges' and litigants' ability to negotiate and forge new legal identities, rights, and rationales over time—a process important to the recognition of LGBT parents and their families. As a cumulative whole, these analyses of identity, rights claims, and judges' dissents also contribute to a growing theoretical understanding of law and social life as mutually contingent and influential. In the final chapter, I forge a link between these two well-documented visions of law, arguing that the indeterminacy in rights, identities, rationales, and custody outcomes shown in this book provide a fertile ground for the revision, negotiation, and eventual sedimentation of new social *and* legal concepts of family, sexuality, and "best interest of the child." Indeed, it is precisely this link between the vagueness of family law and the mutual influence of society and law that has allowed—and will continue to allow—notions of sexual orientation and family to evolve, linking legal innovation with social change.

2

At the Intersection of Sexuality, Family, and Law

It is not the courts that have engendered the diverse composition of today's families. It is the advancement of reproductive technologies and society's recognition of alternative lifestyles that have produced families in which a biological, and therefore a legal, connection is no longer the sole organizing principle. But it is the courts that are required to define, declare and protect the rights of children raised in these families.

—*In re Parentage of A.B.*[1]

It is no longer novel, or open to serious controversy, that lesbian and gay individuals form relationships and exist as families, in varying degrees of visibility, across the United States. Even for those heterosexuals who may not personally know any (out) LGBT individuals or families, they most certainly are aware of their existence, thanks to increased visibility in popular media (such as *Will & Grace* and *The L Word*) as well as to political discourse and public debate such as that over same-sex marriage. These relationships and families did not need public approval or legal recognition to form—even if their existence is made less secure by its absence. In this sense, the epigraph to this chapter is correct: the diversity of the American family, just like homosexuality itself, is something that has preceded legal efforts to protect, dismantle, or even define it.

"Families We Choose" and the Forming of the Modern LGBT Family

The evolution and diaspora of gay and lesbian communities and alternate forms of family are well documented in sociological and historical studies by Kath Weston, John D'Emilio, and others.[2] Having often been kicked out of their homes and families of origin upon revelation of their sexual identity, gay men and lesbians were forced to find and construct new families composed mostly of other gays, lesbians, and sometimes straight supporters in their new communities. These "families of choice," often composed of friends and their families or partners, filled the support gap left by the abandonment of individuals' biological families, and in doing so, eventually rose above the level of friendship circle to the status of kinship network.[3] This sense of expanded and constructed family is not dissimilar to those documented in communities of color by Carol Stack and in other socioanthropological studies.[4] In similar ways, their existence and documentation helped to deconstruct the concept of family by refuting the statistical and normative myth of the ubiquitous "natural" nuclear family. Contrary to nostalgic revisionist history lamenting the recent downfall of the nuclear family, debunked effectively by Stephanie Coontz in *The Way We Never Were*, these extended family networks have existed in the gay and lesbian community for decades.[5]

These gay and lesbian families of choice provided a framework in the LGBT community for families formed on the basis of something other than genetics. Yet their transition into planned families with children, as a widespread trend at least, took somewhat longer. The planned (mainly) lesbian families that began to appear in the 1980s and '90s can be traced to two important developments: the advancement of reproductive technology that allowed women to reproduce without a male parent's involvement; and the rise of the gay and lesbian rights movement, which allowed gay men and lesbians to exist openly as couples and families and prompted a shift in adoption agencies' willingness to place children with gay and lesbian parents.[6] This trend was soon dubbed the "gayby boom"—as discussed in chapter 1, a reference to the increase in planned gay- and lesbian-headed families as a result of new reproductive technologies that allow a woman to be inseminated and become pregnant outside the context of a heterosexual relationship. A rise soon followed in planned families headed by gay male couples, through either adoption or surrogacy. These families have increased in number dramatically since the 1980s, though they are still significantly outnumbered by planned lesbian families.[7] More frequently seen are gay male parents who had their children in the course of heterosexual marriages that subsequently broke up. Thus, gay and lesbian families exist in a number of forms: children born during a heterosexual marriage and raised postdivorce by a gay or lesbian parent (and possibly his or her partner); single- or dual-adoptive gay or lesbian parents with no genetic relation to the children they adopt; planned lesbian families in which the children were conceived through donor insemination and raised by either a single lesbian mother or two lesbian mothers; and gay male families in which a child was conceived by surrogacy and was related to at least one father genetically. In each of these categories, the family structure is further complicated by the prospect that a second same-sex parent may or may not be able to adopt the child, depending on jurisdiction, and therefore may act in every regard as a parent without ever being legally recognized as such. Although estimates vary widely, the 2002 U.S. census recorded 162,000 same-sex households that were raising children; other researchers' estimates range from one million to nine million children being raised by at least one gay or lesbian parent.[8]

These multiple examples of family structure, then, allude to the complexity of "family" in both common social understandings and law—and show why family structure must be defined to include both biological ties and such factors as residence, marriage or partnership, financial support, and emotional ties. In their study of gay and lesbian family values, for instance, Elizabeth Say and Mark Kowalewski found that every person they interviewed had a different definition of family.[9] Some suggested the importance of biological ties, but most saw family as a primary support network, defined more by actions than by genetics—a proposition analyzed in depth in chapter 3. Weston employs these same concepts in *Families We Choose* to "examine the ideological transition that saw 'gay' and 'family' change from mutually exclusive categories to terms used in combination."[10] Sociologist Judith Stacey states explicitly what these and other scholars suggest: that there is no longer a "single culturally dominant family pattern."[11]

Although this sociological understanding of family had been growing for some time and the technologies used to create planned gay and lesbian families had already been available for over a decade by the 1990s, it was not until then that the families that had been formed began to be seen in the courts, often as a result of (obviously unplanned) relationship splits and disintegration of these families. As is often the case, the law was not developed in tandem with the medical advances and changing social circumstances that facilitated these planned families, thus creating much of the indeterminacy and attendant difficulties discussed in subsequent chapters. Again, there is no way to accurately count the number of such families, but the first second-parent adoptions for lesbian couples who conceived through donor insemination were granted in Alaska and Oregon in 1985.[12] The first recorded "lesbian divorce" case, in which a planned lesbian family went to court in a custody dispute, was not until 1990.[13] When these cases began to come to the courts in increasing numbers, throughout the 1990s and into the new century, judges were forced to grapple with the definition of something often taken for granted—family—and recognize the changes attendant to the burgeoning gay and lesbian rights movement and the rise of reproductive technology.

These issues were deeply implicated in judges' understanding and recognition of the multiplicity of the family form. As one well-known New York attorney noted in an interview, "if there's any group of judges who have to be aware of changes . . . in the social structure of the family, it's judges looking at family law cases."[14] In 40 percent of the cases (126), in fact, family and parenthood were explicitly treated by judges as institutions or constructs to be defined—in other words, their definitions were not taken for granted or assumed to be settled as a matter of law or linguistics. In 24 percent of the cases (76), the litigants set forth alternative legal theories of parenthood aimed at institutionalizing such redefinitions—and in half these cases, the courts accepted, at least in part, this definition of parenthood. This evolved understanding of same-sex parenthood and the variability of family, however, was only possible because of a foundation laid by several decades of gay and lesbian rights activism and progress in the courts toward recognition of LGBT civil rights as well as privacy rights more generally.

Legal Progress in Brief:
Privacy Rights, Family Rights, Gay Rights

The rise of the right to privacy in the United States is perhaps the most misunderstood issue in constitutional law. A quick read of the U.S. Constitution reveals no explicit mention of a right to privacy in the Bill of Rights. This is because the right to privacy is an invention of case law and broad legal interpretation—what might be called "judicial activism" by conservative pundits in today's vernacular. Ironically, this right, which is at the root of most family law today, was originally articulated in a case dealing with the right *not* to have a family. Arising from a challenge to a Connecticut statute barring the sale of contraceptives, the case of *Griswold v Connecticut* found a right to privacy in the marital relationship in the "penumbra," or shadows, of the Constitution, and specifically derived from the First and Ninth Amendments.[15] This was later expanded to nonmarital privacy rights in the case of *Eisenstadt v Baird* and confirmed most famously in the landmark abortion decision of *Roe v Wade*.[16]

What was essentially a common-law invention, then, became the basis for an entire body of laws governing both sexuality and family. In terms of gay and lesbian rights, the first attempt to apply this newfound right to privacy was in relation to sodomy laws, which—though in literal terms applying only to a particular set of sexual behaviors—in practice were used essentially to ban homosexuality in all or most of its manifestations and to justify legal discrimination against and harassment of same-sex couples and gay and lesbian individuals. It is not surprising, then, that a primary focus of the burgeoning gay rights movement in the United States, from the birth of the Mattachine Society to the Stonewall rebellion to the later founding of national advocacy organizations such as the National Gay and Lesbian Task Force (NGLTF), Human Rights Campaign (HRC), and Lambda Legal Defense and Education Fund (Lambda), was to overturn sodomy laws. The first such challenge to reach the U.S. Supreme Court was *Bowers v Hardwick* (1986), in which the Court's majority upheld Georgia's antisodomy law that made consensual adult sodomy a crime, and decided that the right to privacy under *Griswold* did not extend to homosexuality or sodomy. By the time this ruling was overturned in the landmark 2003 decision of *Lawrence v Texas*, however, the movement had been successful in working at the state level to overturn sodomy laws in all but thirteen states and in securing other legal victories, such as in *Romer v Evans* (1996), which assured certain civil rights protections for gay men and lesbians under the Equal Protection Clause of the Fourteenth Amendment.[17]

The *Lawrence* decision, hailed as one of the most important gay rights developments in U.S. history, was significant both for what it said and what it did not say. In some ways, the decision was much more progressive than had been predicted: rather than relying on the narrow grounds of due process and equal protection to find that sodomy laws that *only* applied to same-sex couples rather than all couples (as five states' laws did, including Texas's) were unfair, it issued a much broader vindication of gay rights by overturning *Bowers* in its entirety and ruling that gay men and lesbians were deserving of the dignity and equality in their personal lives that was denied them by the existence of sodomy laws. The ruling did not, however, specifically address family law or the heterosexist assumptions that made for a marginalized existence for gay- and lesbian-headed families. Most notably, it did not mention (except as critiqued in a vociferous dissent by Justice Scalia) a right to same-sex marriage, nor did it mention any rights related to custody or adoption. In fact, the ruling emphatically stated that *Lawrence* "does not involve whether the government must give formal recognition to any relationship that homosexual persons seek to enter."[18] This may not seem surprising given the dictate that judges adhere to the "case and controversy" before them, but the fact that the issue was raised so markedly in the dissent and that the justices in the majority felt compelled to comment explicitly on it reveals that such future implications must have entered the conversation at some point.[19] Hence, even though Justice Scalia's worst fears were realized barely five months later, when the Massachusetts Supreme Judicial Court relied on the ruling in *Lawrence* to legalize same-sex marriage in its landmark *Goodridge v Department of Public Health* decision, *Lawrence* did not have a sudden and sweeping effect on gay and lesbian parents' custody and adoption.[20] Indeed, those few states that still had adoption bans did not overturn them in the wake of *Lawrence*; and most of the changes occurring in the legal status of gay and lesbian families in the early twenty-first century were already in process by the time the decision arrived.

The irony of the early gay rights movement, which was after many decades successful in overturning sodomy laws and protecting LGBT civil rights under Supreme Court precedent, is that it did not prioritize the other issue that was significantly affecting half the community. Whereas sodomy laws were a priority for the gay *male* population, lesbians were facing the loss of their children in family courts as they came out of the closet in increasing numbers. Family law, then, did not become a priority of the movement until lesbians and bisexual women began to assert leadership and some control over the agenda, beginning in the 1970s. Thus, when gay and lesbian family issues did finally come to the attention of judges and legislators, it was largely within a context of activism on the part of lesbians, who had long been excluded from the major currents of claims-making in both the women's movement and the gay rights movement.[21] Again, although there is no way to know how many children were being raised by lesbians before this, and cases appeared sporadically in the appellate courts as early as 1952, the first activist group dedicated to this cause, the Lesbian Mothers National Defense Fund, appeared in 1974; the major gay legal rights organization in the United States, Lambda, first became involved in a lesbian mother's custody case in 1977. In the same year, the Lesbian Rights Project (later renamed the National Center for Lesbian Rights) was founded in San Francisco, with its main purpose at the time to represent lesbian mothers in child custody proceedings. By 1990, Lambda, the Lesbian Rights Project, and the American Civil Liberties Union (ACLU) had filed "friend of the court," or *amicus curiae,* briefs or provided representation in at least sixteen appellate cases. By 2004, such amicus briefs—from these organizations or others—appeared in 30 percent of the cases, or ninety-three total.

There is, of course, an undeniable link between custody and adoption rights for gay and lesbian parents and legal same-sex marriage or civil unions—particularly in the context of planned same-sex-parent households. In several states, the right to second-parent adoption or parental recognition for nonbiological and nonadoptive gay and lesbian fathers and mothers has been assured only with the advent of domestic partnerships or civil unions in that state. Perhaps not surprisingly from a legal diffusion perspective, in the two states that do have legal same-sex marriage—California and Massachusetts—both the right to second-parent adoption and the right to parental recognition for nonbiological *de facto* parents were secured in case law before, and independent of, the right to marry. But in other states with domestic partnerships or civil unions, such as Washington, parental recognition is one of the hundreds of rights afforded to same-sex couples who do register as partners—and in some cases allows these couples to bypass the lengthy procedure of a stepparent adoption, sometimes involving a year or more of home inspections and legal processes. Perhaps because it is more a product of common law than of statute, however, changes in LGBT custody law, and custody law more generally, have also progressed independent of formal civil union or domestic partnership recognition. Moreover, because such relationship recognition is relatively new in most of the few states that have it (only Vermont's law has been in effect since the start of the twenty-first century), and because it has most often happened in states that already had a record of recognizing LGBT parents' rights, the full potential of these laws for custody, adoption, and parental recognition has yet to be seen.[22] And yet, as will be seen in subsequent chapters, parents' legal relationship to each other remains an important facet in the cases discussed in this book even when no such official recognition exists.

Opposition to the Gayby Boom: Family Values and Assumptions of Harm

Perhaps not surprisingly, the increasing visibility and recognition of gay and lesbian relationships and families has been a lightning rod for religious antigay fervor. Although more recently the religious right has focused its attention and resources on fighting against same-sex marriage, increasing legal parenthood recognition and decreasing barriers to adoption for gay and lesbian parents (or potential parents) flew under the radar in large measure during much of the gayby boom. Quietly and without fanfare, states began repealing one by one their bans on gay and lesbian foster parenting and adoption either in the legislature or in the courts, while people concerned with conservative "family values" and conceptions of morality aimed their critiques at increasing acceptance of homosexuality in popular discourse and media (such as Ellen DeGeneres's coming out on national television in 1997) and Hawaii's brief flirtation with legal same-sex marriage in the 1996 case of *Baehr v Lewin*.[23]

At the same time, despite the purported separation of church and state, these concerns continued to show up in judicial narratives in custody and adoption cases on appeal, depending often on their geographical and temporal contexts. In 34 percent of custody and adoption cases (106 total), in fact, explicit references to morality and religion are found in the judicial decision. The notion of "family values" as referenced by groups such as Focus on the Family and the Family Research Council, and the public debates surrounding morality that it has spurred, have been part and parcel of evolving judicial and public attitudes toward LGBT parents and families.[24] One supervising judge in a conservative county of California noted in an interview that this is not surprising, given that family law "expresses some very profound fundamental values that people may embrace today but change tomorrow." Another more recently appointed judge on the same panel commented, "I think the judiciary is the morality of our government. . . . The judiciary is where the morality of our society lives, does it not? Right and wrong is exactly why people go to court. Yes, morality has changed. And yes, morality is emblazoned in our law."[25]

Yet often the type of morality emblazoned in law has been one that is resistant to changing conceptions of sexuality, families, and family values. In its early days (and to some extent since then), the emerging confluence of homosexuality with the family, one of the most revered and protected institutions in American life, tapped into a deep-seated underlying collective fear. This fear was rooted in two culturally embedded systemic beliefs. The first was that homosexuals, more than just aberrations from the norm, are overly sexualized and promiscuous to the point of depravity. This stereotype, although empirically groundless, is in some ways not surprising, given that the LGBT community is the only minority group largely defined by its sexual practice.[26] This belief encouraged the fear that the presence of gay men and lesbians in family would corrupt it as an institution. The second was the widespread disbelief that LGBT individuals would be interested in or capable of nurturing children and having a family. Gay men and lesbians were (and in some rare cases, still are) not seen as possessing the attributes needed to be a parent—so the two images were often irreconcilable in the eyes of many, including the court—despite their presence in the American population for many years before they came to the attention of the courts.

The intersection of nonnormative sexualities with family was particularly troublesome for the law, then, because homosexuality and family were traditionally thought of as mutually exclusive institutions. Although feminist scholar Martha Fineman discusses the law as being formed around and aimed at preserving the "sexual family" as its normative and empirical base, this sexual family has been distinctly *hetero*sexual.[27] The law and its institutions were neither doctrinally nor ideologically equipped to deal with the possibility of a family whose heads of household look less like "Ozzie and Harriet" and more like "Rozzie and Harriet."[28] The legal (if not public) existence of same-sex parenting couples is in large part a recent phenomenon—only two are documented as having had a case heard at the appellate level before 1990. But the law's ill-preparedness for dealing logistically with the breakup of a family in which there are two mothers, for instance, has been far from merely a problem of novelty. There has also been an ideological and highly moralistic component to the courts' traditional reticence in recognizing the role of gay men and lesbians as parents, which goes beyond their ambivalence (at best) toward homosexuality in general. This component often included normative evaluations of the possible effects, mainly seen as negative, of gay and lesbian parents on their children.

The custody challenges arising from such concerns generally revolved around a set of assumptions regarding gay and lesbian parents and their effects on children. Generally speaking, the four leading rationales for denying custody to a gay or lesbian parent all concern certain understandings of sexuality. First, it was assumed that an LGBT parent's lifestyle was not conducive to having children—that these parents were more promiscuous or deviant, that lesbian mothers would be less "maternal" by nature than their heterosexual counterparts, and that LGBT parents would be more interested in sex than in parenting. This set of concerns might not be unique to gay and lesbian parents—after all, it is not uncommon for sexual activity and promiscuity of parents to be raised in particularly acrimonious heterosexual custody cases. And concerns about how "maternal" a woman will be largely implicates gender roles—indeed, at the time that the "tender years" doctrine of maternal preference was introduced in the nineteenth century, those mothers who did not appropriately conform to traditionally gendered expectations and roles (including those who worked outside the home) were excluded from this preferential treatment. Yet, in the case of gay and lesbian parents, these assumptions were more likely to rest on general beliefs about gays and lesbians as a *class* of people, rather than on any specific trait possessed by the *individual*.

A related concern was that the children would have a greater chance of being molested or otherwise sexually harmed because of their parents' sexual propensities and associations. These concerns were fueled in part by the historical framing of homosexuality as a psychological disorder. In its original version of the Diagnostic and Statistical Manual (DSM) of psychiatric disorders, the American Psychiatric Association (APA) included homosexuality as a sexual disorder—a scientific confirmation of the public's condemnation of alternative sexualities as "deviant" and "perverted." Its deletion in 1973 from the DSM, the result of extended lobbying and debates within the APA, prompted a change in the framing of homosexuality, from a disease to an orientation.[29] Although this move did not result in an immediate cessation of references to homosexuality as deviant in judicial narratives or public discourse, it did have a dramatic effect, over an extended period of time, on such references and on custody and adoption cases.

Second, the fact that some states still had sodomy laws on the books until 2003 buttressed these assumptions and added the potential label of "criminal" to the evaluation of LGBT parents. In effect in every state of the Union at one point, sodomy laws began to be slowly repealed one by one, starting with Illinois in 1961. In most states that still had these laws in effect by the 1990s, they were either rarely enforced or treated as misdemeanors. Interestingly, lesbian mothers were in many cases challenged for custody based on existing sodomy laws at that time in their jurisdiction, though such laws were generally not enforced against women with any frequency (or as often as they were against gay men) outside the context of child custody.[30] In the family law context, however, sodomy laws were used not only to justify the denial of custody rights but also to deny LGBT parents' constitutional claims based on equal protection, due process, and privacy—all principles that have in the past been applied to family law and custody concerns.[31] In all, 13 percent of cases (forty-two) raised the issue of sodomy laws and the resulting criminal status applied to the parents in question.

Third—and most commonly in the modern era—because of the sexualized and moralized traits enumerated above, it was assumed that children would be harmed by contact and residence with an LGBT parent as a result of the stigma associated with the community's disapproval of their parent's sexuality, or others' perception of it. In 18 percent of the cases (fifty-six), in fact, "harm" was defined as stigma borne by the child as a result of having or living with a gay or lesbian parent. This was also a common theme in interviews with current family court judges; as one very senior and well-respected judge in California commented regarding the notion of stigma causing harm, "I suppose on the altar of political correctness is very often sacrificed the psyche of children actually suffering, being required to live in circumstances where they're absolutely ostracized." He went on to note that a societal interest in not abiding discrimination had to be balanced with the child's well-being (defined as free from stigma): "Let's look at it from the child's perspective. Even though it runs afoul of the societal considerations, let's protect this particular child. That's not wrong, nor is the societal perspective wrong."[32] Although these concerns were arguably aimed not at the gay or lesbian parents but at the community that would ostracize them, the result was the same, and essentially validated their sexual identity as a source of stigma.

Finally, perhaps the most discussed (and studied) concern raised against gay and lesbian parents in custody and adoption cases was that the child would become homosexual or develop a nonnormative gender identity as a consequence of contact with a homosexual parent. In fact, in

14 percent of the cases (forty-four) "harm" was defined at least in part as the production of a homosexual child. A related concern, often raised in tandem, was that being raised by LGBT parents would have an adverse impact on the child's moral development—because of a judge's or opposing parent's normative assumption either that being gay set a bad moral example for the children or that contact with a gay parent would conflict with the moral or religious teachings of the other (straight) parent. Thus, this assumption about parents' sexuality and its effects on children was multidimensional: not only did it assume that homosexuality could be passed on from parent to child as a matter of genetics or psychology, but it also assumed that, should such a transformation result, it should be considered a negative development and a "harm" to the child—both propositions to be discussed in more detail in chapter 3.

In response to these claims, psychologists and child development scholars have studied the parenting styles of lesbians and gay men and their impacts on their children and have debunked many of the assumptions surrounding gay and lesbian parenting, as well as those surrounding homosexuality more generally. Following the deletion of homosexuality from the DSM in 1973, both the American Psychiatric Association and the American Psychological Association have submitted *amicus curiae* briefs to the courts refuting claims that LGBT individuals suffer from mental disorders and that they are likely to molest or otherwise be harmful to children.[33] These organizations—as well as many of the other major mental health organizations in the United States, including the National Association of Social Workers, the American Medical Association, and the American Academy of Pediatrics—have since issued general statements in support of gay and lesbian parents based on an accumulation of research in their fields. More recently, in 2002, the American Academy of Pediatrics released a policy statement supporting the custody and visitation rights of nonbiological lesbian mothers, finding not only that it is *not* harmful for children to be raised by two same-sex parents but that children are harmed by being *barred* from contact with gay or lesbian parents who have raised them.

Individual psychologists, psychiatrists, and social workers who are called on to testify in custody cases most often render evaluations of the child's mental and emotional status, his or her attachment and relationship to the respective parent(s), and the parents' fitness. In cases involving gay or lesbian parents, questions raised in court about parental ability and psychological attachment of children are compounded by questions regarding the likely effects of a parent's alternative sexuality on the child's psyche—including, as discussed earlier, gender identity development, future sexual orientation, and harm as a result of the social stigma attached to homosexuality and bisexuality. In general, studies have not found major departures from the norms of good parenting for either mothers or fathers.[34] Most reliable studies have also found that, although children of gays and lesbians do experience some level of stigma due to the community's negative attitude toward homosexuality, they are not adversely affected by this stigma in terms of mental health or general well-being.[35] In fact, psychological research has consistently shown that being raised by a gay or lesbian parent is not harmful to children and that gay men and lesbians are *less* likely than heterosexuals, statistically, to be child molesters.[36] Those few differences in child-rearing practice and developmental outcomes that are noticed, upon closer inspection appear to be ones that would, by many observers, be considered beneficial to the child.[37] Nevertheless, it has become standard practice in child custody cases involving gay and lesbian parents to raise, or dispute, these assumptions regarding their ability and propensities as parents.

The Legal Context:
A Note on Custody, Adoption, and Family Law

The Family Court Process

To appreciate fully the experience of gay and lesbian parents in family court—which culminates in the appellate decisions discussed in the coming chapters—it is important to understand the family court process itself. Obviously, because of the personal nature of family law and divorce (and often out of a concern for children's well-being), there are most often efforts made to resolve custody and visitation issues outside court.[38] Only when out-of-court mediation fails in this regard would the litigants enter a family court proceeding involving a trial by judge.[39] Additionally, in cases involving parties that are not biological or already legally recognized adoptive parents to the child, they must prove that they have standing even to bring the issue to court, before a custody trial can commence. At the trial stage, the proceedings are generally not recorded or published (a standard legal practice in all areas of law), or open to the public, because of the private nature of these cases and concern for the welfare of the children involved. Thus, except for the rare occasions when a researcher or expert is granted access on an individual basis by the attorney or litigant (or in the State of New York, where trial decisions are often published by the court system), the trial-level decisions and transcripts are generally not available except to the appellate court or parties directly involved.

Once a decision is rendered at the trial level, either legally recognized party is entitled to file for an appeal of the decision or challenge any aspect of the custody decision, until the child turns eighteen. There are three aspects of family law, however, that constrain successful attempts to appeal or otherwise revisit custody and visitation decisions. First, judges are generally inclined not to alter a custody arrangement unless one party can prove that there has been a *significant change* in circumstances affecting the welfare of the child(ren). Second, the standard of review in custody law, "abuse of discretion," is itself notoriously vague and discretionary and can vary significantly not only from jurisdiction to jurisdiction but from judge to judge. In other words, a custody case can be appealed and overturned only if the appellate judge finds that the trial judge or judge in a lower appeals court abused the discretion afforded to him or her by rendering a decision that is not legally sound or supported by facts. Finally, the standard that must be met to deny a parent visitation (as opposed to custody) is quite high—rather than simply determining the child's "best interest," it must be proven that the visitation would be *detrimental* to the child. These standards, however, do not always dissuade parents' attempts to change custody and visitation orders—in fact, some observers have argued that because of these vague standards and the high stakes involved, appeals may be more likely than in some other areas of law. Furthermore, the "abuse of discretion" standard for review is not necessarily stringently enforced: 34 percent of cases appealed over the years were overturned at least in part, yet only 13 percent of them cited an abuse of discretion.

Legal Developments and Standards of Family Law

Because family law is perhaps the most discretionary area of law practiced in the United States, and because there is a degree of variance between jurisdictions, it is difficult to summarize the contents of family law across all fifty states.[40] A few commonly accepted standards do exist, however. At various periods in history, a number of general principles have been stated and adopted to govern custody decision-making.

In early U.S. law (as adopted from British law), children were treated as property of their parents, and as such, custody was given to the father in the event of a divorce, since women did not yet have the right to own property. Later, the "tender years" doctrine was adopted, which held that, because of women's "maternal nature" and nurturing capacities, they should be given presumptive custody if the child was still of "tender years," that is, a young age.[41] Although historical reliance on the "best interest of the child" in judicial decisions significantly overlaps with the "tender years" doctrine, the former having been first introduced in 1813, it was not until the mid- to late twentieth century that the "tender years" doctrine was abolished in most states, leaving a purportedly gender-neutral (though still unsatisfactory to many) "best interest of the child" standard. Starting in 1981, following a major critique of the best-interest standard as it was then practiced, some jurisdictions changed to a "primary caretaker" doctrine, which favored awarding primary custody to the parent who had the most "day to day responsibility for the child."[42] By then, gender-neutral standards, in theory if not in practice, were prevalent in most jurisdictions, but many continued to rely implicitly on gendered presumptions.[43] Eventually the "best interest of the child" standard of today evolved, with the presumption that the gender of the parent is not relevant in deciding which custody situation best meets the child's needs. Many jurisdictions have continued to consider the primary caretaker or, more likely, to default to a presumption of joint custody as being in the best interest of the child, assuming no major risks or failings by either parent. But the best-interest standard is still used to consider which parent will have primary residential, or physical, custody. Regardless of the standard employed, it is more difficult to change custody once it has been awarded since, as mentioned, the challenging parent must show that there has been a significant change in circumstances since the time of the original custody award.

In determining what exactly constitutes the "best interest of the child," there is little formal guidance that is recognized across states, the closest being the Uniform Marriage and Divorce Act, which lists a number of considerations including the wishes of the child and parents; the child's adjustment to the home, community, and school; the mental and physical health of all parties involved; and the occurrence of abuse, among other things.[44] Like all uniform acts of their kind, these guidelines are not mandatory, however, unless formally adopted by the state legislature, and therefore they may be cited or disregarded by individual family court judges. Some case precedents have sought to lay out criteria for determining best interest, such as *Bah v Bah* in Tennessee, which stated that judges should consider, among other things, the parents' "character and propensities as evidenced by their past conduct."[45] Moreover, although the "best interest of the child" standard is the guiding rule across the United States, there is a strong presumption, and most often *requirement*, that custody and deference be given in any custody or visitation dispute to the biological parent or parents (assuming both parties are not equally blood-related to the child).[46] Although sometimes disputed for other reasons, this presumption generally is only discarded when the biological parents' rights have been explicitly terminated in court voluntarily or when the biological parents have been found so unsuitable as to pose a specific severe danger to the child. In some cases, however, even a history of abuse or violence has not been enough to terminate a biological parent's right to custody.[47] Much like the "best interest of the child" standard, then, the notion of "harm" is widely varied and disputed.

In determining visitation claims, as mentioned earlier, the standard is different than for custody. In order for a legal parent to be denied visitation, a judge must find that visitation would be *detrimental* to the child. For this reason, it requires a much higher standard of proof to deny a parent visitation than it does to deny him or her custody. The key here, though, is parental status; visitation rights, over a legally recognized parent's objection, are in no way guaranteed or even subject to the same standard. Although many judges still cite the "best interest of the child" in these scenarios, there is no hard-and-fast rule governing visitation with parent-*like* figures who are not related by biology or adoption. The precedent set by the U.S. Supreme Court in 1999 in *Troxel v Granville*, discussed in more depth in chapter 4, strengthened the rights of custodial parents to the detriment of others seeking visitation and set forth some guidelines in determining these visitation claims.[48] As lawyer Nancy Polikoff has noted, the gay and lesbian community followed this case closely because of its potential ramifications for LGBT parents, particularly nonbiological and nonadoptive co-parents.[49] Because *Troxel* involved grandparents rather than same-sex partners, however, its applicability to co-parenting situations has not been fully resolved.

Unlike custody and visitation, adoptions tend to be largely regulated by statute. Still, the best-interest standard sometimes plays a role in deciding whether to allow the adoption of a child by a single parent or a couple. In order for this standard to be applied in adoption cases, however, both the child and the parent(s) have to be determined eligible—and the requirements for eligibility vary significantly from state to state.[50] In general, a child is only eligible to be adopted if his or her birth parents have given up all parental rights, either voluntarily or by force of law. If only one biological parent's rights are terminated, this does not necessarily mean that the child is eligible for adoption by a second adult. In many states, there are statutory guidelines that govern this situation, which may include requirements that the second adoptive parent be related by marriage to the existing parent or by blood to the child (e.g., as an aunt or uncle) or that he or she not be the same gender as the existing parent. In most if not all cases, it is required that the existing parent consent to the second parent's adoption. It is important to note, however, that in almost all states, the adoption statutes were written without explicit reference to the possibility of second-parent adoptions (and particularly second-parent adoptions by same-sex partners), thus providing for some confusion over the statutory consideration of same-sex parenting dyads—an issue discussed in more detail in chapters 3, 4, and 5. In many jurisdictions, however, the legislature has specified that adoption laws are to be construed broadly so as to serve the best interest of the child—again affording a great deal of discretion to the individual judges and appellate panels. What this means in practical application is that if a second-parent adoption requirement was written to apply to heterosexual stepparents, it could be construed by analogy to apply also to same-sex co-parents—but that this determination is entirely a matter of the court's interpretation and discretion. As of 2005, three states had adoption statutes that specifically allowed second-parent adoptions, seven others (plus the District of Columbia) had case law allowing such adoptions, and there were fifteen states in which these adoptions had been allowed by a trial court, without an explicit law in place.[51]

As with many other developments in family law and civil rights more generally, gay and lesbian parents' adoption claims have built on the gains made by others before them, including single parents, parents of a race or religion different from the adoptee, or parents who were otherwise, at their time, considered "unconventional." Indeed, at the advent of official adoption in the nineteenth century, the typical adoption was one that took place *within* the family, for example, adoption by an aunt and uncle or other relatives.[52] Well into the twentieth century, the goal of adoption was to place the child with the most "normal" family, and one that most closely simulated the child's biological family. Not until 1994 did Congress pass the Multiethnic Placement Act, which explicitly aimed to remove extant barriers to adopting a child of a different "race, color or national origin."[53] Certainly single or unmarried adoptive parents, as well as remarried heterosexual parents and those who had a child using a surrogate or sperm donor, preceded and laid significant groundwork for the rights of same-sex couples and gay singles to adopt or to have children born to their partner recognized as their own. For instance, the 1993 case of *Johnson v Calvert* in California, involving a hetero-sexual couple's use of a surrogate, established the notion that "she who intended to bring about the birth of a child that she intended to raise as her own—is the natural mother under California law."[54] Likewise, the Uniform Parentage Act of 1975, in calling for the elimination of the dis-tinction between "legitimate" and "illegitimate" children, helped to pry parentage loose from the requirement of (heterosexual) marriage.

The eligibility requirements of adoptive parents in general are much more variable and complex than those applying to children, with stan-dards differing greatly between states. In addition to those requirements for second-parent adoptions mentioned earlier, many states require, for instance, that the prospective adoptive parent be over the age of eighteen and that he or she go through an approval process by the local child welfare service or adoption agency or be certified as a foster parent. Two states, Florida and Mississippi, categorically forbid adoptions by gay or lesbian (potential) parents.[55] Other states bar such adoptions indirectly, by either not allowing "unmarried cohabitants" to adopt (Utah), not allowing gay men and lesbians to be foster parents (Nebraska), or allow-ing adoption agencies to discriminate against gay and lesbian parents by relying on moral or religious objections (North Dakota). Again, however, the requirement that adoption statutes be construed broadly to meet the needs of the most children has led some courts to overturn such adop-tion bans in states where they once existed, such as New Hampshire.

When the issue of how a same-sex co-parent who is not biologically related to a child should be treated legally faces courts, the vagueness of custody law, and the requirement of broad interpretation in adoption law, has led to a variety of creative solutions, opinions, and new or reinter-preted legal statuses and arguments. Again, developments in heterosexual family law have often served as the bases for these new arguments. For example, the development of genetic testing to determine paternity has led to a slew of fathers' rights cases in which a "functional" father raised a child that was not genetically his own. When such a father was placed next to a genetic father—often, in law professor Barbara Woodhouse's words, a "fleeting impregnator" whose claim to parenthood is based on biology and not much else—the child's determination of who his or her father was often did not match the law's determination.[56] But such cases eventually gave rise to the notion that parenthood cannot always be reduced to biology (what Woodhouse calls a "generist" perspective), a concept of obvious importance to gay and lesbian families.

In the legal arena prior to the gayby boom, other divergent family forms, such as those involving stepparents or extended kin relations, have necessitated the development of legal statuses and formulations to identify pseudoparental figures and other interested parties for custody purposes. Some of these legal formulations, such as *de facto* parenthood, confer a parent-*like* status to a person who has assumed the day-to-day duties of a parent, such that he or she can participate in court proceedings but cannot generally obtain custody and is not recognized as a legal parent. Other statuses, such as equitable parenthood and *in loco parentis* create parental rights analogous to those of a biological parent. Equitable parenthood is based on a mutually acknowledged parent-child relationship and is often used in situations in which a father has proceeded on the assumption that he is the child's natural parent but later finds out that this is not the case. This type of situation is generally governed by the doctrine of "presumed fatherhood," based on the precedent set in *Michael H. v Gerald D.*, which means that if a father is married to the mother of a child at the time of birth and/or has raised the child as his own, he is presumed to be the father of that child, even if later genetic testing proves that he is not.[57] *In loco parentis*, which creates parental rights for someone voluntarily providing support or care, is often used to confer legal status to stepparents. In some cases, stepparents are allowed to adopt a child to formalize the relationship. Although generally courts and legislatures will only recognize one parent of either sex, as discussed earlier, these adoptions are allowed based on the "stepparent exception" to the rule, which would otherwise require that the biological parent of the same sex have his or her parental status terminated. In addition, contractual parenting agreements are sometimes entered into in an attempt to formally recognize nonbiological parents, but these agreements are not always recognized or validated in courts.[58]

Again, all these legal statuses and definitions were originally formulated to accommodate heterosexual extensions of family, such as stepparents and grandparents, but they have since begun to be used by lesbian and gay co-parents to assert their parental rights and identities in court. Trial courts in some states began allowing second-parent adoptions to gay and lesbian co-parents based on the use of parental contracts or analogies to stepparent adoptions as early as 1985; however, this right was not explicitly institutionalized in case law in any state until 1993.[59] Likewise, some gay and lesbian nonbiological parents had attained visitation as a *de facto* parent or by using the doctrine of *in loco parentis* at the trial level as early as 1984; yet such an argument was not successful in an appellate decision until 1996.[60] Until relatively recently, the courts have been reluctant to apply these labels to same-sex partners or former partners, instead finding that they do not qualify due to their lack of blood or marriage relation.

The most recent addition to the family law lexicon is the concept of the "psychological parent." Referred to by courts alternatively as both a parental status and a custody guideline to succeed the "best interest of the child" standard, the psychological-parent model privileges the child's experience and point of view by asserting that any person who has consistently filled the psychological role of a parent to the child—regardless of blood relation or marriage—may be considered a parental figure in law for the purpose of determining custody, visitation, and adoption. Although this standard is not yet widely adopted in courts as a general rule, it is emerging as the preferred standard of the future by child welfare and gay rights advocates alike and has been cited in some progressive court decisions. In the landmark 2000 *V.C. v M.J.B.* decision in New Jersey, the justices set out a four-part test for determining psychological parenthood: "the legal parent must consent to and foster the relationship between the third party and the child; the third party must have lived with the child; the third party must perform parental functions for the child to a significant degree; and a parent-child bond must be forged."[61] These criteria, or paraphrases of them, have since been used in other cases involving lesbian co-parents to award psychological parent status to the nonbiological parent, such as *In the Interest of E.L.M.C.* in Colorado.[62]

The legal salience of sexual orientation in custody matters, though by no means uniform across states or cases, is guided in some jurisdictions by one of two legal standards. Particularly in the past twenty-five years, a distinction in family law has been made between the "*per se*" standard and the "nexus" standard in determining the relevance of sexual orientation to the determination of harm and best interest of the child. The *per se* standard assumes that having a homosexual parent is harmful *per se*, as a matter of law, and is always contrary to the child's best interest, whereas the nexus standard does not begin with such an assumption. This distinction was first made in the case of *Nadler v Superior Court in and for Sacramento County* in 1967, a landmark decision that was the first to overrule the *per se* standard in defining the best interest of the child and the role of sexual orientation.[63] This case also invented the "nexus test," which requires that in order to show that a parent's sexual orientation is relevant in deciding the child's best interest, it must be proven that there exists a "nexus" between the parent's sexuality and actual harm to the child.[64] Although the nexus test by no means assures that a parent's homosexuality will not be used against him or her, it at least provides a framework for considering sexual orientation within a constellation of factors affecting custody. Whether the *per se* standard or nexus standard is used in a custody case, however, they both carry implicit and sometimes explicit implications for the framing and understanding of sexuality, its forms, and its salience.

The Construction of Sexuality in Family Court

The tradition of studying sexuality through official narratives is well established in the humanities as well as in law and society.[65] In appellate judicial opinions, narratives of sexuality are quite literally written into the law. Although case law cannot change a person's sexuality, it can certainly constrain it in fundamental ways—the well-established legal "apartheid of the closet."[66] Since sexuality is understood both as a private identity and a public construct closely associated with the state's conceptions of morality, legal regulations on sexual behavior have often been justified as interventions on behalf of a legitimate state interest in maintaining public moral standards. And since sexuality is both a practice and an identity, legal regulations based on sexual *acts* or behaviors necessarily have an impact on sexual identities and other aspects of the lives of those identifying with alternative sexualities. Thus, for instance, even if gay or lesbian parents never engage in sex acts that would directly affect their child, the fact of their homosexuality, as a facet of identity or political commitment, has often been seen as relevant, or even controlling, in court. Exactly *how* this relevance is articulated, moreover, reveals much about public and institutionalized understandings of sexuality, both on its own and in its role in the family.

As might be expected, understandings or evaluations of a parent's sexuality were often either the primary focus or one of a few primary issues of consideration in over 92 percent of custody and adoption cases involving gay or lesbian parents that were documented in appellate courts. In nearly three-quarters of the cases (231 total), sexuality itself was analyzed in some sense, apart from merely being a factor in the custody or adoption decision. Yet, although the multiplicity of sexualities and nuanced understanding of sexual orientation is well documented in the academy, often a similar understanding is not revealed in the language of judicial decisions.[67] Almost uniformly, bisexual men and women are lumped into the category of homosexual and treated similarly;[68] or in some cases, a litigant's sexual orientation has been included as yet another item in a litany of sexual misdeeds, including prostitution and adultery.[69] Treatment of transgender and transsexual individuals has been variable, with some courts recognizing their current gender identity (with use of gender-appropriate pronouns, for example) and some not. In one particularly revealing case, *Kantaras v Kantaras*, the court stated, "The words 'sex,' 'male,' and 'female' in everyday understanding do not encompass transsexuals. . . . A male-to-female post-operative transsexual does not fit the definition of a female. . . . the transsexual still 'inhabits a male body in all aspects other than what the physicians have supplied.'"[70] Very few cases, if any, evinced an understanding of sexuality or gender as a continuum—or even something other than a dichotomy—as they have been conceived by many sex and gender scholars both of the past[71] and present.[72]

Indeed, the fact that the majority of custody and adoption cases involving gay or lesbian parents have been borne from divorces of previously heterosexual couples is testament not only to the increasing acceptance of homosexuality, which has allowed individuals to come out, but also to the mutability of sexuality. It is no longer controversial in gender and sexuality scholarship to assert that sexuality can be ambiguous and vary throughout the lifespan—thus escaping easy, dichotomous categorizing as homosexual or heterosexual. Nor is it controversial any longer that one can enact a sexual identity in public that differs from one's sexual behavior or inclinations. Long before the rise of sexuality studies, epidemiologist Alfred Kinsey revealed the gap between common understandings of "normal" or average sexuality and the range of *actual* sexual identities and behaviors.[73] Yet many judges' decisions do not evince a similar understanding and instead compound this erasing of sexual complexity by imputing harmful behavior and personality traits, as discussed earlier, based on the label of "homosexual." For example, a judge may assume that living with a gay father will increase a child's exposure to AIDS or inappropriate sexual role models. Or the reverse may happen: judges assume a parent's homosexuality on the basis of a particular set of behaviors. LGBT parents, their lawyers, and researchers therefore have urged an understanding of homosexual identity as separate from any assumed set of behaviors or characteristics and, in particular, have urged against the tendency to reduce a homosexual identity to the sex acts most closely associated with it (or oversexualizing of any sort). To be sure, some judges clearly make a distinction between act and identity. This bifurcated understanding of sexuality, however, also raises problems for gay and lesbian parents, as it sometimes evolves into an expectation that they may fairly be asked not to "act on" their sexual orientation, thus not repudiating their homosexual identity but effectively confining them to a celibate existence.

Discussion of parents' sexual orientation by judges ranges from specific questions or concerns regarding their actual sexual behavior to broader, more ideological and philosophical questions about homosexuality and bisexuality and its relevance in child custody and adoption proceedings. Nearly 40 percent of cases (124) discussed a parent's or prospective parent's sexual *activity* or imputed promiscuity specifically, whether it was ruled relevant or not. An almost equal number of cases discussed gay and lesbian parents' *association* with other homosexual or bisexual individuals or organizations (122 cases). On a more abstract level, about 13 percent of judicial decisions (41) referenced homosexuality as a "deviant" status; and one-third of them (103) discussed or measured parents' *commitment* to, or prioritization of, their sexual identity or orientation. Bridging the two types of discussions, about 12 percent of judges (39) discussed whether parents' sexual *activity* and sexual *identity* were—or should be—considered separately, distinguished from each other in the case narratives and in expectations of a parent's behavior. The specific implications of these treatments of parents' sexual orientation in the narrative are discussed in more detail in subsequent chapters, but their mere existence has repercussions for how sexuality is understood and represented. Indeed, what judges have to say about gay and lesbian parents, and their families and relationships, speaks volumes about common social understandings and legal consequences of sexuality for parenthood, rights, and identity.

3

Negotiating Parental and Sexual Identity

[T]he concepts of homosexuality and adoption are so inherently mutually exclusive and inconsistent, if not hostile, that the legislature never considered it necessary to enact an express ineligibility provision. . . . Homosexuality negates procreation. Announced homosexuality defeats the goals of adoption.
  —In the Matter of Adoption of Charles B.[1]

To suggest that adoption petitions may not be filed by unmarried partners of the same or opposite sex because the legislature has only expressed a desire for these adoptions to occur in the traditional nuclear family constellation of the 1930's ignores the reality of what is happening in the population.
  —Matter of Adoption of Camilla[2]

Although Domestic Relations Law does not explicitly define the term "parent," we are of the view . . . that the petitioner does not come within the meaning of that term.
  —Alison D. v Virginia M.[3]

It is not common in public discourse that one would think to stop and determine what the definition of "parent" is—or, for that matter, what the definition of "gay" is. These seem intuitive to the average person, if not self-consciously considered often by him or her. At the same time, though, it is not difficult to crack this veneer of simplicity with just a few pointed questions or examples of the variety of sexual

43

and familial configurations that exist in contemporary American society. Consider for example the fallout from the highly publicized scandal in the late 1990s at the University of California–Irvine fertility clinic, where fertile women's ova were implanted in infertile women's wombs, unbeknownst to either party until years later. Or consider the public reaction to the breakup of celebrity couple Ellen DeGeneres and Anne Heche, when Heche went on to marry a man, leaving many people questioning whether she was ever "really" a lesbian. The ambiguity of these identities and their place in an ever-changing social and legal terrain, illustrated in the epigraphs to this chapter, looms quite large in the development of family law pertaining to lesbian and gay parents and would-be parents. Ultimately, these questions of identity not only are crucial to the social understanding of LGBT-headed families but also raise the issue of the role of identity in law, and vice versa.

Recent legal scholarship has noted the particularly potent way in which the law affects people's lives through its power to create, shape, and challenge their legal identities. Many researchers have discussed, for example, the highly consequential and potentially devastating personal impact of being labeled a "criminal" by the legal system.[4] The effects of acquiring such an identity come not only in the form of structural limitations (such as the inability to vote) and institutional requirements (such as requiring one to "register" or stay in contact with a parole officer) but also in more subtle and personal forms—what has alternatively been called "labeling"[5] or "shaming."[6] The process of being cast as a "criminal" and inheriting that identity is an extreme and quite visible example of how the law may shape and impose identities—but it is not difficult to imagine how the same process would apply to parenthood and family.

This process of shaping identities also happens in more subtle ways, under other conditions and in other legal forums. Feminist scholars have noted repeatedly the power of legal institutions to define, delimit, and constrain women's activities and identities in both the public and the private spheres.[7] Groups seeking assistance from the law in asserting their political and legal rights have also been subject to the law's definitional powers. Sociolegal scholar Wendy Espeland notes, for example, how the law can simultaneously represent a group's interest (Espeland's discussion concerns the Yavapai community of Native Americans) and impose on the group an identity that differs from the group's self-constructed identity.[8] In many cases, judges are in the position to decide who are legitimate legal actors and who are not, thus defining some people or groups as appropriate legal subjects and imposing on others a status of legal nonexistence (those who are deemed to have "no standing" or whose problems are deemed to be outside the realm of the legal authority).

In this chapter I analyze gay and lesbian parents' child custody cases as a site of identity formation and negotiation, made possible by the indeterminacy of family law. In this context "identity" refers not only to an individual's own self-image but also to how an individual is constructed as a subject in law and represented in legal decisions and texts. As Espeland insightfully notes,

> The relationship between what is often considered the exemplar of the "public" sphere—law—and what we might suppose is our most "private" realm—our conceptions of self—may seem like a study in oppositions, but like many oppositions, the one often informs (if not requires) the other.[9]

In other words, one's identity as a sociolegal subject is composed in interaction and is necessarily constrained and influenced by the law's categories and processes. This is particularly true in an arena such as child custody, in which frequently the focus is on defining and categorizing, through legal findings and processes, the facets of a person that are often thought to be the most personal: family ties and sexuality.

Thus, the focus of this chapter is how the indeterminacy of family law has allowed judges and litigants, either explicitly or implicitly, to shape and redefine the sociolegal identities of gay and lesbian parents and would-be parents in the context of their custody and adoption cases. At stake are answers to such questions as, How do courts go about defining key aspects of identity whose meanings are often taken for granted, such as "parent," "family," and "homosexual"? How do they identify and categorize members of gay- and lesbian-headed families, who may not fit into the traditional legal family model? How have two identities once thought mutually exclusive—homosexual and parent—been reconciled over time? Examining these questions reveals how sexual and parental identities are negotiated, shaped, and settled over time and in individual cases, such that their vague and unsettled beginnings ultimately result in an expanded palette of options for the recognition and treatment of gay and lesbian parents. The revelation of a parent's homosexuality or relationship status turns from accusation of impropriety to simply a fact of life in a diverse society. Parents who once had to hide any evidence of their sexuality may now be emboldened and find acceptance—even if conditional—in family court. Nontraditional families and nonbiological parents go from being virtually defined out of existence to gradually gaining legal visibility and recognition. But the process of these transformations, and the resolution of questions regarding the role of parental and sexual identity in court, ultimately also begs the question of where identities—both sexual and parental—come from to begin with.

The Etiology of Identity: Essentialism, Transmission, and Labeling

Innately embedded in the study of identity—sexual and otherwise—are questions about its etiology. Certainly in the case of family identity, and in particular nonbiological kinship ties, the law's powers to regulate, create, and deny identity are evident. Gay and lesbian parents encounter this reality when they attempt to legally solidify their parental identity by adopting a child who, in many cases, they may have been raising since birth.[10] These and other gay and lesbian nonbiological parents, when their relationships have broken up, have often been excluded from the legal process and identified not as parents or even as pseudoparents but instead as "third parties" or "legal strangers" who are not allowed to have an interest in the custody proceedings. Yet parenthood is also a culturally articulated and naturalized status with roots that are thought to be outside the law.[11] Although this notion of "natural" parental identity is most often rooted in biology, or "essentialized," there has been over time increasing doubt as to whether biology alone is sufficient to identify a person as a parent. In the well-known New York case of *Thomas S. v Robin Y.*, sperm donor Thomas S. sought paternal rights and visitation with a lesbian couple's child, whom he had helped conceive and with whom he had had no contact until the child was five years old.[12] The lower appeals court judge rejected Thomas S.'s paternity claim, arguing that he had not acted as a parent throughout the child's life, as had the child's two lesbian mothers: "To Ry [the child], a parent is a person who a child depends on to care for her needs. To Ry, Thomas S. has never been a parent since he never took care of her on a daily basis. . . . In her family, there has been no father."[13] In an interview, the two mothers in this case commented, "We were forced to articulate at every step of the way what our family is, . . . [and] biology is not important in our family."[14] Ry herself has commented, "It's such a crazy idea because I *had* parents. I had my mothers and I didn't need another person."[15] Another judge, a veteran of family court, confirmed the notion that parenthood is not solely determined by genetics:

> You have these casual inseminators that disappear, and someone else steps in and raises the child even though there's no genetic tie, man or woman, and they become psychological parents. And the child recognizes them that way. They are parents. So that person should have every right and responsibility of a parent. . . . what does biology have to do with anything? Biology pales in comparison, relative to the psychological parent concept.[16]

Thus, the *Thomas S.* case and others like it suggested that parental identity cannot be biologically essentialized; rather, the acquisition of such an identity must be deliberate and proactive. This is one way in which the indeterminacy of law is implicated in the settling of such identities—if parenthood is socially rather than genetically defined, it must inevitably be subject to change in an ever-changing social world.

The same distinction is useful in discussing the nature and origins of sexual identity. The dispute over the etiology of sexual identity is complex and highly contested. The familiar "nature versus nurture" debate is politicized by the important social and legal consequences its answers have for LGBT communities, individuals, and their families. At stake in particular are two widely significant questions: first, Is homosexuality an "immutable," or born, trait such that it can be protected as a suspect status under equal protection doctrine and civil rights laws (like race)? and second, Is homosexuality socially learned or otherwise communicable, such that it may be transmitted from parents to their children? With regard to the first of these questions, the LGBT community has been hesitant to take a side in the debate because of the possibly troubling policy implications of either conclusion. The point has also been made that sexuality cannot be analogized to race or gender with regard to immutability because it must be *made* visible and therefore may be seen as mutable, or changeable, at least in outward appearance.

The issue is no more resolved in the legal arena. Courts—and often family courts in particular—have frequently been put in the position of debating how one's sexual identity is formed. As early as 1957, the Wolfenden Report, sponsored by the British government, argued that homosexuality was a "'state or condition' that cannot come under the purview of criminal law," while at the same time arguing that a purely biological explanation for its etiology would wrongly absolve these (gay) men of "responsibility" for their actions.[17] The implication of arguing that one is "born" into his or her sexual identity not only simplifies an irrefutably complex social and personal part of human existence but raises the specter of a potential genetic "cause" of alternative sexualities—itself a deeply troubling step toward possible eugenics implications. Yet to argue that sexuality is entirely a socially constructed or learned facet of personality may have the legal consequence of foreclosing on the possibility of adding sexual orientation as a "suspect status" (such as race or gender) to be protected constitutionally—and, as suggested by many of the cases discussed in this chapter, may invite personal criticisms and unrealistic expectations that individuals should be able to "control" or change their sexual identities at will.

The second question—whether homosexuality may be learned or transmitted from parent to child—is equally complex, problematic, and unresolved for both courts and scholars. In 16 percent (48) of the 316 custody and adoption cases since 1952, the judges discussed the possibility of a child's sexual orientation being affected by that of his or her parent(s). The process that this transmission might entail, however, has most often been left unarticulated by courts. Historically, homosexuality has been analogized, by conservative critics and some psychiatric professionals, to a contagious disease, which may infect children by some unspecified means.[18] But often in the legal arena judges and opposing litigants have asserted more specifically that this transmission of sexuality may happen in an active *or* a passive way: children might model the behaviors of their parents and learn their sexual identity, or parents may actively "recruit" their children by making conscious efforts to "convert" them to homosexuality. The primary difference between these explanations is in the level of intent—and therefore culpability—of the parents in contributing to their child's possible alternative sexuality. The second explanation—the "conversion" model—envisions homosexuality as a sort of cult recruiting membership. This model was evident in the Wyoming divorce case of *Hertzler v Hertzler*, in which Pamela Hertzler was accused of "immersing" her children into homosexuality: "the record is . . . replete with Pamela's intensive and unrelenting efforts to immerse the children in her alternative lifestyle, seemingly to the point of indoctrination."[19] Similarly, in *J.P. v P.W.* a Missouri gay father's visitation rights were restricted based on the perception that he had "advocated" his "lifestyle" to his children.[20] This ruling was made notwithstanding the fact that many parents and attorneys commented in interviews that expectations that a gay or lesbian parent—who has no doubt experienced significant stigma, exclusion, ridicule, legal difficulty, and possibly violence as a result of his or her sexual orientation— would want his or her children to experience the same were misdirected, if not absurd.

The first explanation for the transmission of homosexuality to children—the learning model—was less likely to implicate the parent in such "cultlike" behavior but nevertheless assumed that he or she was ultimately responsible as a sexual role model. As an attorney and former Lambda legal director explained,

> The role model concern is almost exclusively about "will the kids be gay?" Like, judges really believe, like most people, that children need strong heterosexual role models in order to be heterosexual. Never mind the sort of slipshod way in which we all say "well, most gay people, of course, don't have gay parents." And you can point that out and it does a bit, sometimes, with judges, "oh."[21]

In the divorce case of *Bennett v O'Rourke*, for example, the Tennessee appeals court revoked custody from lesbian mother Barbara Bennett, after it was discovered that she was in a live-in relationship with another woman. The court based its decision on the belief that her child would "model" her sexual behavior and become a lesbian:

> In light of the fact that here the homosexual parent and the minor child are both female, we consider this factor particularly important because of the increased chance of role-modeling. . . . Common sense dictates that a child should not be exposed to such an unhealthy attitude, especially without the consistent presence of a father to help counteract its ill effects.[22]

In response to such claims, a number of developmental and social psychologists have presented longitudinal evidence both in court and in scholarly forums that refutes the hypothesis that homosexuality is likely to "catch" from parent to child.[23] In addition, as suggested in interviews, many people have pointed out the flawed logic of assuming that gay children must derive from gay parents, since most of the gay parents who were studied or appeared in court were raised by heterosexual parents. As discussed in chapter 2, any evidence of difference between families headed by homosexuals and those headed by heterosexuals generally revealed differences in traits that would be seen as advantageous to the children of gay or lesbian parents, such as open-mindedness and self-assuredness.[24] Some litigants have successfully used this research to counter claims in court that their children will become homosexual as a result of their gaining or retaining custody or visitation. As early as 1985, justices in *S.N.E. v R.L.B.*, relying on the advice of sixteen expert witnesses, for the first time specifically rejected the notion that a child would "catch" homosexuality from his lesbian mother.[25] This was later confirmed by the Ohio court in *Conkel v Conkel*, which stated, "this court takes judicial notice that there is no consensus on what causes homosexuality, but there is substantial consensus among the experts that being raised by a homosexual parent does not increase the likelihood that a child will become homosexual."[26] This change was evident in interviews with judges as well; as one senior family court judge commented with only slight hesitancy,

> My guess, and it's only a guess, is that probably people are the way they are biologically or whatever other reason, very early in life, and I'm not as concerned or worried or thinking that someone by being a parent of a same-sex adoption or living arrangement is going to necessarily take on a particular sexual orientation.[27]

Another judge from a neighboring county claimed, with even more assuredness,

> I've never heard any expert in any court proceeding that I've ever conducted testify that you can change sexual orientation. . . . It's not a learned characteristic: either you are or you aren't. . . . I don't think it's a matter of choice. . . . I don't think you can teach someone to be a homosexual.[28]

Yet such evidence has not always been considered or accepted as relevant in judicial decisions, and the notion of homosexuality as a contagion continued to appear, though with much less frequency, in some judicial decisions well into the late twentieth century. As late as 1999, judges in the Tennessee divorce case of *Eldridge v Eldridge* reflected this line of reasoning in restricting lesbian mother Julie Eldridge's visitation rights based on "sexual orientation and behavior modeling issues."[29]

Negotiating Identities in Court

Beyond the debate over the origin and causes of sexual orientations, however, the process of being identified as homosexual in court is by no means one that should be taken for granted. Far from recognizing sexual identity's fluidity and potential for nuance, change, or inconsistency, judges and lawmakers have tended to see it as a set of fixed, exclusive categories. Bruce MacDougall notes the impact of the various identity labels applied to gay men and lesbians by the law:

> What flows from the use of the term "homosexual," in particular what assumptions are made, what stereotypes are applied once the label is assigned, is . . . significant. . . . Judges have been reasonably content to allow the consequences to be determined by stereotypes, on the whole negative and marginalized stereotypes, the content of which has not been defined by homosexuals.[30]

This labeling process is more than a passive acceptance of extant stereotypes regarding homosexuality, however. By affixing a particular label, depiction, or status, the law asserts discursive control over alternate sexual identities. In other words, the law must have a hand in defining identity in order to regulate nonnormative sexualities. The same determinations also act to regulate and determine family ties and such concepts as "harm" and "the best interest of the child." Thus, the ways that gay and lesbian parents respond to the imposition of these labels, and the process of give and take, action and reaction, and eventual change that ensues is consequential not only for their sexual identities but for how their parenthood and families are understood and treated in law.

The Legal Imposition and Negation of Identity

Undoubtedly, it would be presumptuous to assume that a court ruling would change one's self-image as a gay or lesbian parent. In fact, it is more likely that parents frame their *own* images and identities strategically in family court, as has been noted by historian Heinrich Hartog and others, in different contexts.[31] The court, however, does often impose legally consequential identities, either affirmatively or through negation, on the litigants before it, in both a symbolic and a practical sense. Perhaps the most blatant examples of this are those cases in which the judges, in their written decisions, explicitly denied or contradicted a person's own sexual self-image as he or she articulated it in court. Here, the appeals courts were literally charged with answering the blunt question, homosexual or not?—as happened in a handful of custody cases.[32] The most striking example of such an imposition of identity was evident in cases such as *Guinan v Guinan,* in which the mother involved in the litigation was assumed in the judicial narrative to be a lesbian, despite her denial.[33] Fifteen years later, such imposition was still evident in the case of *D.L. v R.B.L.,* in which a father was assumed to be bisexual based on the fact that he liked to spend time with his male friends and on his "attachment to more feminine-type articles of furniture."[34]

Sometimes, as in *D.L. v R.B.L.,* the imposition of a homosexual or bisexual identity on a person who did not claim such an identity for him- or herself was based on what was perceived to be gender nonnormative behavior or preferences. In most cases, however, it was based on the person's friendships and associations—or on rumors and pure conjecture on the part of relatives, friends, and former spouses. In other words, the imposition of homosexual identity by the court was likely to be the result of a person's friendship with a gay man or lesbian—or with anyone of the same sex with whom he or she spent a significant amount of time—in combination with the active imagination of other individuals and legal actors. Such was the case as early as 1956, in the New York case of *In re Mara,* in which the mother was assumed to be a lesbian based on "evidence of female homosexuality" between some of her friends and her roommate.[35] In fact, this is one trend that, although it does not account for a large number of cases, remained relatively unchanged in frequency in some parts of the country over time; nearly fifty years later, in 2003, in the case of *Taylor v Taylor,* lesbianism was imputed to an Arkansas mother over her denial because she had a lesbian roommate—a year after homosexual conduct was decriminalized in the state by the Arkansas Supreme Court.[36] By imposing a sexual identity in this way, the law was able to accomplish three things: impute sexual meaning to any aspect of a person's life (even one's furniture), regardless of the person's own experiential reality or personal imagination; reify social stereotypes about how gay men and lesbians act and how they relate to others—even in their absence; and redefine one of the most intimate facets of a person's identity against her or his will.

Beyond the basic question of whether someone was in actuality (or in perception) gay or lesbian, sexual identity has also been discussed and interpreted in more normative terms as a form of "deviance." This discussion of homosexuality as deviance took place in forty-two, or 13 percent, of the cases.[37] To be labeled as homosexual in the courtroom, it has often been observed, is to be labeled as "other."[38] As is often the case, this "otherizing" not only marks homosexual identity as nonnormative or unusual but also carries with it marginalization and, often, discrimination. Yet historically, the "otherizing" of homosexuality has taken a different and distinctly more judgmental tone than that of other marginalized identities such as racial minorities, women, and so on. More than just being identified as nonnormative, and often framed as a choice of behavior rather than a born trait, homosexuality has been treated in court alternatively as either pathological or immoral—or as having "pernicious" effects on children.[39] As noted in chapter 2, countless legal and social science scholars have enumerated and presented evidence to counter the multiple ways in which gay and lesbian parents have been assumed to be deviant—by virtue of either excessive promiscuity, a penchant for molesting children, psychological instability, or a desire to "convert" children to homosexuality.[40] Even after the declassification of homosexuality as a psychological disorder, the discourse of deviance was present, though admittedly increasingly rare, in custody decisions as late as 2002 in some states.

The practice of identifying gay men and lesbians as deviant has been, of course, consequential in determining whether they were fit parents. Judges have defined gay and lesbian parents' sexual identity over time as "sexual *dis*orientation"[41] (emphasis added), "abnormalcy,"[42] an "illness,"[43] and a "psychological disturbance."[44] As late as 2002, these types of references were found in the Alabama case of *Ex Parte H.H.*[45] This custody dispute, involving a lesbian mother postdivorce, subsequently gained attention because of the notoriety of Alabama Supreme Court Justice Roy Moore, who was later reprimanded and removed from the bench over an insistence that the Ten Commandments be displayed prominently in the courtroom. Justice Moore, in his concurring opinion in *Ex Parte H.H.*, referred to the lesbian mother's homosexuality as "abhorrent, immoral, detestable, a crime against nature, and a violation of the laws of nature and of nature's God upon which this Nation and our laws are predicated. . . . It is an inherent evil against which children must be protected."[46] These descriptors serve the dual function of justifying the removal of custody from a gay or lesbian parent and also illustrating what a "good parent," in contrast, should be. In 111 cases (37 percent), however, the parents submitted social scientific data and/or expert testimony aimed at supporting their self-representations as healthy and nondeviant. These efforts were met with inconsistent success.[47] In at least one case the court threatened to impose further visitation restrictions on a father if he continued to teach his children that his homosexuality was not immoral: "If the father persists in his vehement espousal to the child of the 'desirability' of his chosen lifestyle . . . the authorities would support even greater restrictions upon his rights of visitation."[48]

In some situations, the departure between the sexual and parental identities attributed (or denied) to LGBT parents and the identities claimed by the individuals themselves took the form of emphasizing traits that the parents themselves did not see as dominant in their identity. Tennessee mother Beverly Collins, whose custody was revoked on the basis of her lesbianism, commented, "I think the court thought they were protecting [my child] from a gay mother—how awful! But, if they had listened to all the facts in the proceedings, the part about being gay was so little compared to all my other qualities." She went on to say,

> The bond my daughter and I had meant nothing. . . . The fact that my daughter did not want to leave her mother meant nothing. Her father's terrible track record meant nothing. All that mattered was that I was a lesbian and he was straight. . . . [My daughter] was forgotten. . . . The only thing that was important was that I was gay.[49]

In this situation the mother experienced a disconnect between her reality and the law's depiction of her not because the law said she was something that she was not but because it essentialized one part of her personhood—her homosexuality—in a way that was not true to her experience. This is one example of how individuals' own self-conceived identity can differ markedly from their official position or identity in law.

Yet, just as the evolution of nearly any type of law can be seen as an incremental "settling," the eventual shaping of certain distinct facets of sexual and familial identity—which although perhaps not conforming strictly to the parents' self-definition, eventually moved toward a closer alignment with them—is apparent in the custody cases as well.[50] One example of this process is the judges' treatment of same-sex romantic relationships. Particularly in pre-1990s custody decisions, the existence of a same-sex partner[51] for anyone involved in a child custody suit primarily functioned as "ammunition" for the opposing party in the custody battle or, at the very least, as fodder for gossip. In 1984's *Wolff v Wolff*, for example, bisexual father Robert Wolff in South Dakota was rumored to have slept with a teenage male babysitter, an assertion that he adamantly denied.[52] Evidence of such relationships was most likely, as in Mr. Wolff's case, to be presented in an accusatory form, putting the target of the accusation on the defensive. Faced with such allegations in court, a gay or lesbian parent would be forced to either reveal the relationship if one existed—with the potential that this revelation would effectively foreclose her or his chances for custody—or deny its existence. As the founder of NCLR recalled, "initially it was just about having the guts to stand up and not being afraid if someone said the word 'lesbian.'"[53] In one early California case, *Immerman v Immerman* in 1959, custody was revoked from a mother (who was not previously identified as a lesbian) after her former husband entered her home unannounced and found her engaging in sexual activity with another woman.[54] In another, later case in South Carolina, *Henry v Henry* (1988), a lesbian mother was forced to move out of the home that she shared with her partner and relinquish contact with her as a condition of partial custody rights—a condition typical of divorce-based custody cases up to that time.[55]

This dynamic shifted, however, in the late 1980s and early 1990s, as a tacit recognition of same-sex relationships became more common. By the 1990s, the relational identity of same-sex partners had evolved somewhat, at least, from a near-uniformly deviant status to a conditionally accepted social phenomenon in family law. As Lambda's legal director at the time commented, "these cases really . . . require the court to move beyond concerns about . . . stability of gay and lesbian relationships and instead focus on what people should focus on, which is the parent-child relationship."[56] This change is evident in the contrast between the earlier cases cited in this chapter and later cases in the 1990s and early twenty-first century—particularly with the rise in cases in which both members of a same-sex couple were litigants, when judges were forced to confront the reality that no matter which party was victorious, the child would be raised by a homosexual parent.

Similarly, the declining impact of homosexuality as an accusation of impropriety in court marks a contemporaneous negotiation of, and change in, the normative evaluation of gay and lesbian parents' sexual identity over time. Although many judges would still fall far short of embracing the homosexuality of a parent or even treating it as a nonissue in custody matters, it is no longer as likely to be referenced as *per se* evidence of pathology or moral unfitness.[57] As one Southern California judge commented in an interview, "I don't believe there's anything in the law that tells me that as a matter of law, a gay relationship, a child being raised in a gay home is, that in and of itself is detrimental to the child."[58] This is quite obviously a change that is not only evident in family court; myriad legal, social, representational, and epistemological factors—too numerous to list—are clearly implicated in the changing perceptions and normative treatment of homosexuality. But a subtler feature of this progression and its impact on the shaping of gay and lesbian parents' identity is evinced in the narratives of the cases. Whereas in earlier cases gay and lesbian parents were forced into a posture of defensiveness, denial, or apology when confronted in court with their sexuality, an expanded range of possible responses and representations was negotiated over time. Even in the face of overtly hostile judges, parents in the post-1980s era were more likely to assert their sexual identities in court and in their social lives (as evidenced in court) without apology or reticence.

The 1995 Louisiana case of *Scott v Scott* typifies this tendency: mother Robin Scott and her lesbian partner, Karri, were open about their relationship, both at home with the children and in court; when asked about the openness of their relationship, Karri "admitted that while she and Robin do not broadcast the nature of their relationship, they do not hide it. Karri further admitted that the boys [Robin's sons] understand that she is their mother's 'girlfriend.'" Robin also added, "the only affection we would display [in front of the children] would be what we would be unashamed to display in anyone's presence."[59] The fact that Karri and Robin were so open about their relationship—at a time when same-sex sodomy was still against the law in Louisiana—is telling of LGBT parents' increased confidence and greater visibility in court. Their honesty was not without consequence, however, as custody of the two boys was revoked from Robin and given to her ex-husband, Robert. In fact, litigants who did present themselves as "out" gay or lesbian parents were less than half as likely overall to prevail in court and retain custody of their children. These numbers, however, shifted dramatically in the post-1990 era. Before 1990, less that 20 percent of gay and lesbian parents who presented an "out" identity in court were successful. After 1990, this proportion rose to close to 50 percent success, and in cases from 2000 to 2004, two-thirds of these out gay and lesbian parents were victorious. In fact, in a handful of cases, such as *Collins v Collins*, gay and lesbian

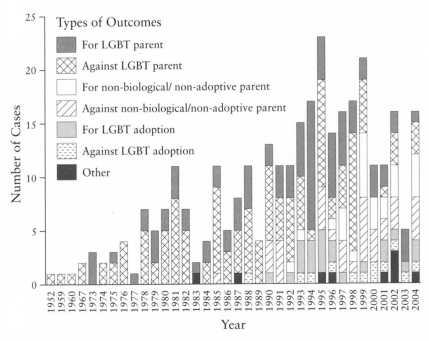

Types of Case Outcomes by Year

parents in relationships were criticized for *not* showing appropriate and honest affection to their partners in front of the children.[60] Such cases resulted in longstanding conflicts in which, eventually, the court began to accept litigants' self-asserted parental and sexual identities.

Negotiating Family and Parental Identity

Sexual identity has not been the only type of identity that has been shaped and negotiated in gay and lesbian parents' child custody cases, of course; these parents' familial identity—as parent, spouse, and so forth—was also at issue in these cases. In Barbara Yngvesson's autoethnographic account of open adoptions, she discusses the process of being defined as either a "real" or an "illegal" parent.[61] The adoptive family, like other nontraditional family forms, is particularly vulnerable to the powers of the law to disrupt and redefine the identities of its members. Because it does not fit within the archetypal framework of "family" assumed by the law—consisting of one parent of each gender who are married and whose children who are biologically related to them—an element of instability is introduced when such familial entities encounter the law. In such cases, in which the actors do not fit into the set of presumed traditional gendered family roles, judges must either create new meaning and new legal categories or stretch the existing categories, forcing nontraditional families into traditional categories—to the exclusion of those for whom the judges cannot find a fit. These labels—or the lack thereof—make evident the court's grappling with the growth of new social identities that lack preexisting correlates in law. These categorizations, in turn, are crucial in the process of shaping and defining the familial identity of the legal actors involved.

Efforts to accommodate the existence of LGBT families have necessitated a recognition of the many ways that courts can define what a family is and who its members are. In 39 percent of the cases (123), there was substantial discussion of how "parent" and "family" are defined. Several judges discussed this issue in interviews as well; as one judge from Southern California commented, "I guess it's rather . . . it's a hard thing to put your finger on when an adult living in a home is acting in a parental way."[62] The question of what constitutes a parent has been at the core of LGBT family law for much of the 1990s and early twenty-first century. That such a fundamental question remains up for debate in many instances speaks to the uniquely indeterminate nature of family law. Familial identity is also unique in that it is a necessarily *relational* status—in other words, it must by definition involve more than one person. Even in cases in which a judge does not consider an individual to be a parent, the individual must still be named in a way that identifies his or her relationship to the other members of the family—whether it is as the "lover" of the other parent, the caretaker of the child, or even a "third party."

Furthermore, these determinations are not merely symbolic. In imposing or denying familial identities, the court can both figuratively and literally dictate a change in the character of one's relationship with one's partner and child(ren). This has been most likely to happen in families that originated outside the context of heterosexual marriage and blood relations, such as those involving a lesbian couple and their children by donor insemination. In all, between 1952 and 2004 there were thirty-five cases involving proposed second-parent or dual adoptions and fifty-six cases involving one gay/lesbian parent against another.[63] In thirty-three of the fifty-six cases involving a split between two gay/lesbian parents, the judges rendered the nonbiological mother a *non*parent, or "legal stranger," by asserting the claim that she had no natural or legal link to the child. Before the year 2000, only seven (of twenty-seven) nonbiological parents were recognized as parents or quasi-parental figures. This is largely due to the legal assumption (especially prior to 2000), discussed in chapter 2, that a child could not have two parents of the same gender.

Thus, most legal formulations of parenthood, though often vaguely defined, have historically been interpreted by judges in a way that has made it difficult, if not impossible, to recognize the parental status of nonbiological lesbian mothers on equal footing with their partners or former partners, the biological mothers—even after the biological mother's death. In the two cases discussed in chapter 1, *McGuffin v Overton* and *Matter of Guardianship of Astonn H.*, the surviving mother in a lesbian couple fought to define herself as a parent for the purpose of retaining custody of her child after the biological mother's death.[64] In the former case, in Michigan, where Leigh McGuffin in her will and power-of-attorney documents had designated her partner, Carol Porter, as guardian of the children, custody was instead given to the biological father, whom the children had never met prior to McGuffin's untimely death. This decision was based on the legal determination that Carol, who had cared for the children their whole lives, was related to them neither by marriage nor by blood and was therefore a "legal stranger." The fact that *Astonn H.*, decided only four days later in New York, resulted in the opposite determination, despite nearly identical fact patterns, is testament to the indeterminacy governing family law and determinations of parenthood, as well as the double-edged nature of this indeterminacy.[65]

More typical than these cases, however, are cases such as *In re Custody of H.S.H.-K.* in Wisconsin, in which nonbiological mother Sandra Holtzman faced her former partner, biological mother Elsbeth Knott, in a custody and visitation battle and enumerated the traditional parental duties she had fulfilled during the child's upbringing,[66] or second-parent adoption cases such as *In re Adoption of Baby Z.*, a groundbreaking case involving the right of the nonbiological mother in a lesbian couple to legally adopt the child, wherein both mothers sought to present the nonbiological mother as an equal participant in deciding to have a child and in the child-rearing process.[67] In the latter case, the Superior Court of Connecticut recognized that second parent Malinda had "shared all emotional, financial, and other parenting responsibilities for Baby Z.," but because the adoption board refused to waive the requirement that biological mother Anne's legal rights be terminated in order to allow

Malinda to adopt, in 1999 the Connecticut Supreme Court ultimately refused to recognize her as a parent or potential parent. The disposition in these cases shows how someone who was identified for years by herself and others as a mother could, at the end of a custody trial, emerge as a "third party" or even "legal stranger." Someone who had a solid parental bond with her child could be renamed as a "lover" or "friend" of the "real" mother, so that, as a result, her identity was defined only in relation to her partner and not by virtue of her connection to her child. As the nonbiological mother in the case of *Liston v Pyles*, Marla Liston, explained in an interview, "because I had no legal connection to Tammy [the biological mother] because I had never married her, which of course, we all know in the United States, you cannot do, and because I had no blood . . . relation to either Tammy or [her son], I had no legal standing as a parent."[68] One attorney and family law scholar further commented that by making such determinations, courts "are narrowing then who can legitimately be seen as primary family from the child's point of view in narrowing it to people who are married to each other or registered domestic partners."[69]

Judges who were interviewed, though ambivalent about the recourse of such parties, were cognizant of the fundamental problem that this lack of recognition posed. As one supervising judge in Southern California commented,

> When the ultimate expectation of being together—they are partner for each other and for the child—and that expectation is no longer realized and that relationship breaks up, the fall-out of that can be very severe for people that are not in a heterosexual relationship that are married and protected by the laws.[70]

She later added,

> these kinds of issues . . . ultimately relate to the very personal question of, if you and your partner break up, are you no longer a parent and more important than that, is that child now permanently deprived of a bonded relationship with a significant, responsible, loving adult? If the answer to that is "yes, that's what's going to happen," that's a heck of an answer.[71]

Yet judges almost unilaterally agreed that this, indeed, was the answer. One relatively new Northern California judge stated with certainty,

"Under the law, there's no standing [for the nonbiological mother]. It is a huge impediment. . . . I think that legally there is no . . . legally I would be very uncomfortable enforcing it [regarding visitation rights]."[72] Another moderately experienced judge, in Illinois, expressed a typically sympathetic but clear resolve: "it becomes a great problem because I'm bound to act according to the law and according to the law, the nonbiological parent has no rights to that child, although morally or ethically you would think they would because they helped raise the child, . . . but as a judge, I have to follow the law."[73]

Several cases exhibited this rationale. In the first case to be decided at a state's highest court dealing with visitation or parental rights for the nonbiological mother in a lesbian-headed family, the New York case of *Alison D. v Virginia M.*—a case that, according to one of the attorneys who tried it, "was brought precisely to broaden the legal concept of parenthood"—the nonbiological mother in the breakup was referenced in court only as the "woman who had a live-in relationship with the child's mother."[74] This was despite the fact that she had raised the children since birth and that the children bore her last name and referred to her as "mommy." Similarly, in the California case of *West v Superior Court*, the judges denied nonbiological mother Pamela Lockrem standing to seek visitation with the daughter the couple had had by donor insemination and confirmed biological mother Barbara West's contention that her former partner did not have the right to "drag" her—the child's only "natural" mother—to court.[75] In reference to these cases and others, NCLR director Kate Kendell commented,

> it doesn't matter if this child looks at his family and says, "I have two moms." . . . you could cut this person out of his life forever based on these legal formulations about whether or not she's got an adoption decree and was the biological parent. And it is unconscionable that the states and courts allow that to happen. It is mind-boggling and it is a travesty.[76]

In the California case of *Kathleen C. v Lisa W.*, the judge came one step closer to a recognition of the status of nonbiological parents in holding that nonbiological mother Kathleen Crandall might have been considered a *de facto* parent were she still living with her former partner but that she subsequently lost her parental status once she was no longer cohabitating with the child's biological mother:

although appellant exhibited the characteristics of a de facto parent during her relationship with respondent, absent any legislative or case authority granting a *nonparent* visitation rights over the objection of the biological parent . . . we cannot grant those rights here. (emphasis added)[77]

Many sympathetic judges noted that this problem could be avoided through official adoption, which, once finalized, tends to be legally binding.[78] Paradoxically, however, judges denied over a third of all second-parent adoptions nationally, based on the lack of an official, legal, or institutionally defined relationship between the couple. As discussed previously, most states have an implicit rule suggesting that the court can only recognize one parent of each gender. This often leads to an exercise in absurdity, such that the nonbiological parent can be recognized as a parent only if the biological mother's parental rights are terminated. Since the only way to circumvent this rule is via the "stepparent exception" (whereby in the event of a parent's remarriage, his or her new spouse can legally adopt the children), the issue becomes one of whether the relationship between the two parents can be defined as a marriage. In most such cases, especially given the political and social fervor against same-sex marriage, the judges were not willing to define same-sex couples as spouses for the purpose of allowing a ruling analogous to a stepparent adoption.[79] As one family court judge noted in an interview,

> you cannot allow a stepparent adoption because there is no marriage. The only way you can accomplish what the parties want is for the biological parent to give up and relinquish all parental rights on that child and to allow the partner to do a single-parent adoption and it's legal.[80]

This problem of the absence of legal marriage was evident in the appellate courts as well, particularly in the 1990s during the height of the gayby boom. Although adoption is the area of family law most defined and regulated by statute, these statutes were not originally written in anticipation of reproductive technology and the rise of gay- and lesbian-headed families, or even of same-sex relationships more generally. Therefore, because adoption statutes' second-parent adoption provisions usually assumed a stepparent situation, the lack of same-sex marriage rights are necessarily implicated. In the Wisconsin second-parent adoption case of *In the Interest of Angel Lace M.*, for example, in which the two mothers proposed a joint adoption of one mother's biological child, the court found that

[s]ince Wisconsin does not recognize same-sex marriages, [the] woman who cohabitated with the child's mother and who shared equally in raising [the] child was not [the] child's stepparent, even though the woman and the child's mother symbolically solemnized their commitment to each other by partaking in [a] *marriage-like* ceremony. (emphasis added)[81]

Similarly, one very experienced California judge commented, "I can't get past the fact that in order to be a stepparent you have to be in a recognizable marriage."[82] He went on to say that to allow such an adoption would be to "ignore the law." Thus, although in certain instances the judges redefined a family member to exist only by virtue of her or his romantic relationship, they were generally not willing to recognize this relationship as a permanent or official bond. Again, the effect of this was threefold: it removed the second parent's identity as a parent, defined her or him out of possible contention for custody, and potentially reinscribed extant stereotypes about the impermanence of homosexual relationships.

Over time, however, the possibility of a normalized same-sex "domestic partner" identity, in many cases socially if not legally analogous to a spousal identity, has been created in many states' family courts, such that it has become much more possible for two parents of the same sex to be legally connected to their children simultaneously, even if not equally so. In fact, one of the most dramatic shifts in family law has been the gradual legal conferral of parental status to nonbiological parents—most often lesbians—in same-sex parenting relationships. Prior to 2000, over 70 percent of cases involving a nonbiological parent were decided against her.[83] In the period after 1999, however, the shift in this pattern became quite distinct: only 36 percent of these cases were decided against the nonbiological parent. By the end of 2004, the number of successful nonbiological parents had quadrupled. This shift was foreshadowed by earlier cases such as *J.A.L. v E.P.H.* in 1996, in Pennsylvania, in which the justices overturned a lower court's decision that a nonbiological mother did not have standing to pursue custody of her children after her relationship with the biological mother ended, and found that she stood *in loco parentis* based on her membership in this "nontraditional family."[84] As Ohio mother Marla Liston noted in an interview,

Clearly, all across the nation, courts are looking at families and saying, you know, "families don't just consist of a married man and woman who

decide to biologically have children." . . . We simply do not live in that narrow, constricted viewpoint of what makes up a nuclear family. . . . The fact
that we no longer live in a society of nuclear families, the court system has
to change to address that.[85]

Although such a contrast to earlier times and cases may have the
effect of eclipsing fifty years of give-and-take struggle and negotiation,
it should be clear that this was a tentative, gradual, and hard-fought
change. As NCLR's founder, now a judge in San Francisco, commented,

Those [the first lesbian co-parent cases] were pretty devastating, but we
weren't surprised by the outcome in court because the courts were in no
way prepared to deal with these issues. I mean, judges hadn't been educated on these issues. They didn't see these as legitimate families. They didn't
see co-parents as truly psychological nurturing parents.[86]

Faced with more and more of these cases over the course of the gayby
boom, however, and through the rise of both legal advocacy organizations for LGBT parents and social scientific evidence refuting common
myths about their effects on children, judges' understandings of planned
gay and lesbian families shifted to greater acceptance, if not endorsement—and this recognition and acceptance is increasingly reflected in
judicial decisions.

Moreover, by the early twenty-first century, a number of states, either
by legislative action or court decision, began to take explicit steps to
acknowledge second-parent adoption as a legal means of recognizing
two parents of the same sex, an innovation that had been easing into
family law between the lines and under the radar for nearly twenty years.
As early as 1996 in New York, for example, the justices acknowledged
that "Courts have long construed statutes to meet the changing needs
of our growing society, . . . [and] the concept of 'family' has expanded,"
as they granted the adoption in question.[87] Eight years later, the Indiana
Supreme Court aptly illustrated the means for making this shift possible
in the case of *In re Parentage of A.B.*: "there is no Indiana precedent supporting [the nonbiological mother's] request and a search for the public policy of this state which might provides guidance provides no clear
path," yet "[t]he Court is also sufficiently prescient to anticipate that the
law will have to extend some form of recognition to gay and lesbian
relationships to create a structure within which a myriad of legal issues

emanating from such partnerships may be resolved." It went on to say, "Case law and commentary on the subject detail the years of litigation spent in settling these difficult issues while the children remain in limbo, sometimes denied the affection of a 'parent' who has been with them since birth."[88] Thus, the courts have begun to admit openly the ability— and even need—for law to stretch the boundaries of who is considered a "parent" because of the absence of any specific guidance or preconceived remedy for same-sex couples in most states' adoption laws.

In this regard, case law in California in the first five years of the twenty-first century was particularly noteworthy. In 2000, a case was brought to the San Diego court, wherein biological lesbian mother Sharon S., who had consented to and begun the process of second-parent adoption with her partner, Annette F., but broke up with Annette before its completion, sought to block the adoption by arguing that the procedure was not legal under California law. In the explicit sense, she was correct: even though many judges in California had been performing second-parent adoptions "under the table" for several years by then, much like in Indiana, there was no formal statute or ruling either allowing or prohibiting them. After losing in the trial court, though, Sharon won an appeal in 2001, essentially arguing that second-parent adoption was not a legal procedure since, unlike heterosexual couples, lesbians and gay men could not marry at that time and therefore could not be analogized to "stepparents"—an analogy that had provided the model, as discussed previously, for second-parent adoptions up to then—and therefore, her former partner was a "legal stranger" who had no right to adopt the child without her consent.[89] The Court of Appeals went so far as to suggest that this precedent might be retroactively enforced such that even *past* second-parent adoptions might be null and void, thus rendering as nonparents even those who were *already* attributed a parental identity.

Annette, the nonbiological mother, then appealed the case to the California Supreme Court in *Sharon S. v Superior Court*. Noting that second-parent adoption, despite its lack of specific legal provision, had become an accepted and even routine way to confer parental identity, the justices ruled that the fact that "[second-parent] adoption procedures . . . have received such widespread acceptance and have been so widely used speaks not only to their utility in the modern context, but to their effectiveness" in maintaining family bonds and aligning nonbiological parents' legal identity with their social identity as parents.[90] Thus, both the ambiguity of California's existing law regarding alternate family forms *and* the resultant years of open interpretation by judges across the state eventually justified and facilitated, for the first time, a formal legal recognition of planned lesbian families in California.[91]

The next wave of litigation in California pushed the boundaries of parental identity and legal innovation further. By the twenty-first century, lesbian parents—spurred by the courts' past reduction of parenthood to biology—had found a way to innovate using reproductive technology and attain biological connection between the child and *both* parents, by implanting the ova of one partner into the uterus of the other. In 2004, one such case, *K.M. v E.G.*, reached California's appellate courts.[92]

K.M. donated her eggs to be inseminated by an anonymous donor and implanted in her partner, E.G., and E.G. subsequently gave birth to a child who was genetically related to K.M. but for whom E.G. was considered the "birth mother" on the birth certificate. Now, even the identification of what constituted a *biological* parent was destabilized and at question. The Court of Appeals ruled that only the "gestational" mother (who gave birth) was in fact a mother and identified the "genetic mother" as an "egg donor," rather than a parent. This in itself demonstrates the indeterminacy of family law because it suggested, in contrast to prior cases, that genetics did not determine parenthood. Ultimately, the case was appealed to the California Supreme Court, which again faced with an issue of parenthood not settled in law, demonstrated the progressive turn toward expanded definitions of parenthood by overturning the appeals court's decision and recognizing both parties as "natural" mothers—a first in American family law and to date anomalous. Yet, in a simultaneous decision, the California Supreme Court extended parental recognition to even those parents who were neither biologically related in *any* sense nor officially related by adoption to the child at the time of the split but who had *acted* as a parent throughout the child's life and had claimed the child as their own.[93]

The Negotiation of Identity:
Reciprocal Processes and Discursive Compromises

The California courts thus demonstrated their willingness to define parenthood as the members of the family in question did, but this was not always the case. Perhaps it should not be surprising that the self-representations of litigants were sometimes directly contradicted by the judicially imposed identities they acquired in court. The tensions, struggles, and negotiations that resulted from these contradictions not only illus-trate in vivid form the process of ascribing parental and sexual identity in law but also mark a newly understood and strategically forged terrain in which once mutually exclusive or contradictory statuses could be rec-onciled, and new parental identities created, due to the flexibility in fam-ily law to give new meanings to existing relationships and identities. This interplay was apparent in moments of negotiation, or in intermediary solutions, when both the law (represented by judges' decisions) and the individual litigants left their mark on the eventual settling of the identi-ties in question. These negotiations happened in a number of ways, both spoken and unspoken.

One particularly interesting site of identity negotiation, though admit-tedly rare, was in cases involving transsexual or transgender parents. In these cases not only the identity of "parent" but those of "man" or "woman" were at stake. Because these were most often cases of first impression in the particular jurisdiction, this area of law was particularly ambiguous and unsettled. An instructive example is the case of *Karin T. v Michael T.* Michael T., a transvestite who was genetically and ana-tomically female, married Karin T. and assumed the role of her husband. Karin was subsequently donor-inseminated so that the two could have a child. Upon the child's birth, Michael signed the child's birth certifi-cate in the space provided for "father" and assumed responsibility as the child's father. When the couple broke up, Karin attempted to nullify the marriage and argued that Michael should not be recognized legally as the child's father since Michael was not actually a man. Instead, how-ever, the court adopted a social constructionist approach and found that since Michael T. had signed the birth certificate and acted as both hus-band and father for the duration of the family's existence, (s)he should be considered a legal parent to the child, "in view of [the] agreement to which respondent affixed her signature as father which stated that the children produced by artificial insemination were respondent's own legitimate children."[94]

This gesture seemed remarkably progressive for a court of the mid-1980s, but because of the unique circumstances surrounding this case, and the indeterminacy involved in such legal questions, its impact on other custody contests between same-sex parents was limited.[95] In fact, family courts did not recognize two parents of the same biological sex again until 1992.[96] Moreover, when courts were confronted with cus-tody cases involving transsexual and transgender parents in subsequent cases, the rulings were generally against those parents. In a case the following year in Nevada, in fact, a transsexual father's parental rights were completely terminated based on the sex change—an unusually extreme measure in modern family law.[97] Over a decade later, in 2004, an appeals court in Florida voided the marriage of transsexual father Michael Kantaras to his former wife, Linda, and rescinded custody because the judges determined that Michael was still genetically (if not anatomically or socially) female at the time of the marriage.[98]

In the previously cited California case of *Kathleen C. v Lisa W.,* although ultimately the court ruled that Kathleen did not have standing to assert parental rights, elements of a different sort of negotiation and arbitration were present in the justices' rationale. Although it may be practically or emotionally untenable for a couple to continue to live together after a rather contentious split, as was the case here, the fact that the court considered Kathleen, a nonbiological lesbian mother, to be a *de facto* parent prior to her move out of the family home when her relationship with Lisa (the biological mother) ended was evidence of the inroads nontraditional families had made in asserting their legal existence. In this instance, Kathleen's self-identification as a mother, her children's recognition of her as their mother, and the community's recognition of her parenthood were confronted with the law's ideal of the heterosexual family, and a sort of legal compromise resulted whereby she was recognized—although fleetingly and retrospectively—as a parental figure.[99]

In another case, *In re Price v Price*, the court issued yet a different type of compromise. In response to the allegation by a divorcing father that the children may be harmed by exposure to their lesbian mother's sex life if she retained partial custody, the court decided to restrict the sexual activity of *both* parents when the children were residing with them:

> We make no moral judgments concerning Mother's lifestyle as it applies to her and her friends. However, we cannot disregard a parent's activity that may have an impact in the developmental stage of a child's life. We feel it is unacceptable to subject children to any course of conduct that might signify approval of any illicit conduct whether it be between homosexuals or heterosexuals.[100]

Attorney Kate Kendell recognized such provisions as a common sort of judicial device:

Cohabitation is often used by courts—heterosexual and gay cohabitation is often used by courts to deny custody on "moral" grounds. Even when the court is pretending it has nothing to do with sexual orientation, they'll use the heterosexual cohabitation cases to say it's just not good modeling for the children to see this person living with another adult in a romantic and sexual relationship.[101]

Thus, instead of accepting wholesale the mother's assertion of self in which her sexual identity was unproblematic, the court located a conciliatory gesture by which it could find the mother and father to be equally suitable parents yet still define her lesbian existence as not entirely acceptable.[102]

The negotiation of identity in court has also often been a function of the law's ability to protect a group, serving its interests and conferring on it certain rights while simultaneously infringing on its powers of self-definition and self-determination.[103] One common theme in the denial of a parent's custody rights, discussed previously, has been the assertion that a gay or lesbian parent might taint the sexual development of her or his child and effectively turn the child homosexual. When social scientific studies that refuted this hypothesis began to emerge in the 1980s, their impact on negotiations of sexual identity in court was complex. Whereas some judges chose to ignore or deny the validity of these findings, others accepted and even embraced this evidence in defense of gay and lesbian parents' custodial rights. In one well-cited Alaska divorce case, *S.N.E. v R.L.B*, the judges rejected the claim that the children's contact with their mother would turn them homosexual, asserting that

> there is no suggestion that this [the mother's lesbianism] has or is likely to affect the child adversely. The record contains evidence showing that the child's development to date has been excellent . . . and that there is no increased likelihood that a male child raised by a lesbian would be homosexual.[104]

Yet this judicial strategy—denial of the gayness-as-contagion hypothesis—can be a double-edged sword. Although its manifest intent and immediate effect has been to allow gay men and lesbians to retain or gain custody and adoption rights in their individual cases, the latent effect has been a reification of the belief that a homosexual identity is inherently problematic. Implicit in the defensive claim that exposure to a gay or lesbian parent will not influence a child to become gay or lesbian is the assumption that such a result is undesirable and in fact would constitute "harm" to the child. So, although *S.N.E. v R.L.B.* was lauded as a victory for gay and lesbian parents' rights, it was premised on the fact that the judges were able to neutralize the perceived threat of what was considered an adverse effect on the child's sexual identity. Similarly, in *Matter of Adoption of Child by J.M.G.*, the judges allowed a second-parent adoption by refuting the proposition that having two lesbian parents would be harmful to the child's "*normal* sexual development" (emphasis added).[105] By premising the decision in this way, the court found a way to affirm the person's self-asserted parental identity while still retaining symbolic control over his or her sexual identity, defining it as abnormal, or at least less desirable. These decisions demonstrated negotiation in the ability of law to simultaneously represent a marginal group's interests while concurrently redefining or finding problematic the group's defining characteristic.

Attorneys specializing in LGBT custody had some other notions of the types of ideological sacrifices that are made when arguing these cases. One common example was the use of the nexus test, which, as discussed in chapter 2, states that in order to deprive a lesbian or gay parent custody on the grounds of sexual orientation, it must be proven that some sort of nexus exists between that sexual orientation and harm to the child. This was hailed as a positive development when it was formulated in 1967 and has been cited religiously by LGBT parents' attorneys, and many judges, in the years since. Yet, upon deeper reflection, many gay and lesbian activists, parents, and attorneys felt that any legal argument that began with the presumption that homosexuality might cause harm was symbolically and ideologically damaging to the LGBT community. As one attorney who has been trying these cases since the 1970s stated,

> we shouldn't be advocating the nexus test; we should be advocating a position that a parent's sexual orientation is *always* irrelevant in a custody dispute. My very short riff on the difference between those two is that as I've read the cases, even the ones who win, if there's any adverse impact on the child, it isn't the parent's sexual orientation that produces the adverse impact. It's something else, which is what it ought to be called. . . . basically I've come to think that any argument that suggests that a parent's sexual orientation could have an adverse impact on a child is missing the point, . . . [and] that has been the strategy we've considered a success for

the last twenty-five years, including me. The cases go down as solid victory if we get that test and if we get a court to apply it. . . . So, you know, it's hard to abandon something that has brought quite a bit of success. . . . But you can read a dozen of the best opinions we've ever had where the gay or lesbian parent wins . . . and still not get any rhetoric that says, "Hey, gay people are a part of life, like, not a big deal that they raise children" or "Gay people have something positive and unique to offer in a culturally pluralistic society." Nothing.[106]

Thus, for attorneys and parents alike, the possibility of sacrificing fidelity to their own ideologies, feelings, and experiences in return for formal legal conferrals of rights was an oft-present dilemma but an inevitable facet of the negotiations attendant to gradual changes in familial and sexual identity.

Similarly, in some situations, parents' representation in court was not consistent with their own images of their family because a particular contrary portrait was more functionally expedient for the legal purposes at hand. A primary example is the use of the "stepparent exception" rule discussed earlier, used in order to persuade the court to allow two parents of the same sex to be recognized as parents. At the time when same-sex second-parent adoptions began coming to court, this was the closest analogy and most relevant legal precedent on which to draw. As one of the first attorneys to work in this area of law commented, "In second parent adoptions, I've kind of thought that whatever theory looks like it will be best in terms of how that particular statute is written and the predilection of those judges in other cases ought to fly. If the stepparent analogy works that's fine."[107] In terms of the families' lived experience, however, it was a problematic analogy. One attorney and lesbian mother from New York explained that the adoptive parents in these situations "were different from stepparents in that they had together decided to have the child in the first place, which seemed like a semantic difference, but . . . when you represent people at this level, you want to make sure you are representing the population in the way that you want them understood."[108] Indeed, this distinction is important not only in the fact that gay parents cannot legally marry each other but also in that the title "stepparent" assumes a person who entered the family at a later date through marriage, not someone who was involved in the family from the beginning and was part of the actual decision to have a child.

In another case, in which two men in New Jersey decided to adopt a child together, state law did not allow them to adopt jointly, so the state arbitrarily chose one of the fathers as the "official" adoptive parent. As it happened, the father that the state chose, Michael, was not the father that the couple decided would act as primary caretaker, and in fact, the other parent, Jon—who would have no parental rights under the court's scheme—had already quit his job in order to stay home with the child. The attorney who represented Jon and Michael explained,

> New Jersey just picked one of the two of them to be the [adoptive] parent and picked Michael, not the person who was staying home, because Jon doesn't have an income. And so, for their paper work, they wanted the adoptive parent to have an income. . . . A lot of it was the symbolism of why can't this couple adopt together.[109]

After a protracted legal battle, the couple was eventually allowed to jointly adopt, but the court's orientation to them as parents stood in stark contrast to their own self-image as a family. These scenarios represented situations in which an ostensibly positive legal outcome (permitting the adoptions at all) could be attained at the cost of having a negative symbolic outcome for LGBT parents, in which they were forced into legal roles that did not represent their reality or self-perceived identity.

Negotiations were also apparent in cases in which a gay or lesbian parent's rights were conditioned on his or her not acting overtly "out" or making known his or her sexual orientation—what was often, in the judicial narratives, called "flaunting." In one case, a lesbian mother was accused of "flagrantly flaunting her relationship with [her partner] in the presence of the minor child."[110] Conversely, in the New York case of *M.A.B. v R.B.*, a gay father was rewarded with custody of one of his children for not having "flaunted" his homosexuality and because his "behavior has been discreet, not flamboyant."[111] Thus, a space of compromise emerged as a result of the reciprocal processes of conflict, tension, and gradual acquiescence, in which a "don't ask, don't tell" approach was taken to sexual identity and a discourse of "outness," or of commitment to identity, became central. The willingness and ability of a parent to conceal, or at least not overtly display, her or his homosexuality is implicated in the question of how *committed* one is to her or his sexual identity.

Commitment to Identity: Prioritizing and "Passing"

The notion of "commitment" to one's identity has been applied, although in different ways, to both sexual identity and parental identity. The central question emergent in the issue of one's commitment to his or her sexual identity is whether such an identity is a constant feature or whether it can (or should) be effectively muted at times. In 115 cases, for instance, a gay or lesbian parent was criticized for even *associating* with others who were openly gay or lesbian. In 35 cases, judges asserted that gay and lesbian parents should be able to separate their behavior from their sexual identity, and not "act on" their homosexuality.

The imperative not to "act on" one's homosexuality must be understood in historical and social scientific context, as homosexuality has most often been defined, in law and in public discourse, by the sexual act(s) most associated with it. In ruling on its criminal status, the Supreme Court referred to sodomy as the behavior that defines the "status" of homosexuals.[112] Yet, as noted earlier, scholars have shown that this rendering of act and identity as mutually defining is problematic for a number of reasons, in particular because of the reality that heterosexuals also engage in sodomy and that not all self-identified homosexuals do.[113] Subsequent decisions such as that of the U.S. Court of Appeals in *Watkins v United States Army*, in efforts to remain consistent with *Bowers*, made a distinction between act and identity by finding that the *status* of homosexuality could be protected under equal protection doctrine even if the *conduct* associated with it was not.[114] Such developments and contradictions have prompted many scholars to adopt what Janet Halley has called a "personhood definition" of sexual identity, in which the classes of homosexual and heterosexual are defined by the form of personality that members of each class may share rather than the sexual behavior in which they engage.[115] But this distinction is not universally accepted, and often these two facets—behavior and personhood—are conflated, particularly in discussions of how one "becomes" homosexual or enacts this identity.

As noted earlier, sexual identity is unique in that it is not a visible trait and must be rendered visible in a "coming out" process. As an attorney and former Lambda director noted, "the legal rulings have a lot to do with how comfortable lesbian and gay men feel about being out and really structuring their families in ways of really being out about who their families are. I think they make choices that are sometimes different and more visible."[116] Evaluations of such visibility are implicit in judicial narratives of a parent's commitment to sexual identity. These narratives involve questions about how sure litigants are about their sexual orientation, how open or "out" they are, and how integrated they are in their lifestyle, in the gay and lesbian community, and in queer politics. For instance, in *Jacobson v Jacobson*, the judges contended that a lesbian mother's sexual orientation was "beyond her control" but that acting on it was not, and she was expected not to express her sexual identity verbally, socially, or sexually.[117] As one judge interviewed in Southern California explained, "It's not a matter that they can choose not to be gay, the issue . . . is whether or not a gay person can practice their gay lifestyle or must they remain celibate for life. That's the debate I have with myself."[118]

This question has been important in child custody decision-making because of the negative effects a parent's homosexuality—or the knowledge of it—has been presumed to have on children. These effects, enumerated in the preceding chapter, include a conversion of the children to homosexuality, the social stigma associated with having a gay parent, and a disruption of the child's "normal" development or gender identity. There has been a sometimes tacit and sometimes well-articulated expectation on the part of family court judges that it was incumbent upon homosexual parents to shield their children from the evidence and manifestations of their sexuality. As one supervising judge in California commented in an interview, "A lot of it has to do with how people handle their lifestyle issues. It's not the lifestyle itself, it is how that is handled."[119] As a result, parents have often been reprimanded for not closeting their sexuality or for being too involved in the homosexual community.

Such was the reasoning of *In the Matter of J.S. & C.*, in which a gay father in New Jersey who had held a position as director of the National Gay Task Force[120] was denied visitation with his children largely because of his gay rights activism and the prospect that his children might be exposed to these activities. According to the judges, the "defendant's total involvement with and dedication to furthering homosexuality has created an environment exposure to which in anything more than a minimal amount would be harmful to the children." The decision went on to refer to the involvement of the father in the gay rights movement as an "obsessive preoccupation."[121] A similar rationale was used again, despite the passage of over two decades, to deny custody to a gay father in Indiana in *Marlow v Marlow*, because of his involvement in gay and lesbian church groups and the organization PFLAG (Parents and Friends of Lesbians and Gays).[122] Yet parents did not necessarily have to be involved with gay rights organizations to incur this critique; in an earlier Pennsylvania case, *Commonwealth ex rel. Ashfield v Cortes*, lesbian mother Justine Cortes had custody of her children removed from her and placed with the children's grandmother because she was "engaged in open, notorious and unconcealed acts of sexual abnormalities" by living with her domestic partner.[123]

Alternatively, those who concealed their homosexuality and promised to continue to do so were praised in court and rewarded with custody or visitation rights, as in the otherwise quite progressive decision of *M.A.B. v R.B.*, discussed in chapter 1, in which a custody award to a gay father was premised on the finding that he was not open about his sexual orientation in public or with the children. Similarly, in 2001 in Colorado, judges in *In re Marriage of Dorworth* restored visitation to a gay father after being assured that "the child had not been exposed to father's gay lifestyle . . . and that the parties had not discussed father's sexual orientation with the child."[124] In the *Eldridge* case, discussed earlier, lesbian mother Julie Eldridge's ability to regain visitation rights on appeal were premised on the facts that she and her partner did not share a bedroom, had "not been sexually intimate" in over a year, and made "no expression of physical emotion or physical contact when [the child] is in the home."[125]

In other cases, parents were portrayed as "flaunting" their alternative sexualities by virtue of their gender nonnormative appearance, behaviors, or preferences. Again, this theme was evident across time periods. In 1979 in *Newsome v Newsome*, the North Carolina justices chastised a mother for keeping *Ms.* magazine in her home, as they saw this as an open sign of radical feminist lesbianism and not gender appropriate.[126] In *Ward v Ward*, judges cited the female child's poor hygiene habits and "prefer[ence] to wear men's cologne" as evidence of disturbed gender identity and harm from having lived with her out lesbian mother and instead awarded custody to her father, who had previously been convicted of murdering his first wife over a custody dispute.[127] In most of these cases there was a sense that the law was encouraging—or even demanding—that parents engage in the normalizing strategy of "passing" as heterosexual or asexual.[128] Through this strategy, homosexuality could be—and was—rendered compatible with parenthood in the eyes of the law.

The commitment of litigants to their own *parental* identity has often been inextricably linked to their sexual identity in the judicial narratives. This tendency has its roots in historical assumptions that gay men and lesbians were either unwilling or unable to also be parents or that the two statuses were somehow mutually exclusive, as discussed in chapter 2. Although this *de facto* presumption of incompatibility has waned in the wake of the gayby boom, it has also been manifested in the imposition of a hierarchy of identities, such that gay and lesbian parents were assumed to value their sexuality over their families. Although it was their parental identity that brought them to family court, their sexual identity constituted a "master status," eclipsing other facets of their lives and personalities.[129] As Julie Eldridge commented regarding the justices' 1999 decision to revoke her custody of her daughter based solely on her sexuality, "if they had listened to all the facts in the proceedings, the part about being gay was so little compared to all my other qualities."[130] One attorney-turned-judge added that, in fact, "it takes a lot of courage and effort on the part of lesbians and gay men to get custody of their kids, to really love their kids a lot, *a lot*, because they are put through such hell."[131] In order to gain or retain custody of their children, gay and lesbian parents were required to prove that their sexual identities and relationships were not—and would never be—prioritized. In *Roe v Roe*, for example, a gay father in Virginia was accused of "choosing his own sexual gratification" over his child because he openly affirmed his gay identity.[132]

Lesbian mothers, in particular, were many times put in the position of "choosing" between motherhood and lesbianism, even as late as 1999. In the cases of *Hall v Hall* and *Bottoms v Bottoms*, for instance, each lesbian mother was chastised for being involved in a same-sex relationship and ultimately had her child removed from her custody. In the former case, the Michigan court found that "the interests of the children could well be subverted by [the mother's] relationship, which was clearly the chief priority in her life";[133] in the latter case, lesbian mother Sharon Bottoms was criticized by the Virginia court because she "felt her individual rights [to live with a companion] were as important as her child's."[134] This theme was evident in much-earlier cases as well. In the Ohio divorce case of *Towend v Towend*, after extensive questioning of mother Larraine and her partner, Vicky, regarding their sexual activities, a judge stated that he was "struck by the primacy that . . . the two lesbians . . . give to multiple organisms [*sic*]. They mean more to them apparently than the children."[135] Conversely, parents who were willing to forgo any same-sex romantic partnership or even social recognition of their sexual identity were found to be appropriately dedicated to the parental role, a theme returned to in chapter 4. Yet even doing this sometimes was not enough for parents to prove commitment to their family identity: in one case, a gay father's award of partial custody was premised on his not being too "out," but at the same time he was called untrustworthy for having hid his homosexuality from family members.[136]

Adoption and Commitment to Parenthood

In the case of adoptive parents, the onus of proving appropriate commitment to parenthood as a status was doubly challenging because of the court's traditional predisposition toward privileging biological family ties. Whereas biological parents can generally have their parental status revoked by a judge only if they are proven to be unfit or abusive, adoptive parents must affirmatively prove their fitness and their ability to forge a bond with the child. This difficulty has often historically been exacerbated in the case of gay and lesbian parents by several structural obstacles, including state laws barring adoption or foster parenthood by gay and lesbian individuals, as well as a lack of legal provisions for dual-parent or second-parent adoption by same-sex couples. One Lambda attorney in the Midwest commented, "[adoption] statutes aren't made with, really, not with any particular families in mind but certainly not with our [LGBT] families in mind. They are meant to give the courts a lot of freedom. It is striking how few states are allowing adoptions by the other individual in the couple."[137]

Even with regard to adoption by a single gay man or lesbian, such impediments still existed in some states well into the 1990s. In one case, for example, *Matter of Appeal in Pima County Juvenile Action*, the court barred a bisexual man from adopting a child based on the criminal status of sodomy in the state of Arizona at that time: "It would be anomalous for the state on the one hand to declare homosexual conduct unlawful and on the other create a parent after that proscribed model, in effect approving that standard, inimical to the natural family, as head of a state-created family."[138] Here, the identity of the prospective parent was marked more as "criminal" than as "father." In New Hampshire, which did not have a sodomy law in place at the time, gay and lesbian individuals did not gain the ability to adopt until 1998—and even then the state continued to restrict same-sex couples from adopting jointly.

These issues, though largely a thing of the past in most states, persist today in others, as the State of Florida continues to enforce a specific ban on adoption by any gay or lesbian individual or couple.[139] This law has been challenged unsuccessfully many times by prospective adoptive parents, perhaps most famously in the case of *Lofton v Kearney*. Mr. Lofton was the foster father of three children who were born HIV-positive and whom he had raised with his partner since birth. Yet when he filed a petition to adopt the youngest of these children, who had since sero-reverted to HIV-negative status, it was denied by the Florida Department of Children and Family Services on the grounds that, knowing the law prohibited gay men and lesbians from adopting, he failed to answer the question on the adoption form asking his sexual orientation. Both the Florida Supreme Court and the Eleventh Circuit U.S. Court of Appeals found that, despite the fact that "Lofton's efforts at caring for these children have been exemplary," Florida exercised a rational interest in "promoting adoption by marital families" by "disallowing adoption into homosexual households, which are necessarily motherless or fatherless and lack the stability that comes with marriage."[140]

Even when these impediments did not exist at the state level, however, there has sometimes been significant resistance in the past to adoption by gay and lesbian individuals or couples. In a case in which an abused and abandoned girl was placed by the New Mexico Department of Social Services in the care of her adult gay brother, for instance, the court barred the adoption and removed the child based on the finding that the home was unsuitable because of her brother's homosexuality.[141] Moreover, the contention that a gay man or lesbian would be willing or able to prioritize a child's needs over his or her own sociosexual activity and involvement—without a preordained obligation to—was often the subject of significant doubt in the judicial narrative. A 1988 decision denying an adoption petition by a gay man reflected the sentiment of many judges: "The so-called 'gay lifestyle' is patently incompatible with the manifest spirit, purpose and goals of adoption."[142]

Evolving Identities and Legal Change

The myriad ways in which identity is represented, imposed, negotiated, produced, and reproduced in these child custody cases at once reveals both diversity and commonality in the sociolegal existence of gay and lesbian parents. This body of cases confirms what has been suggested repeatedly in the past, that the family and its constituent membership is by no means a stable or easily definable institution. Despite efforts to legally define the status of "parent" in some of these cases—and the reticence to name it in others—such efforts to "define down" parental identity do not always reflect the social and personal realities of the people they are meant to describe. The judges' attempts to interpret the law's ill-defined concepts of who is a "parent" and who is a "legal stranger" or "third party" are not immune to the diversity of family forms and types of parental units that exist, however; and in its failure to impose any sort of determinacy, the law even recognizes this diversity and its implications for legal parenthood and social policy at key moments.

At times this analysis might seem to show the power of the law to impose identities and conditions not welcomed by LGBT parents. Yet the construction of parental and sexual identity in family court is not a one-way process. Gay and lesbian parents have put forth self-images that are often contradictory to those imposed by the court and, in doing so, have taken advantage of the ambiguous parameters and definitions of parenthood and same-sex civil rights in family law. At the very least, these parents forced the law to confront and document—if not formally recognize—the existence of gay and lesbian parents and alternative family forms by virtue of their presence in the appellate courts. They influenced family law by necessitating the convergence of two institutions previously thought of as divergent—alternative sexualities and family—in judicial narratives. They resisted the law's closeting tendencies by affirming their sexual identities in court, and they brought their personal realities to bear by naming themselves as parents despite their legal exclusion from the family. Thus, the social world of the parents and the legal world of the judicial narratives inevitably impinge on each other and affect each other. This two-way process is the essence of the negotiation of identity—how legal identities emerge, are contested, and are eventually settled and prioritized—and demonstrates how the indeterminacy of family law has opened opportunities for such negotiation and change.

In identifying the complex processes involved in the negotiation of identity in family court, an emergent sociolegal terrain is revealed where identities once thought to be mutually exclusive—"gay/lesbian" and "parent"—have over time been rendered compatible, deproblematized, and their possibilities expanded. This was accomplished through a decades-long dialogue between LGBT parents and the law, and a variety of mechanisms of compromise: either the construction of an "identity hierarchy" in which priorities and commitments to differing statuses are articulated; "passing" gestures, which require the strategic muting of certain identity traits; or provisional and temporary conferrals of an otherwise unattainable status such as "*de facto*" parenthood. Through these processes, gay and lesbian parents have eventually become legally viable subjects rather than cultural contradictions. The same mechanisms of discursive compromise might be found at work in the merging of other seemingly contradictory identities: "Islamic feminist," "moral criminal," or "elite deviant."[143] But here, it brings to bear a number of issues that affect not only the composition of the family but also common understandings of the origin, character, and mutability (or immutability) of sexual and familial identity, and at the same time, it represents the ability of marginalized actors to harness certain aspects of a vaguely defined area of law to their eventual benefit, precisely because of its vagueness.

This is not to say that the indeterminacy of family law and the vague "best interest of the child" standard have not at times provided cover for antigay bias in the judiciary, or that these identity compromises should necessarily be seen as an end-point for gay and lesbian parents. Although preferable to outright homophobia and denial, these negotiations often resulted in expressions of *conditional* support for gay and lesbian parenthood—custody and visitation rights conditioned on a parents' effectual disavowal or abandonment of her or his sexual identity and partnership, assurances that "harm" will not result in the form of a gay or lesbian child, and recognition of the parental rights of same-sex partners with the proviso that such recognition does *not* constitute support for same-sex marriage rights. The fact that parents were commonly rewarded for not being "too gay"—for remaining appropriately closeted and not identifying with a broader gay rights movement—resulted in a Pyrrhic victory for gay and lesbian parents. Yet these concessions and compromises have also, in recent years, been followed by more fundamental changes in several states, many of which now may not only reject the call to make a parent's sexual orientation a central consideration in their deliberations about custody and adoption but recognize the need to broaden family and parental identity in law as not a point of controversy but a *social reality*. Indeed, only six years after the California Supreme Court offered a compromise by recognizing temporary *de facto* parenthood for nonbiological and nonadoptive mother Kathleen Crandall in *Kathleen C. v Lisa W.*, it issued the broadest expansion of parental identity to date, recognizing two "natural mothers" in *K.M. v E.G.* and releasing the definition of parenthood from both biological constraints and strict statutory construction.

The negotiation of identity in family law is both inevitable and productive. The power of law to impose labels and coercively shape identity is explicit in the experiences of gay and lesbian parents in family court, but so are these parents' efforts to self-identify, to make their existence and their families visible, and to force family court judges to confront new social realities. The interplay between these forces, regardless of their independent successes and failures—along with the indeterminacy that gives rise to them—results in an expansion of possibilities for interpreting parenthood and sexual identity and allows for the emergence of new meanings, new identities, and new sites of contest and compromise. Sociologist Judith Stacey, in her powerful book *In the Name of the Family*, discusses the transformative potential of queer families as something that could benefit the entire institution of family, if we as a society could only "get used to it."[144] The struggles, tensions, and creativity of LGBT parents and family law judges are part and parcel of the gradual procession toward *getting used to* it.

4

Right or Wrong?

The Indeterminacy of Custody and Adoption Rights

The myth of rights . . . seeks to be all things to all people—or at least as many things to as many people as possible.

—Stuart Scheingold[1]

The historical, political, and symbolic importance of legal rights, particularly in American legal culture, is well known in popular consciousness and scholarly thought. Americans have seen the First Amendment right of free speech invoked in high-profile settings anywhere from the Berkeley student protests in the sixties to the gangster-rap genre of the nineties. *Miranda* rights, stemming from the Due Process Clause of the Fifth Amendment, have become ubiquitous through the popularization of television crime dramas such as *Law and Order* and *NYPD Blue.* These most common examples have something in common: the right to be left *alone.* But what of the right to be *connected*? The "myth of rights" may be many things to many people, but it almost always connotes individualism—not the most intuitive fit for a necessarily *communal* institution such as family. Despite a recent upsurge in political dialogue centering on the family, this "fervor over the family" is often spoken of in a distant, individualistic way that does not do much to address the needs of the family *unit.*[2] At the same time, the entirely indeterminate nature of the discourse of rights engenders a legal atmosphere in which the same rights claims made by gay and lesbian parents can be disregarded as "selfish" and "irrelevant" in one instance and held up as "fundamental" and "sacred" in the next.

In this chapter, I examine the successes, failures, and intricacies of rights claims in the context of gay and lesbian parents' custody and adoption cases, analyzing specifically the paradoxical and problematic position of rights in this family law context, which fundamentally sits at the intersection of the individual (i.e., privacy rights) and the collective (i.e., family). How is it, for instance, that the same constitutional rights (e.g., the right to privacy) can be deployed both in defense of and in opposition to a gay/lesbian parent? For that matter, how are the rights of the parent pitted against the rights, or "best interest," of the child or against another parent? This chapter reveals the indeterminacy and therefore complexity of rights as a strategy and a discourse in the family law context, examining in depth the intersection of the collective and the individual and suggesting ways in which this very complexity and open-endedness can lead to new forms and creative uses of rights for gay and lesbian families.[3]

The assertion of rights-based claims, since the civil "rights revolution" of the 1960s, has increasingly become the "rhetoric of choice" in moral and legal claims-making in the United States, serving both instrumental and ideological goals.[4] Even those who are dubious of the efficacy of relying on traditional liberal rights claims to enact social change often acknowledge their symbolic resonance.[5] The resonance of rights, not surprisingly, is particularly potent for populations that have been or continue to be deprived of them—not least, gay men and lesbians. Yet it is undeniable that "rights, like law itself, do cut both ways—serving at some times and under some circumstances to reinforce privilege and at other times to provide the cutting edge of change."[6] For example, the invocation of rights may help a gay or lesbian biological parent retain custody while simultaneously being used to deny such rights to a nonbiological parent. The 1999 Supreme Court case of *Troxel v Granville* and the reaction to it in the gay and lesbian community illustrate this indeterminacy: it was lauded as a victory by parents who lived in fear of having their biological or adopted children removed from their custody by a third party (as happened in the highly publicized *Bottoms v Bottoms* case in 1996), but it also dealt a blow to gay and lesbian nonbiological parents who did not have the opportunity or ability to formally adopt their children, holding the potential to "all but foreclose the claims of legally unrecognized lesbian mothers."[7] Indeed, the years since *Troxel* have shown that even ostensible gains for LGBT parenting rights can sometimes backfire against certain segments of the population.

The Legal Landscape:
Gay Rights, Family Rights, and the Constitution

Despite the imprecision of "rights" and their potential for cooptation or backfire, however, LGBT individuals and communities often find themselves faced with no better recourse—whether because of their ubiquity and nearly universal appeal, their cultural salience, or a lack of alternatives—than to invoke the abstract doctrine of "rights" in their political, social, and legal struggles. Indeed, almost every aspect of gay men's and lesbians' public as well as private lives has been defended with rights claims, either in scholarship, court, or legislative session—including, but not limited to, employment, housing, military service, freedom from violence and harassment, sexual relations, marriage, access to health care, immigration, and, of course, custody and adoption rights. One of the most frequently articulated legal bases for LGBT rights, in family and other realms, has been the right to privacy, a right that has been "vaunted as a *superright*, a trump" (emphasis added).[8] Yet the right to privacy does have its limits, as was shown in *Bowers v Hardwick*, in which the Supreme Court ruled that the right to privacy did not extend to homosexuals and homosexual activity, a ruling that had immense impact on LGBT rights claims, custody included, until it was overturned in 2003.[9] Moreover, the right to privacy falls squarely within the critique of rights as overly individualistic; it is, after all, essentially the right to be left *alone*.[10] Indeed, *Eisenstadt v Baird* solidified the right to privacy as an *individual* rather than *family* right, as had been suggested by the prior precedent in *Griswold v Connecticut*. Thus, despite the commonsensical appeal of the right to privacy for issues of family and sexuality, its actual application to any family, and specifically gay and lesbian families, has been uneven at best.

Yet, despite the sense that any type of rights-based claim in family court may be variably interpreted and even harmful to their own purposes, LGBT parents and would-be parents have not been deterred from invoking their constitutional rights—and neither, in many cases, have their opponents. Indeed, the occasional success of other marginalized populations in applying constitutional rights in family law, together with the high stakes and intense emotional investment involved in custody litigation, has encouraged these appeals to a liberally construed rights paradigm. In addition to the right to privacy, also common are assertions of rights connected to the Fourteenth Amendment's Due Process and Equal

Protection Clauses, and the First Amendment's freedom of association and protection of "expressive conduct." In fact, in slightly over one-fifth of the cases, the gay or lesbian parent made specific constitutional claims of these types in their appeals.

Perhaps the most common assertions of gay and lesbian parental rights were those based on the notion of the "fundamental" rights to parenthood and to raise one's children, established as precedent by the Supreme Court in 1972 in *Stanley v Illinois*.[11] As one family court judge in Southern California stated, "a parent has unfettered access. I think it comes almost from our libertarian roots of the country, that the . . . court . . . should not get involved in those kinds of things. It's a little more sacred. Near and dear areas of our personal life that we would be able to resolve in families."[12] Both the legal director of Lambda in New York and NCLR executive director Kate Kendell agreed and commented on the long-recognized sanctity of the parent-child relationship. Kendell commented in reference to cases in which custody is removed or visitation restricted based on the parents' sexuality, "what you're essentially doing is depriving that parent of the right to continue their parental relationship, and that's protected by the highest level of scrutiny under the Constitution."[13] This right was stated even more ardently in the divorce case of *In the Matter of J.S. & C.*, discussed in the preceding chapter, in which the father contended, and the court agreed, that

> [t]he parental rights of a homosexual, like those of a heterosexual, are con-
> stitutionally protected. Fundamental rights of parents may not be denied,
> limited or restricted on the basis of sexual orientation, per se. The right of
> a parent, including a homosexual parent, to the companionship and care of
> his or her child, insofar as it is for the best interest of the child is a fundamen-
> tal right protected by the First, Ninth and Fourteenth Amendments to the
> United States Constitution. . . . The right of a natural parent to its child must
> be included with the bundle of rights associated with marriage, establishing
> a home and rearing children; as such, it should be viewed as "so rooted in the
> tradition and conscience of our people as to be ranked as fundamental."[14]

The court went on to quote *Stanley* at length, calling the right to raise one's children a "basic civil right," "essential," and "[f]ar more precious than property rights."[15] Yet still, the court decided in the end that the father's rights had been appropriately restricted because of his sexual orientation and that the custody ruling against him was valid. Thus, it is already very clear that the "fundamental right" of parenthood is not quite as fundamental or uniform as the case law might suggest; indeed it was not difficult at all in the judges' narrative in this case simultaneously to recognize the sanctity of this right and still to exempt this particular gay father from it. Neither was this finding anomalous: the same rationale was found in cases for years to come, such as in the 1998 Alabama divorce case of *R.W. v D.W.W.*, in which the court proclaimed that "all other rights are secondary" to the court's interest in protecting children in their best interest—in this case, from visitation with their lesbian mother.[16]

The *Troxel* case in 1999 renewed the debate about the extent of (legally recognized) parents' fundamental rights to control their children's lives, and it strongly suggested a fortification of these rights. Though it weakened the position of co-parents not already legally recognized vis-à-vis their former partners, *Troxel* seemed to be a welcome protection for those gay or lesbian parents who were challenged for custody by third parties, such as grandparents. Unlike in 1996, when lesbian mother Sharon Bottoms lost custody of her son to her own mother, Garth Strome, the gay father in the 2003 Oregon case of *Strome v Strome*, successfully fought off a custody challenge by his mother, the children's grandmother. The court concluded that,

> under *Troxel*, biological parents have a fundamental due process right to make decisions concerning the care, custody, and control of their children . . . [which] supervenes a pure "best interest of the child" analysis in a custody dispute, replacing it with one in which a fit biological parent will presumptively prevail.[17]

Even in the wake of this precedent, however, fundamental rights claims were far from universally successful and still were subject to whatever was considered the best interest of the child. A long string of cases found ways around a strict interpretation of this case and continued to privilege, or at least consider, factors other than the parents' rights.

The courts' reticence in this area is a product of the ill fit between the foundations of the liberal rights paradigm and family law. Whereas rights are generally invoked on the *individual* level, a family is by definition *relational*. This dichotomy is particularly at issue here, as the gay rights movement has often been typified by citizenship claims based on individual privacy rights, as in the struggle to decriminalize sodomy and the *Lawrence v Texas* decision. Furthermore, gay men and lesbians have often, in public discourse, been assumed to be uninterested in or incapable of family life (as discussed in the preceding chapter), thus emphasizing the personal and individualistic appearance of gay rights claims. Although this perception is increasingly challenged in the modern era by the hypervisible campaign for marriage equality, it is still invoked by opponents who see same-sex couples' gayness as *excluding* them from marriage rather than seeing their coupledom as *including* them. Thus, as a growing number of LGBT parents seek to solidify their parental rights in court, they find dramatic evidence of the complexity of rights as a discourse and a strategy.

The complexity of rights in the family context is well illustrated by reference to Henry Sumner Maine's famous assertion that the evolution of law can be traced as a progression from an emphasis on familial status to one on individual contract as the basis for legal rights and entitlements.[18] The claims at the heart of the "rights revolution" exemplify Maine's notion that legal rights in the modern era should not be a function of one's lineage but rather should be afforded by virtue of one's individual citizenship—a contract, so to speak, with the state. In Maine's words, "The Individual is steadily substituted for the Family as the unit of which civil laws take account."[19] In the custody arena, however, the family, for obvious reasons, is once again the significant unit. The relationship between status and contract as bases for rights in the family arena is particularly complicated by the claims of gay and lesbian parents, whose relationships are *not* legally recognized in most states to this day, even if their individual rights as gay and lesbian citizens are. Thus, though rights may be asserted by gay and lesbian *citizens* as members of a marginalized group, their citizenship is not their defining feature in family court. This distinction, then, necessarily complicates the discussion of "family rights" and "parental rights" for gay and lesbian parents and would-be parents.

The contract basis for rights in family law is admittedly less well established than in other areas of law since by definition the family is relational, though it is undeniable that the emergence of new reproductive technologies and the increasing number of adoption and surrogacy arrangements has tended to support Maine's thesis. Neither the individualism framework nor the "contract" framework of rights, however, extends to those gay or lesbian families that are composed of two mothers or two fathers with children who were conceived through reproduc-

tive technology or surrogacy, such that the parents are not equally connected to the children by biology or adoption.[20] When faced with the
challenge of a nonbiological parent seeking custody or visitation rights,
in the past the courts have most often suddenly shifted to a vision of
family as inextricably connected by blood. Rather than recognizing the
individual rights of each member of these nontraditional families, the
courts have traditionally privileged only the tie between the biological
mother or father and the child, to the detriment of the nonbiological
parent, a trend reinforced in legal precedent by the *Troxel* decision and
discussed in more detail later.

Parental Rights: Who May Assert Them and How?

Whether in regard to privacy or a broader idea of "fundamental rights," the invocation of parents' rights has often backfired when
asserted by a nonbiological parent, because the court interpreted those
rights as applying *only* to the biological parent whom the nonbiological
parent had opposed for custody. Here, the court has clearly distinguished
between different types of individuals in their ability to invoke these
rights. In cases in which one parent was not biologically related to the
child, for instance, it was much less likely that the nonbiological parent
would even be granted standing to appear in court to assert these rights.
As one former supervising judge in Southern California commented,

> It would be very difficult I think under the current state of the law to
> give [custody rights to] a nonbiological parent with the biological parent
> objecting. . . . I just don't think you could do that, particularly if the bio-
> logical parent can establish themselves as being a competent parent, and I
> mean, if they're competent, to deprive them of primary physical custody
> would be very difficult, very unusual.[21]

Judges in Ohio agreed in the 1997 case of *Liston v Pyles*, discussed
in the previous chapter. Marla Liston and Tamara Pyles had a child
by donor insemination, and when their relationship ended three years
later, Pyles, who was the biological mother, cut off all contact between
Liston and their son. Having not been allowed to adopt the child under
Ohio law, Liston was left with no parental rights or recourse. When she
appealed the trial court's decision denying her standing to seek custody
or visitation, the Ohio justices wrote,

We agree with [Liston's] premise that the liberty interest in a familial relationship is entitled to the highest constitutional protection. . . . However,
we also agree with the trial court's finding that no United States Supreme
Court case nor our Ohio Supreme Court has extended this protection to
include family relationships stemming from a homosexual union.[22]

Liston responded in an interview,

they're saying there is no venue by which I can even seek justice or by
which my son can seek justice. That's what I just, I simply do not understand. I can't comprehend that, that we live in America and we're told,
there is no remedy for this wrong. There is no way to right this wrong.
There is no one who will even listen to it. How can that be? How can
we live in a society that has the kind of court system and judicial system
that we have and there not be somewhere that you can go to have a right
remedied?[23]

Even some advocates for gay parents' rights articulated resistance to recognizing the rights of nonbiological and nonadoptive parents' rights, arguing that it "opens up the floodgates to others who [would] assert rights" to
a lesbian mother's children, thus threatening her own parental rights.[24]

When the *Troxel* precedent was successfully invoked to protect a gay
or lesbian parent's rights, though more rare than one might expect, it
was often in cases stemming from same-sex unions in which the biological parent was recognized as a parent and his or her partner was not.
The irony here is that, with the shift in the 1990s from custody cases
stemming from former heterosexual marriages to cases involving children conceived in same-sex unions, the results tallied from the cases seem
to suggest that LGBT parents were no longer losing in court. Indeed,
by 2000, it was much less common (though certainly not unheard of)
that gay or lesbian parents, facing a heterosexual ex-spouse, would be
deprived of custody based solely on their sexual orientation. Yet, though
at first glance this would seem to indicate that the courts had become
friendlier to LGBT parents' rights, this was only true to the extent that
these rights overlapped with their biological status as parents and therefore fit with heteronormative understandings of family structure. Therefore, the fundamental rights of parenthood could still be invoked for the
purpose of *denying* an adoption or custody claim by a parent who was
not biologically related, which demonstrates the double-edged sword

of indeterminate rights. In *In the Matter of T.L.*, for instance, the fundamental rights of the biological mother outweighed the rights of her former partner, with whom she raised the child and whom the court recognized as a *de facto* parent, to custody or visitation, as well as the right of the child to have contact with her nonbiological mother.[25] Similarly, in *In re Thompson*, the Tennessee appeals court ruled that nonbiological mother Pamela White would need to have proven that there was substantial harm to the child in order to "overcome [biological mother Patricia] Thompson's constitutionally protected parental rights" and obtain custody or visitation, and she did not.[26] Thus, while the flexibility of rights allows the possibility of adaptation across contexts and cases, it also leaves the door open to unintended and reactionary cooptation of the discourse. Scholars such as Jonathan Goldberg-Hiller have written of the "growing skepticism and uncertainty about the costs and payoffs of rights strategies and civil rights narratives" because of their indeterminate interpretations and consequences, and they point to situations in which rights are "de-mobilized," actually becoming *impediments* to liberty for disenfranchised groups.[27]

Likewise, the right to privacy has been used as a justification to deny custody or visitation to mothers in lesbian parenting dyads who were not biologically related to their children. In cases such as *Kazmierazak v Query*, the court held, "to justify state intervention . . . into a parent's fundamental and constitutionally protected right of privacy, there must be a threshold showing of demonstrable harm to the child." When Penny Kazmierazak, the nonbiological mother in this Florida case, attempted to argue that she, as a psychological parent, "falls within the sphere of those protected by [the] right to privacy . . . and thus, has the same protected privacy rights as the [biological parent]," the court responded with a statement that "unequivocally reaffirmed adoptive or biological parents' right to make decisions about their children's welfare without interference by third parties," thereby relegating Kazmierazak to the status of a "third party" not deserving of privacy rights in relation to the child. The court further emphasized this point by calling Kazmierazak's rights claim an "attempt to circumvent [biological mother Pamela Query's] right to privacy . . . [arguing] that she falls within the sphere of those protected by Florida's right to privacy." Even more bluntly, the concurring opinion added,

> A non-parent's lawsuit involving another's child is an intrusion of privacy. In this aspect of life so protected by the right of privacy, courts should not

create poorly defined relationships such as "psychological parent," which then confer rights on the recipients of the label against a natural parent.[28]

A family court judge in Southern California confirmed this notion: "if the biological parent wanted to prohibit the relationship, they could, period, end of story. The U.S. Supreme Court suggested that that is a constitutional-based, kind of a privacy-based issue."[29] Thus, just as in other arenas of debate involving gay rights and parental rights, judges found themselves distinguishing between those "deserving" and "undeserving" of privacy rights—and using this ill-defined right to very different ends. Indeed, this has been the pitfall of many marginalized groups that seek to invoke laws and protections created without them in mind. Often—and particular to gay rights movements—their rights claims become distorted and reimagined as "special rights" above and beyond what is deserved; or they eventually result in a backlash, leaving progressive groups and would-be rights claimants "puzzled and defenseless."[30] Certainly the LGBT family rights pioneers of the 1970s who first fought for the application of privacy and other rights to gay and lesbian parents' claims did not anticipate that these very rights would be relied on to disenfranchise parents who did not have a biological connection to their children.

This pattern remained the dominant one, however, until shifts in the conception of family, and in who qualifies as a parent in order to claim rights, began to assert themselves in the twenty-first century. Before 2000, only the states of Massachusetts, Missouri, Wisconsin, and New Mexico had established precedent that a nonbiological parent might have standing to seek visitation or any sort of parenting rights and responsibilities. One family court judge in Illinois—where this right had not been established—commented in reference to such situations,

> Well, it becomes a great problem, because I'm bound to act according to the law, and according to the law, the nonbiological parent has no rights to that child, although morally or ethically you would think they would because they helped raise that child—and that becomes a real tough decision, . . . but as a judge, I have to follow the law.[31]

Another judge, in California, concurred: "[if] the nonbiological parent had not gone through that legal step [of adoption], then they [have] absolutely no rights."[32] By 2007, the list of states granting standing to nonbiological parents included Minnesota, Rhode Island, Colorado, California, Indiana, Pennsylvania, New Jersey, Washington, and Maine, though in only five of these states was the right established as law by a state supreme court. Furthermore, over half of these laws provide only for visitation by a nonbiological *de facto* parent, not full or equally shared custody; and ironically, in a Minnesota case, the same judicial panel that allowed a nonbiological mother visitation rights also granted them to the sperm donor who had helped the lesbian couple to conceive.[33] This Minnesota case illustrates both the ability of parental rights to be co-opted by those outside the social movement that pushed for them and the worst fears of those who are critical of casting too wide a net in redefining "family" and parental rights, thus reinforcing the dual-edged nature of indeterminacy in the interpretation of these rights.

Similarly, in cases in which the nonbiological parent in an intact same-sex union wished to adopt the child (with the partner's consent), the fundamental rights of the parent were not historically recognized or were recognized only for the purpose of denying a second-parent adoption. Such was the case in the 1994 Wisconsin case of *In the Interest of Angel Lace M.*, discussed in the preceding chapter:

> This relationship, between a child and her mother's nonmarital partner, is not one that has traditionally received constitutional protection . . . While [the child's] relationship with her mother . . . is constitutionally protected because the two form a "unitary family," her relationship with [the nonbiological mother] is not.[34]

Even pairing the rights of two co-parents to a second-parent adoption with the right of the child (to be adopted)—a strategy that would generally broaden the appeal of the rights framework by focusing on children's rights—found little success in the 1990s. The 2000 Pennsylvania case of *Adoption of C.C.G. and Z.C.G.* was typical of cases over the previous decade in this regard; in response to the parents' argument that the "constitutional guarantees of equal protection of the laws" required that the children not be "denied the benefits of adoption by their second parent solely because of their parents' marital status [or lack thereof]," the court adhered to a strict literal interpretation of the adoption statute, claiming that there simply existed no right to adoption when the biological mother had not given up her rights and the two were not married (which of course, is not legal in Pennsylvania).[35] In an interesting example of self-reversal, when the Pennsylvania Supreme Court did legalize second-parent adoption two years later in *In re Adoption of R.B.F. and R.C.F.*, the court relied on the exact same logic it denied in the earlier case, that the rights of children to be adopted were served by allowing the nonbiological parent to adopt.[36] This reversal was thanks in large measure to the growing reinvention of rights in family law as protecting not individuals but *relationships* between individuals.

One area where the transformation of rights claims and their reception in court was quite visible was in the First Amendment right of freedom of association. Since the 1970s, many gay and lesbian parents have asserted arguments based on the First Amendment to protect their relationships with their children. In the 1976 Ohio case of *Towend v Towend* and later in the Illinois case of *In re Marriage of Diehl* in 1991, for instance, the lesbian mothers both used the same commonly applied right to freedom of association to argue that their custody and visitation with their children could not be restricted.[37] Despite the passage of fifteen years between the cases, however, the courts in both cases found this argument not compelling, stating in the latter decision that "[f]reedom of association is not absolute and must yield to sufficiently important government interest."[38] Even as late as 1998, in *Marlow v Marlow*, Mr. Marlow argued that a restriction prohibiting him from taking his children during visitation to "activities sponsored by or which otherwise promoted the homosexual lifestyle" (he belonged to a predominantly gay church) was unconstitutional under the First Amendment; as was typical of the time, however, he failed in court.[39]

By the turn of the twenty-first century, however, a change was perceptible, in part facilitated by the gradual state-by-state repeal of antihomosexual sodomy laws throughout the 1980s and '90s (culminating eventually in the 2003 *Lawrence* decision) as well as the first Supreme Court confirmation of LGBT civil rights in *Romer v Evans*. In the 1999 Mississippi divorce case of *Weigand v Houghton*, the same First Amendment argument, based on the freedom of father and son to associate freely both with each other and with father David Weigand's male partner, was successful in overturning several visitation restrictions that had been imposed on him (such as not being able to visit with the child around his domestic partner or in the home that he shared with his partner).[40] A similar conclusion was reached in 2004 in Tennessee, in the case of *Hogue v Hogue*, in which not only had Mr. Hogue been restrained from exposing or talking to his son about the "gay lifestyle" or visiting with him while his partner or any other gay individuals were present, but he had actually been slapped with a contempt charge for having told his son that he was gay. The Tennessee Court of Appeals did not explicitly cite *Lawrence* or *Romer* but overturned both the contempt charge and the visitation restriction, on the grounds that there was no harm and that the boy benefited from a continued relationship with his father.[41] This line of reasoning foreshadowed one particularly important way in which the indeterminacy of rights allowed them to be repositioned and reimagined over time as relational rather than individualistic—and therefore entirely relevant to the goal of keeping parents and their children together.

Rights Claims Based on Sexual Orientation: The (Ir)Relevance of Civil Rights in Family Law

The observations in the preceding section show how the language of rights as an individualistic discourse, even in the context of *parents'* rights, has been problematized in family law. When several of the same constitutional principles that have been invoked to assert or defend parental rights, such as freedom of speech, freedom of association, and privacy, were applied to parents' sexual orientation (as a minority status), they were met with even more aversion in most cases. This is in part because LGBT family rights, and gay rights claims in general, are limited by their opposition in popular discourse, in which they are often framed as "special rights" rather than equal rights. Suggesting that gay men and lesbians are seeking entitlements that the average citizen does not enjoy, the discourse of "special rights" authenticates certain "real" rights (such as those attained during the civil rights movement of the 1960s) while painting these specific actors (gay men and lesbians) as at once not deserving and not needing equivalent protections.[42] Again, when applied to gay and lesbian rights in the family arena (especially but not exclusively pertaining to same-sex marriage), this "special rights" discourse of deserving-versus-not is particularly ubiquitous—and indicative of the potential for "rights talk" to backfire due to its "open texture," as its critics warn. Clearly, then, there is an upside as well as a downside to the ability of rights to be "all things to all people."

In several cases around the same period, such as *Marriage of Diehl* in Illinois in 1991, *Thigpen v Carpenter* in Arkansas in 1987, and *T.C.H. v K.M.H.* in Missouri in 1989, parents argued that the court "engaged in unconstitutional sexual orientation discrimination" or that "the trial court's order denying custody and restricting visitation on the ground that the appellant is a homosexual violates the appellant's rights under the federal Constitution";[43] in all three cases, these civil rights arguments were not successful. The results were not dissimilar to cases as early as the 1970s, such as *In re Jane B.* in 1976, in which a lesbian mother in New York argued that the revocation of her custody and visitation restrictions imposed because of her lesbian relationship violated her First Amendment freedom of speech and freedom of actions.[44] In this case, the judges rejected this rationale on the grounds that although precedent supported such an argument on the basis of other minority statuses such as race, it had not yet been applied to homosexuality. Yet even decades later, judges were similarly prone in interviews to reject such arguments in the face of visitation restrictions based on parents' sexual orientation and relationships; one judge from Southern California, when asked about a case in which a lesbian mother's visitation was cut off because she shared a home with her partner, commented with characteristic simplicity that "you eliminate the visitation portion of it [the custody order] with the new girlfriend being there, then there isn't a problem."[45]

A resistance to arguments based on equal protection and due process was evident in judges' evaluations of parents' claims that they were discriminated against because of their sexual orientation. Particularly noteworthy was the denial in 1987 in *Thigpen*, in which the justices stated that they "disagree[d] that the [mother's] rights were violated, or that due process requires a showing that there be a nexus between the parent's activity and harm to the child."[46] This rationale broke with a principle established in precedent in 1967 and adopted increasingly throughout the country (but not in Arkansas, where this case took place) that such a nexus was *required* to be shown before a parent's sexual orientation could be considered in a custody determination—a precedent that soon became known as the "nexus test" and contrasted with the "*per se*" standard (which, as discussed in chapter 2, found parents' homosexuality *per se* harmful to children).

Yet, consistent with the "myth of rights" and its ubiquity in social movements and law, LGBT parents, attorneys, and activists were not dissuaded from insisting that sexual-orientation *discrimination* was indeed a relevant consideration in child custody. In the introduction to her book *Rainbow Rights*, Patricia Cain emphasizes the importance of the invocation of "rights" in order to reflect the notion that gay men and lesbians are *citizens* and legal persons under the law.[47] Indeed, the founder of

NCLR, now a judge in San Francisco, pointed out that when litigating a gay or lesbian parent's custody case, "it wasn't just a family law case, it was a civil rights case."[48] Others, such as NCLR director Kate Kendell, argued similarly that

> when it comes to lesbian and gay parents, constitutional issues are always implicated because if you're restricting their parenting simply based on sexual orientation, you're restricting a fundamentally protected right. So, we make constitutional arguments [based on equal protection] all the time.[49]

An attorney in the case of *Kathleen C. v Lisa W.* concurred that it is "absolutely, 100 percent an equal rights issue."[50]

This designation is particularly important to advocates for gay and lesbian rights, who are often accused of trying to secure undeserved "special rights," as discussed earlier. Combined with the experience of being exempted as a class from the ubiquitous right to privacy until 2003, this presumption puts gay men and lesbian in the position of being deprived of that which they feel, as citizens, should be most theirs but yet is most taken away. This perception may be well founded, according to recent research on public opinion regarding gay rights in the United States, which finds consistently that, while the majority of Americans continue to find homosexuality morally wrong, they support the extension of basic civil rights and nondiscrimination policies to gay men and lesbians.[51] It is not surprising, then, that most LGBT activists continue to invoke and rely on civil rights language. Not only do rights strategically make sense, but they carry important symbolic meaning, connoting full citizenship for gay men and lesbians. Even among attorneys who have worked for gay rights, however, there is still ambivalence. One, who practiced as an attorney for many years before becoming a judge, commented that "a lot of people who litigated some of these kinds of cases focused too much on the 'gay' part and not enough on the 'child' part."[52] Even a prominent lesbian activist and attorney commented, "I think that there just isn't enough support for equal protection theory that would be good for gay and lesbian parents to really want to chance it."[53]

Interestingly, even applicable Supreme Court precedent did not make judges more amenable to gay and lesbian parents' rights claims based on equal protection. For example, the issue of equal protection was applied specifically to the contention that the children would be damaged by the stigma associated with having a gay or lesbian parent, and the accompanying response that such a basis for a custody decision was impermissible due to the Supreme Court's 1984 precedent in *Palmore v Sidotti*.[54] In *Palmore*, a divorced and remarried parent was denied custody because of the stigma associated with her cross-racial marriage to her second husband. The Supreme Court ruled, based on the Fourteenth Amendment, that the private racial prejudices that produced such stigma should not be abided and could not be used to deny her custody. In the *Marlow* case discussed earlier, Mr. Marlow argued, based on *Palmore*, that the restrictions imposed on him were based on "a private bias and therefore violate[d] his constitutional right to equal protection." However, in response to the father's contention that "the law is clear: visitation restrictions based on bias and prejudice are incompatible with the concept of equal protection and must be vacated," the court disagreed, concluding that "the trial court's foremost consideration in this case was the children's best interest, not [the father's] homosexuality."[55]

The result had been similar in a Missouri case argued eleven years earlier, in 1987, involving a lesbian mother, *S.E.G. v R.A.G.* There, the court responded to the rights claim by arguing that "[h]omosexuals are not offered the constitutional protection that race, national origin, and alienage have been afforded," suggesting that the equal protection application in *Palmore* was contingent on the issue of race specifically and that homosexuals are not deserving of similar equal protection.[56] This ruling was particularly striking in that an Alaska court had ruled only two years prior, in the nearly identical case *S.N.E. v R.L.B.*, that societal stigma of homosexuality could *not* be used as a rationale for denying a gay or lesbian parent custody, a decision that relied specifically on the precedent set in *Palmore*. Still, as late as 2002, attorneys also recognized that, as one stated, "*Palmore v Sidotti* is a race case, and race is a suspect classification under the Equal Protection Clause and sexual orientation isn't. . . . I wish that language had caught on more [in reference to sexual orientation and parents' rights], but it hasn't."[57] One judge from Southern California expressed this ambivalence:

> here we're looking at it from a societal perspective that invidious discrimination should not be abided, as a function of the civil rights movement, the gay rights movement, and other movements. We can all understand that, and there's nothing wrong with looking at it from a societal standpoint. But I guess you have to rationalize that you're gonna be sacrificing a few [children's] souls, collateral damage.[58]

Aside from rights claims based on the Fourteenth Amendment, gay and lesbian parents commonly asserted their right to privacy in custody proceedings in which their sexual orientation or practices were at issue. As early as 1976, in *Towend v Towend*, lesbian mother Larraine Towend asserted that her right to privacy had been transgressed by the Ohio family court, when the judge compelled her to answer detailed questions regarding her sex life with her current partner. Such lines of questioning, in fact, occurred commonly in lesbians' divorce trials before the 1990s (and to a lesser extent, have continued since), though they were less frequent in gay men's custody cases, in which public behavior (such as appearing at a gay-pride event or attending a predominantly gay church) rather than intimate behavior seemed to be more at issue.

In the pre-*Lawrence* years, often the right to privacy was linked to the criminal status of same-sex sexual activity and, by extension, the criminal (or potentially criminal) behavior of a gay or lesbian parent. This narrative, because it was likely to be linked to the existence of a specific sodomy law in that state, was more prevalent in the earlier years, prior to such laws being struck down in many states (and later by the U.S. Supreme Court), yet the narrative still persisted in twenty states through the 1990s. In 1982 in *L. v D.*, for instance, the Missouri court found that "homosexual activities have been condemned since the beginning of recorded history. Such practices are not within the privacy of a marriage as discussed in *Griswold v State of Connecticut*. Nor are such practices protected by the constitution."[59] Although such narratives might be expected in relatively early cases such as this one, a similar rationale was also found twenty years later in *Ex Parte H.H.*, discussed in the preceding chapter. Only one year before the *Lawrence* decision overturned sodomy laws nationally, this Alabama Supreme Court decision described the mother's homosexuality as a "crime against nature"—and clearly, then, not protected by the constitutional right to privacy.[60]

Yet even before *Lawrence*, judges occasionally found ways to exercise LGBT parents' privacy rights without bucking the law entirely. In the 1985 Pennsylvania divorce case of *Constant A. v Paul C.A.*, the justices cited at length the importance of the right to privacy, noting that

[t]he personal intimacies of marriage, the home . . . and the family have been held "fundamental" by the Supreme Court and, hence, have been encompassed within the protected rights of privacy. Marital intimacies in the privacy of their bedroom are within the protected right of privacy . . .

[and] although an activity (sodomy) is a crime, it is protected by the privacy requirements of marriage.[61]

Despite using their discretion to ignore sodomy laws in the context of heterosexual marriage, however, courts were unwilling to extend this requirement to the conduct between a mother and her postdivorce lesbian partner; the judges therefore denied her custody on the basis of her sexual relationship with this partner, which they deemed to be "criminal activity." Likewise, nearly a decade earlier in *In re Jane B.*, the court even found that the right to privacy protected homosexuals' right to engage in sodomy but reasoned that "these cases do not, however, extend the protection to innocent bystanders or children who may be affected physically and emotionally by close contact with homosexual conduct of adults" and therefore rescinded custody from the lesbian mother.[62] Thus, this "superright" was apparently universal neither in its applicability nor its effects.

Because privacy is specifically an individual right, it would be difficult for it to be reinvented in relational terms. However, the fact that no single right—whether based on sexual orientation or parental status—is uniformly interpreted or universally defined in such a way as to categorically exclude any particular situation opens a door to the potential creative reframing of civil rights paradigms already in place. In that sense, the indeterminacy of rights saves us from having to create *new* rights to protect nontraditional families—an admittedly difficult task in a common-law system and conservative legal environment—in order to extend them to new situations and family forms.

Indeed, by the late 1990s, this creative potential began to yield results. In *In the Matter of T.L.* in 1996, the justices asserted,

> The Court will not avoid its constitutional duty . . . by bowing to the hypothetical effects of prejudice; to refuse . . . homosexual parents, as a class, the rights and protections afforded . . . heterosexual parents is . . . violative of the Equal Protection Clause. . . . [Therefore,] sexual orientation, standing alone, is not a permissible basis for the denial of custody or visitation.[63]

This rejection of social stigma against homosexuality has become increasingly common, and the successful use of such stigma as a rationale for denying or restricting custody for gay and lesbian parents has become increasingly rare. Although not entirely absent from judges' minds—witness the 2002 Alabama case *Ex Parte H.H.*, discussed previously, and the Florida Supreme Court's use of the stigma argument, in part, to continue to bar adoptions by gay and lesbian parents in that state—by the twenty-first century such rationales had plummeted in frequency, as had success in those cases in which they were attempted. In fact, these two cases were the only ones in which such findings were upheld after the turn of the century. Even in Florida, the Court of Appeals found in the 2000 divorce case of *Jacoby v Jacoby*,

> even if the court's comments about the community's beliefs and possible reactions were correct and supported by the evidence in this record, the law cannot give effect to private biases. Moreover, even if the law were to permit consideration of the biases of others, and even if we were to accept the assumption that such would necessarily harm the children, the bias and ensuing harm would flow not from the fact that the children were *living* with a homosexual mother, but from the fact that she *is* a homosexual. The circuit court's reliance on perceived biases was an improper basis for a residential custody determination.[64]

One of the other most noticeable changes over time was judges' inclination to adopt the nexus standard discussed previously, requiring harm be shown before considering a parent's sexual orientation to determine custody, although they still did not address equal protection or other rights claims raised by the parents. The 2001 Colorado divorce case of *In re Marriage of Dorworth* never mentioned the word "rights" once in the decision and yet found that "the court may not restrict parenting time merely because of a parent's sexual orientation."[65] In the 2003 divorce case of *Damron v Damron*, the North Dakota Supreme Court more explicitly stated that it would not even be considering Valerie Damron's claim that removing custody of her children from her based on her sexual orientation violated her rights under both the federal and state constitutions. It did, however, find that "[o]ther courts have generally recognized that, in the absence of evidence of actual or potential harm to the children, a parent's homosexual relationship, by itself, is not determinative of custody" and that "[father] Shawn Damron failed to meet his burden of proof to justify a change in custody . . . [because] he presented no evidence that the relationship was causing actual or potential harm to the children."[66] This finding is particularly noteworthy in that the same court had ruled twenty-two years earlier, in the case of *Jacobson v Jacobson*, that a parent's homosexuality created a presumption against the child's best interest and *must* be taken into account in deciding custody. The *Damron* majority, without compunction, stated, "to the extent that *Jacobson* can be read as creating such a presumption, it is overruled."[67]

The next year, in *Hogue v Hogue*, the Tennessee divorce court went even further, reaching beyond the nexus test to suggest that sexual orientation is *always* irrelevant in custody determinations. This was also surprising, given that the same court had ruled only five years earlier that it was appropriate to remove custody of Julie Eldridge's daughter from her, based on her lesbian relationship.[68] Thus, even when arguments against restrictions based on sexual orientation were not framed as constitutional or equal rights issues, courts began to roll back such restrictions and with increasing frequency to adopt a nexus standard—a standard that, according to most legal analyses, is based on the Fourteenth Amendment right of equal protection. And yet, even in the course of this development, arguments that rest solely on a platform of parents' rights have been seen as ill fit to custody and family law.

The Children's Rights Paradigm

Following the popularization of the "best interest of the child" standard in the second half of the twentieth century, claims based on children's rights, rather than parental rights, became increasingly popular in the 1980s and '90s. The invocation of children's rights, by both the court and the litigants, was a dramatic example of the way rights discourses could be strategically and creatively employed to a variety of ends. If rights are susceptible to multiple and opposing interpretations in other legal contexts, they are especially so in family law, where the guiding principle is as ideologically loaded a term as "best interest of the child."[69] The case stories that follow illustrate the myriad contexts, purposes, and outcomes of legal claims based on children's rights—some supporting the position of gay and lesbian parents, and some opposing them.

The children's rights paradigm of family law is one example of the misguided application of individual rights to the family—specifically, the representation by some children's rights advocates of children as individuals needing protection rather than as members of a family unit needing connection to parents or parental figures.[70] As legal scholar Lawrence Tribe has argued, the law treats families simply as a collection of individuals, and what are often named "family rights" are actually the rights of individuals whose ties to one another are, in law professor Mary Ann Glendon's words, "increasingly fluid, detachable, and interchangeable."[71] This individual-rights-based orientation begins to explain why sexual orientation or involvement in a same-sex relationship can be used as justification to deny a parent's contact with his or her child(ren). By focusing on only the purported *individual* rights of the child, such an approach does not consider the importance of relationships between child and parent to children's development and, indeed, to their best interests.

Because of this problematic tendency to treat the individual as the basic social unit, there is often, in discourse as well as in practice, an implicit assumption that if parents are asserting their rights, they are subjugating children's rights and best interests. And, conversely, a rhetoric of children's rights that portrays children as victims in need of protection from their parents is often used to curtail certain parents' or would-be parents' rights. It tacitly implicates parents as harmful or selfish while at the same time emphasizing children's rights as *individuals*, rather than their place in the family unit. Although this framing of rights is ironic in that children were not actually considered rights-bearing citizens when most individual rights were conceived in American law, it can be difficult for parents to respond to in any meaningful way, as no one wants to be labeled "antichild."

Commonly, the judges have put rights claims in an ideological and discursive hierarchy, positioning what they perceive to be the rights of children clearly over those of the parents. Some judges, such as one interviewed in Southern California, expressed this concern as one of balance: "It's a matter of how can the court ensure, as much as possible, the right balance of both the child's right to have a loving, intimate relationship with both parents with the least interference from the parents' rights to function as parents."[72] Other judges were more specific in their prioritization of children's rights *over* parents' rights. One supervising judge in Northern California observed, "I don't think that the superiority of the parent is a new issue. . . . You know, a parent, 'we do not trample on parental rights.' And unfortunately there's never a counterbalance about the children's rights. It's always the parents' rights."[73] Even more vehemently, another judge proclaimed, "We see that all the time, typically the mother, who believes that she owns this human body of a child and she gets to decide where the child is going to be at any particular time. . . . It's just an ownership issue and it's a power play, isn't it?"[74] Even attorneys for gay and lesbian parents recognized this hierarchy of rights. One, who later became a judge, commented in regard to making rights-based arguments for parents, "yes, we used them, but we always made it secondary to the children's rights."[75]

In the appellate decisions, this sentiment was even more evident. As early as 1976, in the case of *In re Jane B.*, the court ruled, "Here by statute there is governmental interest in the welfare of children which supersedes the rights of parents. . . . The best interests of the child is the predominant criterion, to which, in the event of conflict, all others must be made to defer."[76] Similarly, in the 1988 Tennessee divorce case of *Collins v Collins*, Beverly Collins was ordered not to live or be romantically involved with any other woman as a condition of visitation. The judges justified this infringement on her civil rights by stating, "the court must assert itself as the guardian of the moral and physical welfare of these children. The rights of the children take precedence over the rights of the parents."[77] In an interview, Collins responded that denying her custody of her daughter, "affects civil rights issues. It affects children's rights [too]," but she was ultimately unsuccessful in retaining custody or reversing the visitation restrictions.[78]

Conversely, parents were credited if they clearly subordinated their own interests and rights to those of the children. Attorney Steve Drizin, who became involved in these custody cases through a children's rights legal clinic in Illinois, commented on the effect of his lack of affiliation with a gay rights organization in arguing the appeal in *Pleasant v Pleasant*, a 1993 case in which a lesbian mother's custody and visitation rights had been revoked:

> I think one of the reasons . . . why we were able to create such a strong opinion [on appeal] was that it was coming from a legal clinic that was associated with children's issues, rather than from an organization or a party that was clearly representing one parent's issues over another. . . . the court clearly look[ed] to the fact that this was a legal clinic involved in it and . . . [that] this doesn't appear to be part of a legal strategy aimed at getting increasing rights for gay and lesbian parents.[79]

Likewise, in the 1996 case *In re Adoption of Baby Z.*, the court of appeals ruled in favor of a second-parent adoption in Connecticut because it determined that "[i]t was apparent to the court that neither [mother was] pursuing this adoption for a particular cause or to advance the greater good as they see it."[80] In such cases, the notion that the rights of parents and their children might mutually reinforce one another was rendered essentially impossible.

In some cases, a distinctly different children's rights framework was apparent, in which the assumed best interests of the children were not just balanced with but justified an outright *denial* of the parents' rights to custody and visitation. This narrative was apparent particularly in cases in which the issue of stigma was raised as evidence that the child(ren) would be harmed by residence or association with a gay or lesbian parent, such as in *Marlow* and *S.E.G. v R.A.G.*, discussed earlier. In *S.E.G*, for instance, the judges' "wish to protect the children from peer pressure, teasing, and possible ostracizing they may encounter as a result of the 'alternative lifestyle' their mother has chosen" necessitated, in their rationale, a rejection of her due process and equal protection claims, denial of custody, and limitations on her visitation.[81] Likewise, eleven years later in *Marlow*, Mr. Marlow was told that "the restrictions were based on the children's best interest" and that his constitutional rights claims regarding sexual-orientation discrimination were therefore irrelevant.[82] Indeed, most judges agreed with this sentiment in interviews; as one commented:

> Did it discriminate against [the parents] and cause [them] to be thought of differently as a result? Okay, probably. She [a lesbian mother] obviously was put in a different situation because of her choice. You'd have to do it for the kid. I mean, that's the way it would be. So that's why it's hard to engraft into the family code that kind of value system.[83]

Another well-experienced judge agreed: "Even though it runs afoul of the societal considerations, let's protect this particular child."[84] Yet the judges in the divorce case of *Conkel v Conkel*, decided in Ohio the same year as *S.E.G. v R.A.G.*, pointed out the logical flaw with such rationales: that even if primary custody is denied or visitation is restricted, the fact that the children have a gay parent remains unchanged and may lead to the same level of stigma. As the judges in *Conkel* reasoned, "This court fails to see why the extension of visitation would exacerbate this issue [of stigma]. The children will have to come to terms with the fact that their father is homosexual."[85] Thus, it was not necessary to abridge the parent's rights in order to serve the best interests of the children.

Again, however, especially prior to 2000, the court distinguished between different parents' ability to assert rights on behalf of their children, with nonbiological parents lacking standing to do so—once more demonstrating the practical difficulties in determining the appropriate source of a well-respected but poorly defined right. In *Kathleen C. v Lisa W.*, discussed in chapter 3, Kathleen asserted that denying her custody of or visitation with her two daughters violated both her and her daughters' freedom of association with one another. Even though she included the children, this argument was denied by the court, as they found she had no status to assert the rights of the children. In *Liston v Pyles*, Marla Liston argued that, by not granting her standing to seek visitation, the trial court "erred in its failure to find that [her] relationship with [the child] is constitutionally protected, and that [the child's] interest in continuing his relationship with [her] is constitutionally protected." In response, the court "question[ed] whether [she] may properly assert [the child's] rights, given that she is not his parent."[86] Liston commented in an interview, "I think that we have to have legal rights for our children, and really, the juvenile court system is not set up to ensure the rights of the children."[87] In *Adoption of T.J.K.* in 1996 the two Colorado mothers seeking simultaneous adoptions of each other's biological children asserted that the rejection of their petition, based on the mothers' position as "unmarried cohabitants," constituted a violation of their children's due process and equal protection rights and that their children were at a disadvantage relative to children whose parents can legally marry. The court reasoned, however, that biological connection was a precondition for being able to argue rights claims on behalf of the child:

> This relationship, between a child and her mother's non-marital partner, is not one that has traditionally received constitutional protection. . . . Even if we assume . . . that a child has a corresponding liberty interest in care from his or her natural parent, we find no indication of such an interest regarding the relationship between a child and a *potential* adoptive parent. (emphasis added)[88]

Success was even more elusive when the arguments that unrecognized parents made on behalf of their children were accompanied by rights claims of their own. *In the Interest of Angel Lace M.*, discussed earlier, was one such case; the two mothers argued that the denial of their second-parent adoption petition violated both the nonbiological mother's and the child's due process rights. In this instance, the court did not address the claim made on behalf of the child at all and effectively immobilized the rights claim of the mothers by concluding that it was in the best interest of the state to protect "the traditional family" by not recognizing a household with two mothers. The *Lofton* case challenging Florida's gay adoption ban was another example in which the judges were able to sidestep the children's rights claim presented alongside the assertion of potential parents' rights. The U.S. circuit court's decision in 2004 in *Lofton*, in fact, stated that children actually have no fundamental right to be adopted; and furthermore, in addressing the right of gay parents to adopt, the judges circumvented the *Lawrence* decision's precedent in favor of LGBT rights by claiming that it applied only to *privacy* rights and not to a "public" right such as adoption.

Such cases raised questions about the relationship between children's best interests, rights, and judges' interpretations of statutory schemes and case law—and, perhaps more important, questions about what these guidelines left unsaid. One Southern California judge stated the dilemma this way: "are we going to be governed by rules, or are we going to be governed by the equity of the people's decisions, what is fair?"[89] Because "children's rights" is not a specifically defined legal entitlement, it has the capacity to be redefined or interpreted in new and different ways. This is particularly important in resolving the dilemma of how to deal with a solitary construct such as rights in a necessarily collective institution such as the family. The indeterminacy of rights discourses that are as loosely defined as children's rights allows us to think of creative ways to resolve this conflict, such as arguing that children's rights to develop autonomous self-definitions and relationships require the protection of the parent-child bond, however that bond is defined. Reconceptualizing parents' rights and children's rights as compatible, and focusing on a right to be together rather than one person's rights versus another, shows that rights can also be relational, or collective.

For instance, many custody and visitation cases, such as *Weigand v Houghton* and *Hogue v Hogue*, discussed earlier, raised questions about the relationship between the rights of children and the legal regulations sometimes imposed on their parents. In the *Conkel* case discussed earlier, the court found that interference with or restrictions on the gay father's visitation were "not only an infringement on the other parent's right to visitation but also an infringement of the child's right to receive the love, affection, training and companionship of the parent."[90] This finding was an anomaly at the time but became increasingly common later. This notion was confirmed in interviews with judges; one, who had worked in family law his entire career, commented, "The law clearly says that the child has a right to frequent and continued contact with both parents, and what the law really means is that the child is entitled to a loving, nurturing relationship with both parents as long as the parents are willing to give it."[91] Similarly, in *Weigand*, the court in Mississippi agreed with David Weigand that an order banning visitation when his life partner was present "burden[ed] and violate[d] the fundamental rights of both father and son to an ongoing relationship."[92] The attorney in this case commented in an interview (in reference to both this case and the *Bottoms* case), "we wanted to make constitutional arguments about the fact that it's unconstitutional to impose this kind of a burden on . . . the parent-child relationship."[93]

In some instances, though rarely prior to 2000, the recognition of the right to the parent-child bond extended to adoptive or nonbiological parent-child relationships as well. In *In re Custody of H.S.H.-K.* in 1995, the court agreed, on due process grounds, that "the child has a liberty interest in continuing his relationship with both parties and in avoiding the harm from separation from one of them."[94] A San Francisco supervising judge summed up, "There is a strong philosophy in this court that this is not in the best interest of children to have winners and losers."[95] Thus, a recognition developed, sometimes explicit as in *Weigand* and other times implicit, that the rights of a parent and those of the child can often be considered co-determinative, or at least coincidental.

The strategy of invoking parental and children's rights simultaneously is suggestive of a new way to look at family rights, privileging the bond between the two, rather than one person's rights over another, a strategy that is apparent in later decision-making. Some such rights claims, for instance, were aimed at the right to adopt or to be adopted, invoked both by the parents or would-be parents and on behalf of the children. In the landmark case *Sharon S. v Annette F.* in 2003, the California Supreme Court asserted that, contrary to the dissenter's opinion that the precedent "trivialized family bonds" by recognizing alternative family forms, its decision "encourages and strengthens family bonds" and that the law "bases parent and child rights on the existence of a parent and child relationship."[96] The Indiana second-parent adoption case of *In the Matter of Adoption of K.S.P. and J.P.* in 2004 found, "the relationship between parent and child is a bundle of human rights of such fundamental importance that adoption statutes . . . should be 'strictly construed in favor of a worthy parent and the preservation of such a relationship.'"[97] Such evolving views culminated in formal recognition of the right to a parent-child bond, even for those in nontraditional and nongenetic relationships, in many states, such as California, Pennsylvania, and others, and they may be indicative of the future of rights in the family law context. Yet the traditional conception of rights as individualistic, and of rights-bearers as deserving or undeserving, continues to inform courts in many parts of the country.

Are Rights Wrong? Rejection of Rights Discourses in Family Law

Are rights-based arguments *universally* futile or irrelevant in gay and lesbian parents' cases as a strategy, as would be expected based on the critiques of rights by Critical Legal Studies and other modern schools of sociolegal thought?[98] Certainly not. Based on Maine's theoretical continuum described earlier, in fact, one might expect the legal claims-making of gay and lesbian parents to be more successful in recent decades because of an anticipated understanding of family rights based on contractual arrangements rather than biological status.[99] This, however, was not necessarily the case. Not only did status-based determinations of family rights remain relevant, but rights discourses of *any* sort were often less than successful. Attorneys, such as the legal director of Lambda, summarized aptly this reluctance to decide family law cases within a paradigm of parents' rights, and the conflict therein:

> In family law cases, constitutional arguments are rarely successful. You know, courts aren't accustomed to using constitutional law to decide family matters. [But] we make those constitutional arguments for a number of reasons. Number one, we firmly believe that the Constitution applied, even in the context of family law. And some of what happens in family disputes and family court decisions is from our perspective unconstitutional.[100]

NCLR director Kate Kendell agreed: "in family law, judges are so used to applying fact-based analysis, it's really hard for them to think about applying a rights-based analysis, which sometimes should be applied. But they just don't do it. They don't do it."[101]

In fact, in many of the cases in which parents chose to articulate their claims in terms of rights—whether relying on specific constitutional principles, an overarching concept of fundamental rights of parents, bio-logical status, or contractual ties—the discourse of rights was rejected as altogether unacceptable and irrelevant in the child custody context. There was a subtle but distinct suggestion, in both interviews and writ-ten decisions, that judges interpreted rights claims on the part of parents to be selfish and not aimed at meeting the needs of their children. One Southern California judge commented in reference to rights claims,

> Does that come up? All the time. Selfish people will seek their own needs and along the way forget the needs of the children. As far as the custody cases, the people really aren't thinking about the children, what's best for them. . . . I think they have totally lost sight of best interest of the child.[102]

Similarly, in the consolidated 1978 Washington cases of *Schuster v Schuster* and *Isaacson v Isaacson*, in which two women in a relation-ship each divorced their husbands and sought to retain custody of their children, the justices responded to their equal protection and due process arguments by stating, "there is more involved than the rights of these two women. The lives of six children are at stake."[103] Twenty-one years later, in *E.N.O. v L.M.M.*—the first case in Massachusetts to recognize the parental rights of a nonbiological mother in a former lesbian par-enting duo—the Massachusetts justices granted visitation rights to a nonbiological mother over the objection of the biological mother, com-menting, "Parental rights . . . are not absolute. . . . We must balance the defendant's interest in protecting her custody of her child with the child's best interest in maintaining her relationship with the child's de facto par-ent."[104] Even a judge who had formerly litigated for gay and lesbian par-ents recognized that "your best chances are always to stay focused on the child and not argue about your client. . . . your rights are not the issue. The best interest of the child is the issue."[105]

This judicial narrative was intensified when the court perceived that gay and lesbian parents wished to use their child custody cases as a plat-form for furthering gay rights—indicative, again, that their rights as gay *citizens* are not relevant in family court. Marla Liston, for instance, was told after she was denied standing to seek visitation with her nonbio-logical son, "you need to keep low key because people know your name, they associate whatever you were doing with a gay issue."[106] A Northern California judge, who had also previously litigated on behalf of gay and lesbian parents, agreed that certain advocacy activities in support of a gay or lesbian parent have made judges "feel like they were making this a political issue, not about the kid, so I think [one should] also say to the judge, 'this is not about politics, this is not about any of those things.'"[107] This perception by judges was most likely to occur when the parents relied on the legal assistance of gay rights and civil rights organizations. In the 1982 case of *J.L.P.(H.) v D.J.P.*, the Missouri justices chastised a gay father in the decision for enlisting the help of a gay rights organization, Lambda, to represent him: "The appellant father's brief and oral argument indicated a desire on the father's part to convert this appeal into a wide ranging inquiry into the constitutional and marital rights of homosexual fathers."[108] Even those judges who were sympathetic to the civil rights of gay and lesbian individuals generally saw it as an issue that had to be addressed by the legislature and one that did not have a place in family law. One such judge, with over a decade of experience on the bench, noted,

> in terms of envisioning a statute where it's like your typical statute and somebody shall not discriminate on the basis of gender, race, sexual orientation . . . I can't see such a statute being engrafted in this area [of family law] because I think it would be too rigid because most of the factors that are already in here are child focused.[109]

Such a tendency did not go unnoticed by the interviewed attorneys working on behalf of organizations that represent gay and lesbian parents in court, including the former and present legal directors of Lambda and NCLR. NCLR director Kate Kendell commented,

> sometimes the judge, when we get involved in these cases, will say, "see, this is a political issue." And in fact, its interesting because, well, that may or may not be the case given culturally the discourse around lesbian and gay parents. What we really have to come in and say is, well, that may or may not be the case but we don't care about that. What we care about is ensuring that the process by which the parent is determined to be a proper custodian of the children is fair and objective. . . . And so, you know that's going to be used . . . because we are a legal advocacy organization, and organizations and institutions generally are not trusted in this country— everybody questions motives.[110]

NCLR's previous director agreed:

usually family law judges don't appreciate intervention from civil rights organizations. . . . if it appears to the judge that you are trying to make this a political issue as opposed to a discussion about what's actually in the child's best interests, then they really . . . it's a fine line that you have to walk.[111]

Indeed, as the prevailing and only consistent rule in child custody across all fifty states, the best interests of the child—or whatever the judges deemed constituted such best interests—could often be treated as something of a universal trump over all other rights and interests. The best-interest standard is, in fact, an emblem of the indeterminacy of family law and rights discourses therein. One Washington, D.C., attorney even posited that "best interest" could be used specifically to obscure rights violations:

if the motivation was purely, you know, animus against gay people, then its unconstitutional. But it's way too easy to get away from that in any kind of custody case, where all they have to do is reframe it as the best interest of the child and they would get away with it being about animus, and there isn't any guarantee that it would actually require . . . anything we could call proof.[112]

This seemed to be the case in the 1978 South Carolina case of *Cook v Cobb*, in which paternal grandparents Arlene and Glenn Cook successfully removed custody from bisexual mother Janet Cobb on the basis of her "rather bohemian lifestyle." The court found, "The welfare of the child and what is in his/her best interest is the primary, paramount, and consideration. . . . the rights of even a fit parent are merely presumptive and must yield when the best interests of the child would be subserved. . . . the right of the parent is not absolute and unconditional." The court's decision that the child's best interest would be "subserved" with her mother was based on its observation that Janet had "exercised poor judgment" in the past in her romantic life with both men and women, that "among her associates were homosexuals," and that therefore the environment she proposed to raise her daughter in was "far from ideal"—despite the fact that she had since remarried and settled down with her current husband.[113]

Later, in the 1989 Missouri divorce case of *T.C.H. v K.M.H.*, even the children's right to decide who they wanted to live with was subverted, paradoxically, in the name of "the best interest of the child." Even though the children wished to remain with their lesbian mother, the court argued that "a child's preference is 'followed only if the welfare and interest of the child . . . are consistent with that preference' [and] their preference is not consistent with their best interest and welfare."[114] The court also denied the mother's claim that her due process rights had been violated in removing the children from her custody by claiming that this would only have been the case if her parental rights were terminated entirely, which they were not.

One notable exception to the dominance of best interests over rights was the 1994 New York case of *Thomas S. v Robin Y.*, discussed in chapter 3. In a Court of Appeals decision to grant the sperm donor parental rights, the court prioritized the sperm donor's due process rights over what had been determined to be the best interest of the child by both the lower court and the court-appointed psychologist:

> The asserted sanctity of the family unit is an uncompelling ground for the drastic step of depriving petitioner [the donor] of procedural due process. . . . we regard the determination of this matter in any manner that departs from the express procedures delineated in . . . the Family Court Act [discussing the rights of unmarried fathers] as a violation of petitioner's statutory and Constitutional rights.[115]

The mothers in this case commented in an interview that this result, and indeed the tenor of the entire hearing, was that this was "an old-fashioned father's rights case. . . . the family court judge immediately related to this guy" as a father, rather than as a sperm donor.[116] Interestingly, this decision—which stands as case law in New York State—ran contrary to the best interest of the child (who, at the time of the decision, was suffering nightmares and panic attacks at the thought of having to fly across the country without her mothers to spend time with a man she barely knew) at precisely a time when "old-fashioned father's [or mother's] rights cases" were becoming more rare and giving way to broader conceptions of rights and greater reliance on the best interest of the child.

A newer trend has been the recognition that children's best interests and parents' rights are not necessarily mutually exclusive. Several litigants and attorneys pointed out in interviews that the rights being asserted by parents were actually in tandem with the children's best interest, so to deny one would be to deny both. Marla Liston commented,

Let's take the whole gay issue out of the equation, and let's look at the children. And that's not what's being done. People [the judges] are making a political statement, and . . . what's happening as a result of that is that the children are being hurt. Now, clearly, as an adult I am being hurt, too. But I am an adult, and I make my own decisions, and this child has . . . does not even have the ability to say, "okay, yeah, but I want to be with her. I want to be able to see her." . . . So this is not just a gay issue; this is a children's issue. . . . The court system is not acting in the best interest of the children of the state of Ohio.[117]

The attorney for Kathleen Crandall in *Kathleen C. v Lisa W.*, whose California case was very similar to that of Marla Liston, also pointed to this confluence of parents' rights and children's best interest:

It would be refreshing to have them say this isn't about rights, it's about kids, since they never give the kids the benefit of a . . . two parent family. So . . . I don't see a conflict at all between these two issues. It's never in the best interest of the children to deny them access to a parent, *never, ever, ever.* (emphasis in original)[118]

Some judges, even if they did not call them mutually determinative, recognized that both discourses had a place in custody cases. One, from Northern California, commented,

Well, they [rights] certainly have a place. So, can they be used to obscure the best interest? I suppose so. In most cases is there a good faith and belief that the arguments the parents are raising are necessary in determining their lifestyle? I'd rather take the position those people in good faith take that position.[119]

This evolution in conceptualizing parents' rights and children's best interests can be seen in case law as early as 1998, in the Maryland divorce case of *Boswell v Boswell*. Robert Boswell, a gay father whose visitation with his children had been restricted based on his same-sex relationship, argued successfully that this restriction was not only unnecessary but a violation of his parental rights. The court recognized that parents have a fundamental right to the care and custody of their children (a right later affirmed in *Troxel*) but also that the best interest of the child may take precedence over this right. Rather than positioning these two interests against each other, however, the court concluded, "the best interest standard does not ignore the interests of the parents and their importance to the child. We recognize that in almost all cases, it is in the best interest of the child to have reasonable maximum opportunity to develop a close and loving relationship with each parent."[120]

Increasingly, in the years following *Boswell*—and even following the *Troxel* case, which purported to strengthen traditional parents' rights vis-à-vis others who were not related by blood or adoption—judges began to agree that parents' rights in many situations were not necessarily contrary to the rights or best interests of the children and were, in fact, entirely appropriate to consider in this context. Specifically, in new forms of family in which a biological—and in some cases adoptive—relationship with both parents is not possible, this novel way to approach rights and best interest—as connected rather than diametrically opposed—may be indicative of the future of rights. Indeed, since the start of the twenty-first century, such frameworks have increasingly appeared in the rationales of decisions determining shared custody, visitation, and second-parent adoption for previously unrecognized co-parents in same-sex families. The Rhode Island Supreme Court's 2000 decision in *Rubano v DiCenzo* was indicative of this trend. In this case, biological mother Concetta DiCenzo had intentionally fostered a close relationship between the child and Maureen Rubano, her former partner and the child's nonbiological mother, and agreed in a previous co-parenting agreement to permanent visitation rights for Rubano, because she agreed it would be "in the best interest of the minor child." Instead of defaulting to the presumption that DiCenzo held the only rights claim that could be recognized under *Troxel*, or that Rubano's claim of parental rights was irrelevant under the best-interest doctrine, the court reasoned,

> the mere fact of biological parenthood, even when coupled with . . . that parent's fundamental right "to make decisions concerning the care, custody, of control of [her] children" does not always endow the biological parent with the absolute right to prevent all third parties from ever acquiring any parental rights vis-à-vis the child. Thus, the fact that DiCenzo not only gave birth to this child but also nurtured him from infancy does not mean that she can arbitrarily terminate Rubano's de facto parental relationship with the boy.[121]

This rationale by the Rhode Island justices was no longer anomalous by the early twenty-first century, and it has been increasingly adopted by courts in other states faced with similar situations. The 2004 Colorado case of *In the Interest of E.L.M.C.* arose from a dispute between two lesbian former partners who had entered into a co-parenting agreement, with court-ordered shared custody. Because the child had been adopted from China, and the Chinese government refused to allow both parents to adopt (and generally refuses adoption to anyone in a known gay or lesbian relationship), only one mother was legally related to the child by adoption. When the couple broke up, the adoptive mother moved to void the court-ordered shared custody agreement and terminate visitation between the child and her former partner, based on her rights as a parent under *Troxel*. The court disagreed and found that there was a parental relationship between the nonadoptive mother and the child, which was good for the child and in need protection:

> every ruling on parental responsibilities that protects a child from harm also furthers the child's best interests. . . . proof of the close and substantial relationship between McLeod [the nonbiological mother] and E.L.M.C. [the child] and proof of threatened emotional harm to the child should parental responsibilities be denied to McLeod are, in effect, two sides of the same coin.[122]

The Washington co-parenting case of *In re Parentage of L.B.*, decided two months earlier, suggested how the two sides of the coin—parents' rights and children's best interests—might be related in legal analysis: "The decision in *Troxel* [protecting biological parents' rights vis-à-vis other parties] is not a barrier to [nonbiological mother] Carvin's claim. Instead, it provides a roadmap to constitutional application of the statute determining Carvin's [parental rights] claim."[123] In other words, the recognition of a parent's rights in *Troxel* is exclusive of neither competing parental claims nor the child's best interest; it simply provides guidance as to how to navigate these claims to serve the best interest of the family unit, however that is defined, to the benefit of the child and his or her familial relationships.

The "Status" of Rights

In the 2003 landmark gay rights decision of *Lawrence v Texas*, Justice Kennedy remarked, "Had those who drew and ratified the Due Process Clauses of the Fifth Amendment or the Fourteenth Amendment known the components of liberty in its manifold possibilities, they might have been more specific."[124] Yet, as Scheingold's statement at the start of this chapter suggests, such specificity is not found in the "myth of rights." Far from the "trump" that rights in American political and legal discourse are purported to be, their ambiguity and wide-ranging interpretation ensures that their position in family law is anything but static. At the same time, given the ambiguity of family law itself and its predisposed antipathy toward prioritizing individual rights, it is perhaps no wonder that the two would be awkwardly paired and in need of some creative reinvention to ease the fit. The indeterminacy of rights is evinced by the tendency for the same rights to be deployed in opposing and often contradictory ways— such as using the right to privacy, on the one hand, to protect a gay or lesbian parent from incursions into their family or romantic life and, on the other hand, to justify a denial of visitation or custody to a nonbiological co-parent. Some scholars have even suggested that it is precisely this ambiguity and flexibility in the meaning of rights that afford them the rhetorical force they carry in sociopolitical discourse.[125] Indeed, it is precisely this flexibility that has allowed for the assertion and transformation of civil rights discourse by successions of marginalized groups and, most recently, by lesbian- and gay-headed families.

Yet, in a historically sensitive and contextualized understanding, it is important to recognize that those rights discourses that bred great success in the past—such as due process, equal protection, and privacy— have not generally been a panacea for gay and lesbian families. Because of the particular stakes and goals in custody disputes—as embodied in the ubiquitous "best interest of the child" standard—individual rights do not carry the same resonance as they do, for instance, in criminal law. Even attempting to assert rights-based arguments, in many cases, has led in the past to parents being judged selfish and inappropriately focused on themselves rather than on their children, leading many family law actors to seriously rethink the rights frameworks in this particular arena of LGBT civil rights. Such ambivalence was evident in the comments of interviewed family court judges and in cases such as *Collins v Collins*, and it exemplifies the problematic nexus of the two seemingly oppositional paradigms at stake here: that of individual civil rights and that of the family collective.

In the past, this opposition not only has bred ambivalence in the application of rights in the family law context, where they were often positioned in opposition to the best-interest standard, but has also unambiguously backfired in several cases. Sociolegal scholar Helena Silverstein discusses, for instance, the emergence of rights-based arguments raised on behalf of fetuses in challenges to pregnant teenagers' petitions (based also on the best-interest standard) to waive parental consent requirements for abortion.[126] A similar dynamic was present in cases in which nonbiological parents sought custody, visitation, or adoption of the children whom they co-parented with their partners, as in the cases of *Liston v Pyles* and *Kazmierazak v Query*. Here, based on the existence of biological ties, parents' rights once again became the dominant discourse, as the nonbiological parents' rights as well as the best interests of the children took a backseat. In the case of second-parent adoptions prior to 2000, such as *In the Interest of Angel Lace* in 1994, even the biological parent's support for the adoption was not enough to overcome the presumption that his or her own parental rights would somehow be compromised by the conferral of rights to the second parent. Thus, the best intentions of the early crusades for gay and lesbian biological parents' rights, based on the best interests of their children and their own civil and parental rights, were co-opted and reinterpreted in the infancy of the gayby boom and the rise of reproductive technology to legitimate the denial of these rights to other gay and lesbian parents. The complicated deployment (and often refutation) of status-based rights in the cases analyzed here illustrate that the *particular* status involved is of essence when talking about rights and their bases.

Nevertheless, "rights talk," in its many permutations, has persisted as both a strategy and a concept in family law, in large part because of the legal and cultural capital they bring. McCann, for instance, has argued that "rights are invested with meaning by cultural practices themselves, by the repeated acts of citizens using those conventions to negotiate material relations with each other."[127] In other words, irrespective of their roots and their effects in formal legal doctrine, rights have taken on deeper meaning and resonance by virtue of the meaning that people invest in them in their daily lives. This suggests that rights are powerful precisely *because* they can mean so many things to so many people, a testament to both their ambiguity and their resonance, as well as their ability to be reinvented.

The implication is that the very indeterminacy cursed by family law scholars over the years may not, in fact, always be so detrimental: "The flexibility and plurality of our rights traditions allow for adaptation over time, and for continued contests over the legitimacy of prevailing arrangements."[128] Indeed, over time, the individual and contrary conception of rights has yielded to their creative potential to respond to new types of family ties. Within the family law arena, even the "best interest of the child" standard no longer forecloses on the deployment of status-based rights discourses completely, as was posited in interviews by Marla Liston, the attorney for *Kathleen C.*, and others. Indeed, alongside the growing trend toward shared custody in divorce cases and an emergent sense that children are best served by continued contact with both of their parents, the increasingly common phenomenon of same-sex co-parents either seeking second-parent adoption or breaking up and adjudicating visitation and custody for the nonbiological parent gives judges an opportunity to rethink the relationship between children's best interests and parents' rights. Although prior to 2000 it was rare that courts allowed second-parent adoptions outside a handful of states—and even more rare that those who were not granted a second-parent adoption would be recognized as parents in the event of a breakup—more recently judges have been increasingly prone to challenge previous traditional conceptions of family and rights. This was evident in the 2002 Ohio case of *In re Bonfield*, in which the court allowed both mothers to be recognized as parents—notwithstanding their inability to do a second-parent adoption in Ohio—because it recognized that a lack of parental rights for the children's nonbiological mother was contrary to their own well-being or the well-being of the family.[129] Likewise, two years later, in *In re Parentage of L.B.*, the Washington court maintained the position that the best interest of the child and the rights of parents—in this case, the rights of nonbiological parents to be recognized as such—can be mutually compatible and serve one another.

Moreover, this development advances the possibility of new forms of status arguments, for instance, those aimed at protecting rights based on the status of the parent-child connection. The right to such a relationship, it has been argued, "is critical to the formation of the relational self" of the child and must therefore be protected.[130] Indeed, the right to a parent-child relationship is exactly what was prioritized in co-parenting cases involving nontraditional LGBT families, whether in the context of a second-parent adoption, as in *In the Matter of Adoption of K.S.P. and J.P.* in 2004 in

Indiana, or a split between parents and the subsequent recognition of both parties as equal parents, as in *Kristine H. v Lisa R.*, decided later the same year in California. In the former case, the justices went so far as to call the protection of a parent-child relationship a *"human right . . .* of fundamental importance"—language rarely ever used in adoption cases—and chastised the trial court that had denied the adoption petition, charging, "The only immediate threat to preservation of family relationships in this instance is the harsh application of the [strictly construed] divesting statute [claiming a parent must give up parental rights in order for the child to be adopted by a person of the same sex]."[131] In the latter case (which was later appealed to the California Supreme Court and went on to make California family law history), rather than relying on a contractual basis for shared parenting based on an agreement signed prior to their breakup—or denying custody to Lisa based on her lack of biological status—the court ruled her a parent based on her *intent* to mother the child and hold the child out as her own—in effect, based on the "status" of the parent-child bond.[132] This orientation toward the protection of family bonds themselves, rather than individuals, also has implications for the related issue of same-sex couples' rights to be legally connected to each other.

Just as the existence of gay and lesbian families themselves, as a function of their relative novelty in the judicial vocabulary, were at one time challenges to (and sometimes victims to) family law and its indeterminacy, so too are rights, with their "open texture" and complex evolution, indicative of an invitation to reimagine status and its role in determining family relationships and the rights that accompany them.[133] Indeed, although family law, because of its lack of rigid statutory guidelines, is constantly shifting and has not fully adopted new definitions of family and rights, a change is perceptible. This change—a greater awareness of the multiplicity of family forms and a need to reenvision rights to apply to relationship bonds between those who consider themselves family—would not be possible if the Bill of Rights had been written at the level of specificity suggested by Justice Kennedy. It is exactly their indeterminacy that, though proving a hardship in many cases in which parents' rights were pitted against each other or presumed different from the best interest of the child, has since allowed LGBT families and their advocates to strategically *work* this indeterminacy—and to redefine the *relational* rights that ultimately protect their families.

In the policy realm, this redefinition might mean, as suggested earlier, that the *social* status markers that connect family—interdependency, mutual commitment, and caring—replace biology as the primary indicator of "status" as a basis for rights and, indeed, for parenthood itself. In practice this conception would apply equally to all families, but it would hold particular salience for gay and lesbian families, since biological connection to both parents is generally not a possibility. At the same time, the lack of consistently applied second-parent adoption provisions across all fifty states, and the tendency for some courts to read gender-specific adoption statutes literally, precludes the possibility in some cases of a contract basis for all parent-child relationships—and certainly for same-sex parents' relationships to each other, for those living in all but a handful of states that allow same-sex civil unions or marriage. Even though most adoption statutes are written with the intent that they be broadly construed, application of these statutes and the contracts they involve often requires some creativity and a sense that the arrangement will benefit the family unit. Thus, Maine's dichotomous conception of rights advancing from status to contract bases over time—with contractual rights seen as the more "modern" and equitable way to dispense rights—seems far too simplistic and not adequate to tell the story of LGBT family rights. Although certainly adoption contracts are the most durable way to connect families not related by blood, the experience of LGBT families across all fifty states suggests that this approach alone is neither feasible nor possible in all situations. Given the ill fit of family law and individual rights, as well as the exigency of preserving family bonds, then, it behooves family law actors to revisit the use of rights based on something other than this type of contract. For example, though ideally all states would open the possibility of second-parent adoptions, in the absence of that the court could recognize a nonbiological and nonadoptive co-parent as a "psychological parent" based on his or her behavior as a parental figure and relationship to the child—in other words, based on their *relational status* vis-à-vis the child—and preserve the family bond even in the event of a breakup.

Indeed, this recognition and even more all-encompassing legal forms of parenthood and recognition based on a privileging of the preservation of family bonds seem to be the coming trend in family law as it relates to nontraditional families, as is a greater recognition that parental rights do not always negate the best interest of the child. A 2005 landmark California Supreme Court precedent illustrates this point well and may pave the way for future conceptions of family relations and rights. *Elisa B. v Emily B.* is actually a consolidated opinion applying to three sepa rate cases of lesbian co-parents and their children.[134] In *Elisa B.*, the state sued to have Elisa recognized as a parent to the twin children born by her ex-partner, Emily, who was unemployed and dependent on state aid after their breakup; the state sued for the purpose of forcing Elisa to pay child support to Emily for the children whom she had had with her partner but for whom she now claimed no parental obligation. In *Kristine H. v Lisa R.*, the two parents had obtained a prebirth judgment declaring them "joint intended legal parents" of the child born to Kristine by donor insemination, but the couple later broke up, at which point Lisa was not recognized as a parent for the purpose of visitation and custody.[135] Although the court of appeals dismissed the prebirth contract between the two, it left open the possibility of other routes to recognize Lisa as a parent based on her actions since the birth. Finally, in *K.M. v E.G.*, discussed in chapter 3, K.M. sued for partial custody of the children born to her partner with the eggs that she had donated. Although the facts in the three cases varied somewhat, they all raised the question of the validity of a prior contract and of the status of a mother who was not the birth parent. In the consolidated California Supreme Court decision, the court found that the most important determinate was not the parents' status vis-à-vis each other, their biological status, *or* their individual rights as LGBT citizens and parents, but rather, it was the fact that they had *intended* to be parents, that they had bonded as such with the children, and that the biological parents had encouraged their parent-child relationship. It was, in other words, a decision based on the right to family *bonds*, rather than the rights of parents or children as individuals or a wholesale rejection of rights altogether.

The examples of gay and lesbian family law depicted here are a cautionary tale, warning of the dangers of assuming a unitary normative position on rights discourses that ignores their indeterminacy and their nuances, either in the affirmative or the negative. Their capacity for reinvention, particularly in the context of family and sexuality, allows for both conclusions: that rights are "wrong" and that they are "right." Yet more importantly, this capacity allows rights to transform as needed, whether by the strategic framing and adaptation of parents and their advocates or by a more organic development process responsive to social change. As it becomes increasingly apparent that neither biology nor contract is a sufficient way to determine who is deserving of parental rights—and that children's rights are not necessarily disserved by maintaining bonds in alternative family formations—rights in family law take on a new meaning: the right to be related.

5

Talking Back
Judicial Dissents and Social Change

[D]issenting opinions may be the symptom of life in the law of time.

—Roscoe Pound[1]

A dissent . . . is an appeal to the brooding spirit of the law, to the intelligence of a future day.

—Charles Evan Hughes[2]

How do most people come to understand what the law is and what it says? Certainly not by researching decisions handed down by appellate courts or by delving into the family code or penal code. The recent spate of sociolegal scholarship focused on narratives and storytelling, especially in everyday language and experience, adds a new twist on traditional legal analysis by decentering the privilege of official discourse, such as case law.[3] Rather than relying on the "law in the books," such scholarship focuses on both the "hegemonic tales" and the "subversive stories" of regular citizens interacting with the law.[4] This might mean, for instance, exploring ways in which people enact the veneer of legality outside the bounds of formal legal recognition, by taking part in same-sex marriage rituals where such unions are not legally sanctioned or by constructing a family not bound by blood or marriage but still using the official terminology, such as "brother-in-law."[5] The point is that a complete analysis of the role of law in the social world, and vice versa, must focus not just on judges' and legislators' interpretations of the law but also on ordinary peoples' understandings of the law in action and in their day-to-day lives, which may contradict, resist, or subvert the "official" understanding of law. Normally one would look outside institutional legal sources to find these oppositional stories. Yet, unlikely though it may seem, they are also found in the official language itself—there, it is called "dissent."

In this chapter, I investigate the role of dissenting opinions in the development of judicial narratives and in the flux in meaning attached to gay and lesbian families over time.[6] As institutionalized and readable proof of the flux and unsettled nature of law, it is not surprising that dissents might play a role, or at least be present, in cases dealing with gay and lesbian rights and the changing family form, one of the most contentious social issues of our time.[7] Given the public disagreement as to the legal position of gay- and lesbian-headed families, it seems only natural that this dissention would be manifested in judicial records as well—and it is, in the form of widely varying majority and dissenting opinions in appellate cases involving such families. Not only do dissents reflect the flux, instability, and eventual change of gay and lesbian family law, but in certain instances, they may actually play a role in *catalyzing* that change by affecting majority opinions and the future of family law in this ever-changing area.

The Relevance of Dissent in LGBT Family Law

The custom of writing and recording dissenting opinions in appellate courts, when appraised objectively, would seem to be an odd convention in law. This practice might be compared to a professor "trashing" all of his or her own concepts and arguments at the end of a class—it is, at the least, counterintuitive and, at most perhaps, counterproductive.[8] Yet so poignant and deeply felt are the dissents in some cases that, on occasion, the minority opinion is the only one published, as in the Georgia parental-visitation case of *In re R.E.W.*[9] In some cases, the dissent is actually longer than the majority opinion. In the Vermont divorce case of *Nickerson v Nickerson*, the dissent is twice the length of the majority decision.[10] In *Schuster v Schuster*, the two dissents written account for over two-thirds of the length of the record of the case. In the 1999 Connecticut Supreme Court case of *In re Adoption of Baby Z.*, in which the majority declined to allow the second-parent adoption, as discussed in chapter 3, one judge wrote a forty-page dissent, which, among other things, listed the twenty-four *amicus curiae* briefs that had been submitted but were never mentioned by the majority and gave a detailed constitutional analysis of why the state's adoption statute should be construed to allow second-parent adoptions such as the one proposed in the case.[11]

Moreover, dissents, when read with the majority opinion, are uniquely revealing of the whole of the judicial panel deciding the case and of the judicial process itself, an observation made by several attorneys in interviews. As one New York–based LGBT family attorney noted, "what a dissent usually indicates is that the justices have all had a discussion about it too. . . . You know for a fact they had the conversation." She added, "dissents play a very critical role for lawyering and litigating. . . . they give you an insight into . . . a range of judicial thinking on the court, so if you are a lawyer . . . it gives you some guidance."[12] Thus, because of dissents' ability to reveal something about the deliberation process not included in the majority, they are able to lay bare the workings of the law in a way that unified decisions often do not by revealing where disagreement or weak arguments exist on the judicial panel. In that sense, they are helpful to lawyers in considering appeals and strategizing future cases. As the New York attorney went on to comment,

> It gives you a sense, and depending on who else joins the dissent, you have a sense of what the judges are thinking and how, what might be helpful the next time around if the case comes up later on. . . . dissents . . . are very important because the judges are staking out their own views, which are very helpful for the next cases that come around.[13]

Beyond helping in future cases, the dissent can be a valuable source of new information about the case or legal issue at hand, by including testimony or facts left out of the majority opinion, as was evident in the aforementioned *Baby Z.* case. Indeed, in more than a quarter of all the custody and adoption cases with recorded dissents, new information not included in the majority's opinion was revealed in the dissent. In the 1995 Wyoming divorce case of *Hertzler v Hertzler*, for example, the dissenting opinion discusses and quotes at length the testimony of an expert who had been chosen, then rejected, by the heterosexual father. In the dissent, in fact, is included a two-page portion of the trial transcript in which this expert is questioned regarding her opinion about the children's welfare and contact with their lesbian mother; this expert is never cited by name, nor is her testimony quoted or paraphrased in the majority opinion.[14] Were it not for the dissent, the public and scholars of family law would not know of this expert's existence or her role in the trial decision. In *Weigand v Houghton*, the majority ruled against gay father David Weigand's custody bid and instead granted continued custody to the child's mother and stepfather, despite allegations that the stepfather was abusive to the mother and had been arrested twice, for simple assault and domestic disturbance. In the dissent, however, it was revealed that, in addition to these two events (which the majority found not as significant a factor as the father's homosexual relationship), the stepfather had been convicted of multiple misdemeanors and felonies, both violent and drug related, that he abused alcohol and drugs, that he had beaten the mother repeatedly in the child's presence, and that he had threatened to kill the child.[15]

In *S.B. v L.W.*, a 2001 Mississippi custody case involving a biological mother and father who had never been married and appeared requesting custody when the child was seven, the dissent argued that the majority had taken out of context many of the facts of the case and statements of the trial judge. To demonstrate, it reprinted verbatim nearly the entire transcript of the trial judge's rendering his opinion in court. It became clear only with this reprinting in the dissent that the trial judge had glossed over or given short shrift to many legal factors that would have weighed in the lesbian mother's favor and had exaggerated the importance of other factors that the majority took to count against her. These included a determination that the mother was the less "morally fit" parent because in the seven years since the child had been born, she had had two nonmarital relationships (the trial court used the term "lovers," true to the sexualizing of relationships discussed in chapter 3), including that with the father (for whom it was also, obviously, a nonmarital relationship) and her current domestic partner, with whom she had been raising the child.[16] There was no mention of the father's sexual history. Similarly, the lengthy dissent in *Strome v Strome* revealed many aspects of father Bobbie Strome's prior behavior, including some abusive language toward the children, which had been left unspecified and given little weight by the majority because of the time that had passed since.[17]

Dissent as Foreshadow and Catalyst of Change

One of the most intriguing and important functions served by dissenting opinions is that of foreshadowing and even playing a role in legal (and perhaps social) change itself. As recently as April 2007, Supreme

Court Justice Ruth Bader Ginsburg issued a dissent outlining what many believe to be the future of women's right to an abortion, one that pre-eminent law professor Cass Sunstein believes might well be "[i]n the long run, the most important part of the Supreme Court's ruling on 'partial birth' abortions."[18] Indeed, it has been said, "The majority exercise all the powers of the Court, but the minority have a curious concurrent jurisdiction over the future. For a dissent is a formal appeal for a rehearing by the Court sometime in the future, if not on the next occasion"; in other words, dissents may play a vital role in the likelihood and possible success of appeal in a particular case or on a particular issue.[19] Legal scholars have noted in general that dissents may embolden counsel in later cases to try again, even signaling on what grounds their efforts at reversal will be most effective.[20] Indeed, interviews with family court lawyers suggest that this may in fact be the case. As one attorney noted in an interview, "when you have one of their own peers raising it [the counterargument in the dissent] that's a very good thing, even if they don't win in that particular case."[21]

This function of dissent was apparent in the 1983 divorce case of *Matter of Marriage of Cabalquinto.* Bisexual father Ernest Cabalquinto had moved to California after the divorce, while the mother, Cheryll, remained in Colorado (later moving to Washington upon remarriage). Despite the fact that the initial custody decree allowed Mr. Cabalquinto liberal visitation, the court later placed visitation restrictions—including barring visitation at his home in California, which he shared with his male partner—based on his sexual orientation. The trial judge remarked, "a child should be led in the way of heterosexual preference, not be tolerant of this thing [homosexuality]" and "it can[not] do the boy any good to live in such an environment. It might do some harm." The dissenting justice responded, "the majority has given judicial condonation to the personal feelings of the trial judge. . . . The State [of Washington] may not restrict a parent's reasonable visitation rights merely because that parent's lifestyle is not within the societal mainstream."[22] Three years later, this dissent was vindicated, when the case was reheard at the Washington Court of Appeals, and the visitation restrictions were overturned, allowing Mr. Cabalquinto to visit with his son in California.[23]

The case of *Matter of Adoption of Charles B.* also aptly illustrates this potential.[24] In 1988 in *Charles B.*, the Ohio Court of Appeals reversed the decision of a trial court to allow the adoption of Charles B., a disabled seven-year-old boy who had been bounced between five foster homes in the first four years of his life, by "Mr. B," a gay man, social worker, and Charles's caretaker for the previous three years. The majority decision, quoted in part in chapter 3, was scathingly antigay and categorically foreclosed on the possibility of any gay man or lesbian adopting in the State of Ohio. The dissent pointed this out, as well as a concern for the best interest of children like Charles B., who would be deprived of the most significant parental figure he had. It pointed out that by denying the adoption the majority was actually acting against the best interest of this child: "the majority has been so blinded by the dazzling lights of the antipodal stars of 'homosexuality,' 'gay rights,' and 'gay lifestyle' that they strayed from the polestar of the welfare of this particular child"[25] and, in doing so, set the stage for the Ohio Supreme Court's reversal two years later.

A similar reversal happened in Pennsylvania in *Adoption of R.B.F. and R.C.F.* In 1998, a trial court refused to allow nonbiological mother "B.A.F." to adopt the twins planned by the couple and born to her partner, "C.H.F.," the previous year. When the couple appealed this decision, the Superior Court in 2000 opted for a strict construction of the adoption code that did not allow the nonbiological mother in this lesbian family to adopt as a second parent because the two were not married. The dissent, however, criticized "the Majority's wooden application of [the adoption code]" and noted,

> the reality is that a lesbian couple is parenting the children. It is doubtful that our decision here will have any affect [*sic*] on this reality. However, our decision here does affect the children's interests. Regrettably, the Majority turns a blind eye to the children's interests by choosing to ignore the reality of non-traditional families. Indeed, the Majority goes so far as to denigrate the family before us.[26]

This dissent set the stage for an appeal and was redeemed two years later in 2002, when the Pennsylvania Supreme Court overturned the ruling and issued its landmark decision formally legalizing second-parent adoption.[27]

Some dissents even set the stage for future majority opinions in *other* cases, by virtue of either a change in attitude among the jurists or an influx of new judges who are more convinced by the dissent's logic than their predecessors had been. It is admittedly not routine that the text of a dissent reappears verbatim in a subsequent majority opinion, directly effecting a change in law. But upon close inspection, many of the significant shifts in judicial opinion and family law as it pertains to gay and lesbian divorced parents' rights and second parents' visitation and adoption rights, in particular, were foreshadowed in particularly cogent and memorable dissents in previous cases. Justice Cardozo, himself a frequent dissenter, viewed the contents of dissents as "the best inspiration of the time" for information and instruction on sociopolitical viewpoints and issues not yet generally accepted.[28] A New York attorney concurred in an interview: "dissents have their way of working into being a majority opinion over time, particularly on major social issues [such as LGBT parenting]."[29] This observation is astute, given that approximately one-third of the dissents either noted or marked the need for significant legal, social, or legislative change regarding the rights of LGBT parents and would-be parents. Indeed, eleven of the seventy-six dissents in this study were later cited verbatim in majority decisions that adopted their reasoning; and an additional six majority opinions in this time period cited and adopted reasoning from dissents in other family law cases, not involving LGBT parents.

One illustrative example of such use of dissents is the 1991 case of *In re Interest of Z.J.H.*, involving the custody and visitation claim of a lesbian co-parent that had been denied.[30] The dissenting justices urged both the legislature and the court to adopt a legal change that would allow her these rights, thus heeding the call of legal scholars that law must be responsive to a changing world. As Peter Simmons notes, "The law is not static. It grows—and the dissenting opinion is one of the processes that aids in that development as the law meets and solves new situations."[31] The dissent in the lower appeals court decision, in fact, was one of the first published appellate opinions anywhere in the United States to articulate a strong argument in favor of recognizing these new "nontraditional" families. At the Wisconsin Supreme Court, the dissenting justice argued,

> The legislature could not have intended such an absurd and cruel result, but that is what the majority of this court has determined. . . . The legal façade adopted by the majority cannot withstand scrutiny. . . . Accordingly, I cannot accept the majority's opinion as a prediction of what the holdings of this court will be in future cases involving children of non-traditional relationships. . . . I would also urge the legislature to act to rectify the unjust disparity created by today's decision, a disparity that will victimize children who have had nothing to do with their lot.[32]

Indeed, four years after this decision, the same court adopted the rationale put forth in this dissent and ruled in favor of nonbiological mothers' visitation rights (recognizing their status as *de facto* parents) in the landmark 1995 case of *In re Custody of H.S.H.-K.*, discussed in chapters 3 and 4, the first case in the State of Wisconsin (and one of the first in the nation) to grant such rights to a lesbian nonbiological mother. Moreover, the justices in *H.S.H.-K.* cited not one but *three* previous dissents—*Z.J.H.*, *In the Interest of Angel Lace M.*, and one other dissent in a heterosexual divorce case.[33]

A similar reversal was seen in Missouri, where analogous dissents were filed in the divorce cases of *J.P. v P.W.* in 1989 and *G.A. v D.A.* in 1987, challenging visitation denials and restrictions on gay and lesbian parents. In the former case, the dissenting justice stated, "As I read the majority opinion, no homosexual parent should ever have unsupervised custody of his child even for a relatively short period." Citing as evidence the outcome in the earlier case, *G.A. v D.A.*, he went on to say, "This is the type of generalization that courts should not make, although that appears to occur in this type of custody matter."[34] Both dissents argued for the abandonment of the "*per se*" presumption that gay and lesbian parents are unfit as a matter of law. Nine years later, in 1998, this position was finally officially adopted by the Missouri Court of Appeals, in the case of *Delong v Delong*. In the *Delong* decision, the judges quoted the dissents from both of these prior cases at length. First, the *Delong* majority quoted the dissenting justice in *G.A. v D.A.* verbatim:

> If there has been any doubt as to the issue of homosexuality being an absolute or conclusive presumption of detriment, the result in this case on these facts dispels that doubt. . . . To say it is in the best interests of this little boy to put him in the sole custody of the [heterosexual] father, who was pictured leering at girly magazines, solely on the basis of his [lesbian] mother's sexual preference, would be and is a mistake.[35]

The decision then went on to quote the excerpt discussed earlier from the dissent in *J.P. v P.W.* and cited its conclusion that "each custody case, whether a parent is homosexual [or not], is different and should be determined on its own facts,"[36] a conclusion that was finally reached and made law in this 1998 decision.

Some judges have even established a legacy as dissenters who later saw their minority opinions become the majority opinion and the law of the land. Alan Barth has called these judges "prophets with honor" for their ability to prophesy social change and the need for corresponding legal change, writing "what the law ought to be, or what it might some-day be."[37] Oliver Wendell Holmes, for example, is famous for having written particularly prescient dissents, nearly all of which later became majority opinions. In the context of recent LGBT family law, New York's Chief Justice of the Court of Appeals, Judith Kaye, is thought by some to be the contemporary corollary of these "prophets with honor."[38] Indeed, Judge Kaye delivered opinions in most of the significant New York LGBT custody and adoption cases in the 1990s and 2000s. In the landmark case *Alison D. v Virginia M.*, Judge Kaye wrote a powerful dissent underscoring the need to decide such matters with an eye toward the "modern day realities" of the family, laying the groundwork for later decisions across the country that would adopt a more reflexive definition of "parenthood" and "family."[39] Indeed, the attorney who represented the nonbiological mother, Alison D., noted in an interview,

> Knowing that Judge Kaye in the *Alison D.* case had set out a very differ-ent framework . . . was very critical. I mean, we knew where Kaye stood, we know that she's obviously very influential to the court because she's chief judge now and . . . she hasn't won on everything she's wanted but she has been very consistent over the years in sort of striking out on different grounds.[40]

In Judge Kaye's own jurisdiction, this dissent was later cited, and Judge Kaye's interpretation adopted, in the case establishing second-par-ent adoption rights in New York in 1995, *Matter of Dana*, as well as in at least three other cases' majority opinions.[41]

Simply by virtue of dissents' being recorded, they can also preserve an issue or argument for future consideration or "salvage for tomorrow the principle that was sacrificed or forgotten today."[42] In *Matter of Appeal in Pima County Juvenile Action*, discussed in chapter 3, the dissent chal-lenged the majority's finding that a bisexual man could be barred, based on his sexual orientation, from adopting a child in the State of Arizona. The presiding judge issued an ardent dissent, claiming,

> It is clear from the record that both the trial judge and the majority of this department have no intention of ever letting a bisexual adopt a child. I refuse to participate in such a decision. I, therefore, set for the facts which

merit a reversal of the trial court's order. . . . While there is not case law particularly applicable to the situation at hand, I believe the proper rule to be that homosexuality or bisexuality standing alone does not render an applicant unfit as a matter of law to adopt children.[43]

Although this dissent has not yet been directly incorporated in a majority opinion in Arizona specifically articulating adoption rights for LGBT individuals, it did point out the inconsistency between the court of appeal's decision and the adoption statute for the state, which holds that any adult may adopt, regardless of his or her sexual orientation—thus leading the way to legal adoption rights in the future for gay, lesbian, and bisexual parents.[44] Indeed, the case of *Thomas v Thomas* in 2002 demonstrates that this is so.[45] The child at the center of this case was born to the sister of Jayme Thomas, a lesbian, who adopted the child at birth, and was raised by Jayme and her partner, Lisa. The issue was not the original adoption by Jayme but the trial court's decision to grant joint custody to Jayme and Lisa after their breakup. Although the court of appeals ultimately overturned this decision and rescinded Lisa's custody based on her lack of legal parenthood or adoption, the notable fact is that the child's adoption by Jayme—an out lesbian—had happened to begin with. Clearly, then, the *Pima County* dissent's argument came to the fore in Arizona law, even if not explicitly and even though Arizona shied away from legally recognizing *two* same-sex parents simultaneously.

The influence of dissents and the transformation they portend can happen in more subtle and indirect ways as well; for instance, dissents may add to the collective of jurisprudential thinking by pointing out flaws or weaknesses in the majority opinion and providing a palette of differing ideas on which to draw. Supreme Court Justice Ruth Bader Ginsburg has pointed out that, "[t]he prospect of a dissent . . . pointing out an opinion's inaccuracies and inadequacies strengthens the test [and] heightens the opinion writer's incentive to 'get it right.'"[46] In addition, dissents affect the law by virtue of their language circulating generally in the legal community as a source of education and ideas, as well as the fodder they sometimes supply for possible appeals. Several interviewees noted that, just as courts are not bound by the precedents established in other states but nevertheless often adopt their language or reasoning, so too can the content of dissents affect later cases in other jurisdictions simply by making their language available. As a very experienced

LGBT family law attorney in Washington, D.C., noted, "theoretically it can [have an effect] because in another state, neither the majority nor the dissent is binding on a judge. So, you can say to a court, 'Look, I know this was a dissent, but the majority was wrong and I want you to go with the language there.'"[47] The supervising judge in one California jurisdiction, who had previously practiced as a family law attorney, similarly commented, "I'm not necessarily bound by a court of appeals decision in [another jurisdiction in California], if the issue hasn't been decided by my district. So in some cases, I could use a dissenting opinion from another district."[48]

Marla Liston, the nonbiological mother who had lost custody of her son in *Liston v Pyles* and subsequently became an activist for lesbian parents' rights in Ohio, pointed to the educative function of dissents from Ohio as well as other states in leading to social and legal change: "[They] will certainly play a part in that [legal change] because that is educating our politicians to understand that people's mindset is no longer staid on the fact that a child has to have a mother and a father. . . . I think ultimately yes, it will have an effect."[49] Indeed, the appearance of dissents is evidence, in a sense, that some aspect of the law is no longer settled (or may never have been) and that changing social conditions require a reshaping or at least reconsideration. Certainly, the profound changes in the family as both a legal and a social entity—to which Marla Liston and others attest—require such adaptation. In still other cases, the dissent could have an effect on the reasoning of the next court to hear the case. Lesbian mothers Sandy and Robin, who were challenged for custody by their sperm donor in *Thomas S. v Robin Y.* (discussed in prior chapters) commented in an interview that the dissent written at the lower level court "definitely had an impact at the Court of Appeals" and that, as a consequence of the strong dissent, they "didn't have to beg for an appeal." Furthermore, after the court did grant Thomas S. paternity rights, the mothers found that the dissent was imperative to their being granted a stay on that order, because, as they said, "the judge who granted the stay had read both decisions."[50]

The appearance of dissents such as those in *Thomas S.*, *Interest of Z.J.H.*, and *Alison D.* is evidence that the judiciary had begun to respond to and recognize the changing face of the family as a social construct, even if the majority or the legislature had not entirely embraced or adapted to these changes. Certainly, the profound changes in the family as both a legal and a social entity require such adaptation. At the same time, dissents are an almost tangible manifestation of the indeterminacy of law, particularly evident in the notoriously vague area of family law. Despite the norm of *stare decisis*, "A reasoned dissent is proof positive that the law is not an accumulation of worn concepts and beliefs."[51] Dissents, then, it might be argued, are an inevitable marker of the dynamic nature of judge-made law.

Resisting Change: Regressive Dissents

Just as some dissents, such as those discussed in the preceding section, call for—and sometimes lead to—legal and social change in the recognition and treatment of LGBT parents, others are written with the purpose of *resisting* such changes. Progressive majority decisions inspired these regressive dissents in somewhat fewer instances than the reverse, but the tendency to write very strongly worded dissents was nearly equal. One judge's dissent in the 1992 divorce case of *Chicoine v Chicoine* distinguished itself from the majority's ruling, arguing that lesbian mother Lisa Chicoine should have *no* visitation rights, rather than restricted visitation, and asserted,

> Lesbian mother has harmed these children forever. To give her rights of reasonable visitation so that she can teach them to be homosexuals, would be the zenith of poor judgment for the judiciary of this state [South Dakota]. Until such time that she can establish, after years of therapy and demonstrated conduct, that she is no longer a lesbian living a life of abomination, she should be totally estopped from contaminating these children. . . . There appears to be a transitory phenomenon on the American scene that homosexuality is okay. Not so. The Bible decries it. Even the pagan "Egyptian Book of the Dead" bespoke against it.[52]

In this case, it was not strong progay sentiment in the majority decision that prompted such an extreme regressive dissent; the majority had already denied Lisa primary custody and placed restrictions on her visitation because of her homosexuality. Thus, the fervor of a dissent has not necessarily always been a reaction to a fervent majority, and even conservative decisions could breed even more conservative dissents.

In other cases the dissent's language was perhaps less flamboyant but equally resistant to change. In the landmark 1999 case regarding nonbiological parents' rights, *E.N.O. v L.M.M.*, the dissenting justice wrote, "In light of the denigration of [biological] parental rights and the judicial infringement on the province of the Legislature effected by the Court's decision, all without an acknowledgement of the novelty of that decision, I must respectfully dissent."[53] It is unclear that the dissenter would have had a different opinion had the court acknowledged the novelty of the precedent it was setting; yet this was an antiprogressive dissent in the truest sense: an objection to the court's role in accommodating, or facilitating, social change. Similarly, the dissenting justice in the groundbreaking New York second-parent adoption case *Matter of Dana* (whose majority was headed by Judge Judith Kaye) cited the 1991 majority opinion in *Alison D. v Virginia M.* in order to reject the majority's "expansionist judicial definition of 'de facto parent' or 'functional family,'" going on to assert, "we derive a diametrically different lesson from [*Alison D.*] . . . Yet, today's majority, only four years later, revives and applies that rejected de facto methodology [from *Alison D.*] using another nonstatutory, undelineated term, 'second parent adoption.'"[54]

Here, the dissent appealed to the principle of *stare decisis*, arguing that the holding in former cases must be adhered to strictly. But the resistance to change in regressive dissents took a number of forms and tactics. In other cases, the dissents argued that the court should defer to the judgment of the trial judge, rather than enact change.[55] This argument was employed in approximately 13 percent of the cases with a dissent, and these dissents generally did not include much more of an argument than, "The majority's decision is wrong, because the Trial Judge is vested with wide or broad discretion in matters of child custody and parental visitation," "The majority's judgment is wrong because the credibility of the witnesses is within the province of the trier of fact [the judge]," and "The majority's judgment is wrong because the Trial Court's findings are entitled to a presumption of correctness unless the preponderance of the evidence is otherwise," as in the case of *Eldridge v Eldridge*.[56]

Another common tactic for resisting social and legal change in the dissents (as well as in majority opinions) was to argue that such issues are the responsibility of the legislature, rather than the courts, to decide. In one of the first second-parent adoption cases in the country and the first in Massachusetts, *Adoption of Tammy* in 1993, the dissenting justices argued that the co-parent adoption approved by the majority should not be allowed because Massachusetts's adoption statute did not allow for it. They claimed that their views "are not motivated by any disapproval of the two petitioners here or their life-style. . . . I am firmly of the view that a litigant's expression of human sexuality ought not to determine the outcome of litigation"; however, they argued, "[The children's] interests can be accommodated without *doing violence* to the statute" (emphasis added).[57] This type of resistance was most apparent, for obvious reasons, in situations such as second-parent adoption, since these situations were most likely to be governed by statute; the fact that same-sex adoptions were not in the public consciousness at the time the adoption statutes were written ensured, in fact, that any such adoption in the future would be faced with resistance by strict constructionists such as the dissenter here.

For similar reasons, the 1999 New Jersey visitation case of *V.C. v M.J.B.* evoked a comparable dissent. In this case, discussed in chapter 2, the issue was not a second-parent adoption but whether a nonbiological lesbian co-parent who had not adopted was eligible for shared custody and visitation as a "psychological parent." This case eventually went on to break new ground for the recognition of lesbian co-parents at the New Jersey Supreme Court, but not before evoking an explicit dissent opposing such "legislating from the bench":

> In my view, evaluating changes in social mores and how those changes are to impact our social policy as reflected in our statutes, is more properly addressed by the Legislature as opposed to the courts. . . . Applying the factors set forth by the Wisconsin Supreme Court, as the majority does here, undermines the rights of all natural and adoptive parents and leads to more litigation concerning the rights of individuals claiming to be parents. This is an issue for our Legislature and not our courts.[58]

The court's mention of "factors set forth by the Wisconsin Supreme Court" refers to the previously discussed case of *In re Custody of H.S.H.-K.*, which also involved visitation rights for a nonbiological mother and was cited by the *V.C.* majority. In *H.S.H.-K.*, a similarly resistant dissent had been written, drawing on both the principle of *stare decisis* and the responsibilities of the legislature:

> Neither marriage nor blood ties justifies this court's creation of an arrangement not recognized until today. There was no marriage—the ceremony gone through by the mother and the former companion is a nullity—it is completely unrecognized in our law. To give any importance to the "ceremony" by these two women should require an act of the legislature, not an

aberrant opinion by this court. . . . [The court] create[s] its new vision of family law in a way that should only be done by the legislature. Changes in family law as drastic as those created here should only be done by the legislature following full hearings and debate.[59]

An additional dissenting justice added,

A state court functions at its lowest ebb of legitimacy when it not only ignores constitutional mandates, but also legislates from the bench, usurping power from the appropriate legislative body and forcing the moral views of a small, relatively unaccountable group of judges upon all those living in the state. Sadly, the majority opinion in this case provides an illustration of a court at its lowest ebb of legitimacy. . . . The legislators of this state, representing the views of their constituents, have consciously decided not to protect or promote non-traditional, non-legally binding relationships, apparently believing that such relationships are not basic to morality and civilization. . . . The majority disagrees with this legislatively declared social policy and, therefore, rewrites the law to reflect its own moral views and to facilitate its predetermined legal conclusion. . . . apparently, the . . . majority does not place much stock in the doctrine of *stare decisis*.[60]

These cases demonstrate not only the vast differences of opinion that are revealed by dissents but their power to facilitate *as well as* retard social and legal change—paradoxically, providing both stability and flux at the same time.

Sedimentation, Settling, and "Talking Back": Family Law as Conversation

The dissenting opinions discussed in the preceding section, in their resistance to change, are also a part of the sedimenting or "settling" of law; while they seemingly resist the necessity of change to adapt to new family forms, they nevertheless illustrate a push-and-pull that is perhaps not surprising in an area of law subject to such flux and contestation. But this sedimentation and eventual settling of gay and lesbian family law, in part through the vehicle of dissents, can also be seen in other patterns and mechanisms. The dissent serves as an avenue for the settling of law by reflecting in law the societal differences in opinion and debates regarding parental recognition and rights for LGBT parents, through the offering of legal and discursive compromises, and by simply "talk-ing back" to the majority, not only in one particular opinion but over time. Because of dissents' responsive nature and positioning as funda-mentally "different," they can be instructively thought of as one half of a conversation in law, wherein the other half of the conversation is the majority opinion. In other words, if the judicial decision is a statement of what the law is, the dissent is a counterstatement, a potential correc-tive offered in response, of what the law *should* be. This is frequently seen in situations involving new and nontraditional family forms, when the legal issue to be settled is a novel one or was not considered when the statutes that might apply to the situation were written, and when the judges must interpret the law with little guidance. In some instances, this conversation is drawn out over decades, during which the issue at hand remains persistently unsettled, as with the issue of parental recognition for lesbian co-parents not related by blood or adoption.

In the Wisconsin second-parent adoption case of *In the Interest of Angel Lace M.*, for instance, the dissenting justice observed, "Much has been written about the nature of the canons of construction and the fact that contradictory canons exist that would lead to opposite results if applied to the same statute."[61] The writer goes on to add that the com-mon wisdom and guiding principle in such cases is to construe broadly the adoption statute in order to serve the best interest of the child; how-ever, as has been noted elsewhere, what exactly the "best interest of the child" is and what type of interpretation of law best serves it are also persistently unsettled issues. Therefore, whereas this particular dissent-ing justice argues that "[a]lthough strict construction of a statute is often seen as an exercise in judicial restraint, in the present case such construc-tion [not allowing the adoption] is precisely the opposite and flouts the legislative will,"[62] other justices view strict construction of adoption stat-utes (reading them as inapplicable to households headed by two lesbians) as entirely appropriate. Indeed, this point is aptly made in *In re Custody of H.S.H.-K.*, in which all three dissents offered solutions to the case dif-ferent from those arrived at by the majority and from one another.

Across the United States, furthermore, the issue of second-parent adoption for lesbian couples remains unsettled in over half of the states and continues to provoke strong dissents in both directions, encourag-ing as well as discouraging second-parent adoption. Indeed, there are just as many dissents calling for liberal construction of adoption stat-utes, so that the law can grow to include nontraditional families, as there are those arguing against such inclusivity. In the Connecticut case *In re Adoption of Baby Z.*, for example, the dissenting justice argued that "a reasonable construction of the statutory scheme governing adoptions" must, in fact, allow for the two mothers in such a situation to be legally recognized and goes on to assert that

> the majority's narrow interpretation of the relevant statutes creates grave constitutional infirmities with the statutory scheme regulating adoptions in the state of Connecticut, and the disingenuous reasons advanced to justify the refusal to reach these constitutional issues cannot withstand scrutiny. . . . [This sort of] hypertechnical eighteenth century analysis . . . has no place in the jurisprudence of the twenty-first century. Future generations will look back upon the majority's decision today with the same opprobrium with which we regard the draconian absurdities of the early English common law. Unfortunately, this observation will provide little solace to young Baby Z., his family, or those who are similarly situated.[63]

This type of progressive dissent speaks back not only to the majority, then, but also to the regressive dissents quoted earlier, which argue for a cementing of traditional notions of family in law. In speaking back in this way, such dissents sediment yet another layer of legal thought, one that draws on traditional notions of justice and common historical references to put forth a new vision of family law.

In some instances, the progression and settling of law can be seen in quite literal legal conversations, in which the majority and the dissent speak back to each other in the text of the decisions. In this same *Baby Z.* case, for instance, the dissent critiqued the majority, as was quoted above, regarding its strict construction of the adoption statute. This conversation went both ways, however, as the majority also offered a prologue critique of the dissent. In fact, before the dissent itself is introduced in the text, the majority opinion spends seven pages of its analysis responding to it, point for point, beginning with the assertion that "rhetoric aside, the dissent's arguments do not hold water."[64] Refusing to give up the last word, the dissent then concludes with a lengthy footnote,

> In a lengthy discussion at the end of its opinion, the majority struggles to either dodge or deflect the force of my dissent. I feel that I have addressed adequately the majority's efforts to poke holes in my arguments. Nonetheless, I will in the interest of clarity address these claims once again. . . .[65]

The dissenting judge then went on to address each of the majority's responses to the dissent's own claims.

A similar back-and-forth conversation is apparent in *Rubano v DiCenzo*, a case of first impression in Rhode Island in 2000. Within the very first page of the decision, the majority was already quoting and responding to the dissent at length. At one point, the decision exclaimed, "The dissent espouses several rather extravagant assertions about what the majority of the Court supposedly has determined in this case. Without responding to each of these assertions, we would simply caution the reader that our silence does not imply our acquiescence or agreement."[66] Nevertheless, the majority went on to list the claims of the dissent that it considered "baseless." An example was the dissent's argument that "all roads from [the statute governing custody for "presumed parents"] lead directly to the 'father' of any child born in, or out of wedlock"[67] (implying that rules governing "presumed fathers" did not apply to lesbian co-parents), to which the majority replied, "[this] overlooks the maternal-relationship superhighway running down the middle of [the statute]."[68] Later, the dissent argued that the majority's statutory interpretation was faulty because it drew on different sections of the family code dealing with children out of wedlock and with standing in cases concerning a mother and child relationship, what the dissent calls "a strange mix." To this, the majority responded preemptively, "whatever 'strange mix' the dissent envisions concerning these two provisions is a cocktail that it alone has shaken and stirred," arguing that each section of the code provides a separate basis for nonbiological mother Maureen Rubano's claim.[69] These exchanges can be understood in the context of judicial deliberation, in which judges circulate their opinions to the rest of the panel before the decision is rendered. In these cases, it is clear that the dissent and the majority were familiar with each other's arguments and felt compelled to respond to them in their respective opinions, thus shaping and making explicit the processes of reaction and dialogue in the law.

Perhaps one of the most noteworthy back-and-forth exchanges was in a petition to the Eleventh Circuit U.S. Court of Appeals to rehear the Florida case *Lofton v Department of Children and Family Services* (previously *Lofton v Kearney*) *en banc* (in front of the entire panel of justices). As discussed in chapter 3, the petitioners in this case challenged the Florida law banning adoption by gay men and lesbians. Like most petitions for rehearing, the majority's decision to deny the rehearing was very brief: one sentence. In a twenty-seven-page dissenting opinion joined by just two other justices, however, Judge Barkett thoroughly critiqued the substance of the majority decision, both the denial of the rehearing and the original decision in *Lofton v Secretary of Department of Health* (2004). The dissent argued that there was no rational basis for the Florida ban and that the decision to support this ban and deny an en banc review of the decision defied prior Supreme Court precedent and the right of equal protection. Determined not to allow the dissent to go unanswered, Judge Birch, who also joined in the majority, wrote a special concurring opinion, seemingly for the sole purpose of rebutting and talking back to Judge Barkett's dissent. The dissent countered Judge Birch's opinion in a footnote:

> I do not believe Judge Birch has offered any plausible explanation for Florida's categorical determination that homosexuals are inherently and always unfit to serve as adoptive parents. I fail to see how any objective observer could think such a law is rational and consistent with the most basic, minimal notions of equal protection under law.[70]

Settling through Compromise

These conversations and reciprocal influences happen in other, less explicit ways as well, akin to the "discursive compromises" in identity discussed in chapter 3. In *Liston v Pyles*, for example, the dissent attempted to compromise with the majority opinion denying Marla Liston custody, visitation, or *in loco parentis* status by focusing on her desire to pay child support. In other words, the dissent expressed a non-traditional vision of family, one not accepted by the majority, but emphasized the benefit that the child would enjoy by allowing Liston to pay child support, rather than focusing solely on the custody issue, which clearly the majority rejected. Although the majority in this case did not accept the dissent's vision, its intermediary move provided flexibility for future rulings. Similarly, in 1988 in *Matter of Adoption of Charles B.*, the dissenting justice agreed with the majority in that he "just as strongly as [his] colleagues, announce[d] that [he did] not sanction, encourage, or look with favor on homosexual adoption, and agree[d] that it is 'not the business of the government to encourage homosexuality.'"[71] Yet he offered a compromise between the opposing factions by emphasizing the best interests and wishes of the child to be adopted in refuting the majority's conclusion that the gay adoptive father in question, who was also a social worker and the child's foster father, may not adopt him. In doing so, in this case, the dissenting justice actually did set the case up for an appeal at the Ohio Supreme Court, where the court overturned the decision and allowed the adoption, thereby legalizing LGBT adoption in Ohio.

In the 2002 Nebraska second-parent adoption case *In re Adoption of Luke*, the dissent again attempted to find common ground with the majority, which had ruled against the adoption, by agreeing that the constitutional claims made by the litigants were not relevant and that that issue of whether second-parent adoption is allowed ultimately was "not affected by the gender or sexual orientation of the biological or prospective adoptive parent."[72] This claim is somewhat curious, since the substance of the dissent argued that the second-parent adoption in this lesbian-headed family was analogous in every way *except* gender—and therefore in access to marriage—to a heterosexual stepparent adoption, which is allowed in Nebraska. Nevertheless, the conciliatory gesture is clear, that the dissent's analysis—"and that of the majority—is not premised on any distinction involving the gender and sexual orientation of the couple seeking a second-parent adoption" and that "the efforts of the parties and various amici to turn this appeal into a forum for or against gay and lesbian rights" were misplaced and irrelevant.[73] Although this dissent has not yet led to a reversal in Nebraska law, by forging common ground on the point debated so fiercely in other cases—as discussed in the preceding chapter—it increased the chances of such a reversal in the future.

In other instances, the dissent offered a middle ground by arguing not against the ultimate policy point decided by the majority but against the legal means by which it was to be accomplished. This most typically occurred in cases dealing with the interpretation of adoption and visitation statutes and their applicability to individual LGBT parents or same-sex couples, cases in which there was a disagreement about how liberally the statute should be construed and what matters were better left to the legislative branch of government rather than decided by the judiciary. For example, in *T.B. v L.R.M.*, the dissent and majority disagreed as to how liberally to construe the doctrine of *in loco parentis*. The majority ruled that T.B., even though she was not the biological or adoptive parent of the child in question, was entitled to parental rights and visitation because of her standing *in loco parentis*.[74] The dissent disagreed, not necessarily with the notion of a child having two parents of the same sex but with the court's interpretation of the family code allowing for such a decision and with the idea that it was the judiciary's job to make this call. Instead of arguing against even the prospect that a same-sex partner could have parental rights outside of adoption and blood relation, as many others have, the dissent offered a compromise by proposing the issue be taken up by the legislature.

Settling through Pendulum Swings

Dissents also "talk back" by embodying a pendulum-swing approach, in many cases, by responding in equal but opposite force to the majority. Lawrence Douglas notes this tendency of opposite pulls: "the law presents its efforts at constitutional exposition in a rhetorical form that orchestrates this performance through *measured subversion* . . . by presenting a majority opinion along with its systematic refutation in the form of a dissent" (emphasis added).[75] This function of the dissent could be seen as "institutional disobedience," analogous to civil disobedience at the judicial level, a "quiet, symbolic act . . . aimed at peaceful revision of attitude."[76] Yet this disobedience is not always so quiet; because dissents are by definition an explicitly oppositional force, they many times employ very strong, blunt, or unpopular language, providing an antidote for, and an opposite pull from, the often measured and negotiated language of the majority opinion.

This tendency is true of the majority of LGBT custody and adoption cases with dissents, regardless of the specific substance or political leaning of the dissent. In the 1998 Alabama divorce case of *Ex Parte D. W. W.*, for example, in which visitation restrictions and a denial of custody were affirmed against a lesbian mother, the dissent began with the following reproach:

> Because the main opinion seems to be more interested in providing social commentary than in protecting the best interests of these parties' two children, I dissent. In an apparent attempt to play to public opinion, the main opinion has ignored the sound reasoning of the Court of Civil Appeals and has mischaracterized much of the evidence presented in this case.[77]

After listing a litany of charges against the father, charges that were entered into the record but not considered by the supreme court's majority—including a history of alcoholism and violence, several criminal charges including drunk driving with the child in the car and domestic violence, threatening to kill the mother, and locking his infant son in the clothes dryer—the dissent concluded,

> I cannot support a judgment that appears to be influenced more by prejudice than by the facts. Prejudice is not within the discretion of the trial court and, in reviewing the record, I find no reason, other than prejudice, to explain the trial court's willingness to ignore [father] D.W.W.'s outrageous conduct while so severely restricting [mother] R.W.'s visitation.[78]

Similarly, in the 1990 Mississippi case of *White v Thompson*, the dissenting justice charged the majority with arriving at its conclusion to take custody from the lesbian mother, Andrean White, and give it to the child's grandparents on the basis of "prudish prejudice," rather than "positive proof."[79] In *Titchenal v Dexter*, the dissent unabashedly responded to the majority's critique that it (the dissent) "stretch[es] the doctrine . . . beyond recognition in an effort to provide relief to this particular plaintiff" by suggesting that the majority's position regarding the nonbiological mother's visitation claim is so archaic as to be irrelevant: "These are the same old stale and discredited charges that 'law' has brought against 'equity' since the days of Henry II."[80] In the previously cited divorce case of *Weigand v Houghton*, the dissenting justice began by bluntly pointing to the inequities of the majority's decision denying custody to gay father David Weigand:

> The chancellor and majority believe a minor is best served by living in an explosive environment in which the unemployed stepfather is a convicted felon, drug-taker, adulterer, wife-beater, and child threatener, and in which the mother has been transitory, works two jobs, and has limited time with the child. . . . The chancellor and majority are blinded by the fact that [the child's] father is gay. . . . The issue is that [the child] is living in a psychologically and physically dangerous environment from which he should be saved, not blindly forced to remain. I dissent.[81]

He went on to state that the majority's decision to deny Mr. Weigand custody "boggles the mind" and is "contrived by the majority for the purpose of punishing [the father] for his lifestyle."[82]

This type of extreme candor is also evident in dissents that were arguing not for a progressive view of gay and lesbian parental rights but for the reverse, in cases in which the *majority* chose to recognize these rights and expanding definitions of family and children's well-being. In *Matter of Dana*, for instance, the dissent chastised the majority's broad interpretation of the New York adoption statute to allow second-parent adoptions: "the majority in the instant [case] violates the very canon it invokes. It ultimately also transgresses another overriding canon, that courts should not legislate under the guise of interpretation."[83] Likewise, in the landmark California second-parent adoption case *Sharon S. v Superior Court*, dissenting justice Janice Rogers Brown, widely reputed then as the most conservative member of the California Supreme Court, wrote a scathing dissent picking apart the majority's decision claim by claim. In one passage, she exhorted, "if it is true that you can't get where you're going if you don't know where you've been, then it should come as no surprise the majority finds itself in uncharted territory."[84] In rebutting the majority's claim that second-parent adoptions were already established as routine at the local level in California by 2003, when the case was decided, Brown responded, "Unless 'established' is redefined to mean 'very recent,' the historical claim made by the majority cannot be defended."[85]

In *Chicoine*, the dissenting justice was harshly critical not so much of the majority's statutory construction but of its acceptance, albeit marginal, of homosexuality *per se*. He opened with the admonition, "For years, [Lisa Chicoine] has followed a life of perversion and openly flaunted it before these children. At the hour of judicial atonement, she now pretends to have changed. This present facade is of transitory mood and a cunning plan, by employing a psychologist, to wrest away good judgment from the judicial officers hereunto attending this case."[86] Similar concerns, with regard to the endorsement of nonheteronormative families made by the majority opinion, were raised in the aforementioned *Sharon S.* dissent, which warned that "the majority all but guarantees new and even bizarre family structures." Although Justice Brown stated, "my own views as to whether children should be allowed to have three or more legal parents are not relevant here," she went on to title an entire section of the dissent with the heading, "THE MAJORITY TRIVIALIZES FAMILY BONDS," leaving little doubt as to what her own views were.[87]

The pendulum-swing effect of dissents is also seen in their propensity to include unlikely or unpopular arguments that most likely would not have withstood the scrutiny of other judges as part of the majority decision. This should perhaps not be surprising, since the dissent is, in essence, a completely institutionalized mode of rebellion, what Justice Potter Stewart called "subversive literature."[88] For example, in some cases judges actually argued *against* the nearly universally accepted guiding principle of "best interest of the child" in their dissents. While the preceding chapter illustrates instances when the "best interest" had to be balanced with—or against—parents' rights, these dissents were absent even that countervailing consideration. Not even a constitutional rights framework was offered as justification to abridge children's best interests in *Adoption of Tammy*, in which the dissenting justice argued, "the court's decision [allowing the adoption], which is inconsistent with the statutory language, cannot be justified by a desire to achieve what is in the child's best interest."[89]

In other cases, the dissenting opinions made morally or religiously based arguments that, were they majority opinions, might have been deemed inappropriate and in violation of the separation of church and state. In the 1997 Nebraska divorce case of *Hassenstab v Hassenstab*, for example, the dissent refers to the "practice of homosexuality" as "morally wrong" and states, "At school and at home, [the child] will eventually be taught that her mother's [lesbian] conduct was morally wrong. . . . With regard to this family's moral code, [the mother] has obviously set a horrible example."[90] The dissent in *Schuster v Schuster* is similar in this regard, admonishing, "The state ought to be concerned that if allegiance to traditional family arrangements declines, society as a whole may well suffer."[91] In perhaps the most blatantly religious and morally charged argument, the dissent in *Chicoine* expresses its condemnation of the lesbian mother in no uncertain terms: "It appears that homosexuals, such as Lisa Chicoine, are committing felonies, by their acts against nature and God. . . . even the pagans, centuries ago, before the birth of Jesus Christ, looked upon it as total defilement." The dissent went on to argue,

> Every judicial decision of consequence, in my opinion, reflects a moral judgment. For those who advocate that exercising a moral judgment is a violation of separation of "church and state," may I express: Those advocates would turn the First Amendment on its head proposing, in effect, that any belief can be fully exercised except religious belief. Judges have values, or should have. We need not be value-neutral.[92]

And in at least one instance, five years earlier in Alabama in *J.B.F. v J.M.F.,* a short conservative dissent helped embolden perhaps the most religiously fervent judicial decision of the post-2000 era, that of Judge Moore in 2002's *Ex Parte H.H.*[93] Whether conservative or progressive, these candid, fervent, and often outspoken dissents extend the scope of judicial reasoning by providing counterpoints to the majority opinions, which are often not as strongly stated, by stretching the limits of acceptable legal discourse and by injecting the opinions (and the law) with a dose of candor and audacity.

The same can be said of dissenting opinions that reflect, as one can imagine most would, the deeply felt convictions and duties of their writers. In *Weigand v Houghton,* for example, the dissenting justice concluded his written opinion against placement of the child with the abusive stepfather by remarking, "justice *requires* that I dissent" (emphasis added).[94] In the equally impassioned dissent in the case of *Matter of Marriage of Cabalquinto,* the dissenting justice asserted, "In making the father's homosexuality its primary consideration, the trial court lost sight of the duties owed both to the child and to his father. . . . I cannot agree with the majority's disposition of the visitation issue [against the father]. I therefore *must* dissent" (emphasis added).[95] In *Alison D.,* Judge Kaye wrote in her oft-cited dissent, "The majority's retreat from the courts' proper role—its tightening of the rules that should in visitation petitions, above all, retain the capacity to take the children's interests into account—*compels* this dissent" (emphasis added).[96]

This latter opinion also exemplifies the deeply felt appeals to the best interests of the child in many impassioned dissents. In *In the Interest of Angel Lace M.,* the dissent argued resolutely for a liberal construction of the adoption statute that would allow for the second-parent adoption sought by the two mothers:

> The majority . . . ignores the legislature's clear statement that the best interests of the child are paramount. . . . Given the shrinking percentage of children that are raised in two-parent families, and the shrinking percentage of children who receive even minimally adequate care regardless of family structure, the public interest is enhanced by granting legal recognition to two-parent families that do further the express objective . . . of "providing children in the state with permanent and stable family relationships."[97]

In the New Jersey case *V.C. v M.J.B.*, discussed earlier, the dissenting justice countered both the majority and a separate dissent, arguing, based on a similar framework, that the nonbiological mother should enjoy not only visitation but also possibly joint custody rights. Accordingly, the justice asserted,

> The controlling best interest standard has never been applied to the facts of this case, because the trial judge concluded, contrary to the overwhelming weight of the evidence, that V.C. was not a psychological parent. . . . In my view, granting V.C. visitation and remanding for consideration of custody would effect a reasonable application of existing statutes and common law to reality; families today take many forms, and we must protect all relationships between parents and children.[98]

Thus, through bold moves, impassioned pleas, and appeals to future wisdom such as this, the dissent is able to respond to majority judicial decisions, illustrate the pendulum-like process of settling law, and reveal, in effect, the other half of the legal conversation. This dynamic is particularly important because this flux reveals an elasticity in the law that allows it to respond to and grow with changes in the social world, including the emergence of new family forms.

Dissent and the Process of Legal Transformation

The study of dissents offers a rare glimpse of judicial panel decision-making at work; in effect, they are the half of the deliberations that may have otherwise been obscured from public view. They add nuance to our understanding of judicial decision-making by showing the range of opinions on the judicial panel and what ideologies and legal arguments the majority may have been responding to. In that way, the dissent provides a behind-the-scenes glimpse of judicial decision-making, helping to demystify law and lawmaking by revealing the processes of negotiation and the variety of conflicting viewpoints that underlie judge-made law as a human product. The fact that so much indeterminacy exists in family law ensures the fullest and widest canvassing of alternative viewpoints and can include novel ways of defining family, parenthood, and the role of sexual orientation.

Just as previous chapters have revealed the negotiation of identity and rights in family law, this chapter reveals judicial opinions themselves as negotiated documents. This is evident in cases in which the dissent suggested a compromise position that would nevertheless shift the law's take on gay and lesbian parenting, as in *Liston v Pyles* or *In re Adoption of Luke*, as well as in dissents appealing for a liberal construction of statutes that would negotiate spaces for recognizing nontraditional parenthood and family forms while still working with foundations of law already in place, such as in *Titchenal v Dexter* and *V.C. v M.J.B.* Contrasted with the majority opinion, which is also often the result of compromise and negotiation but does not reveal itself as such in the final product, the dissent lays bare the raw materials, so to speak, of the processes of negotiation and institutionalization in law.

Dissents also reveal the law as a dialogue, with contradictory and complementary elements constantly speaking back to one another. In this sense, they allow the law to be understood as a dialectical process of judicial action and reaction, evolving over time into a synthesis of new legal thought. This process is particularly important to understanding an area of law as hotly contested, and as ever evolving, as LGBT family law. In some cases, the dialogue between alternative visions of law is explicit, as in *In re Adoption of Baby Z.* and *Rubano v DiCenzo*; in others, it is more subtle but nonetheless identifiable, as in *Matter of Adoption of Charles B.* But the back-and-forth dialectic of law is emergent over time and across decisions, as well as in cases in which the dissent resembles a "pendulum swing" whose aim and eventual result is to destabilize existing assumptions about law, family, parenthood, and sexuality by presenting a strongly stated and often extreme alternative vision, as in *Weigand v Houghton* and *G.A. v D.A.* These pendulum-swing dissents impel the consideration of competing theories and, inevitably, the eventual settling of new theories and findings, a dynamic process that allows law to respond to social change in a thoughtful way. This dialogue is both a symptom and a fundamental component of the indeterminacy of family law, and it is one important mechanism—both strategically in individual cases and more broadly—by which the possibilities of family law can be transformed and expanded.

The dissent's initial and most fundamental role in this dialectical process is that of a challenge to conventional wisdom, and a signal that the majority's way is not the sole way to view an issue. As was noted in interviews, one practical effect of this role is that it enhances the likelihood of appeal, and success on appeal, by signaling to lawyers the grounds on which they may succeed in front of a different panel, or in the future, using the dissent as a "springboard."[99] This pragmatic function was apparent in interviews with attorneys but also in cases in which the decisions were appealed and the dissents vindicated, as in *Adoption of R.B.F. and R.C.F.* and *Matter of Marriage of Cabalquinto*. Yet the dissent also is an act of resistance against any essentializing tendencies in family law. Indeed, dissents can act as a catalyst for change, in a Kantian sense, planting the seeds of a paradigm shift. This happened in cases such as *In re Interest of Z.J.H.* and *Alison D. v Virginia M.*, in which the dissent argues persuasively for a shifting of the law's boundaries, pointing out the inadequacies of the current framework and paving the way for a new paradigm of family law. Indeed, in many instances a dissenting opinion has foreshadowed or even catalyzed changes to come in legal reasoning and standards, as in the cases of *In the Interest of Angel Lace M.* and *J.P. v P.W.* and in the powerful dissents of Judge Judith Kaye, whose minority opinions went on to become law and to shift judicial theories of parenthood, adoption, and "best interest."

Yet, as was noted in cases such as *Sharon S. v Superior Court* and *Chicoine v Chicoine*, strongly conservative dissents can also be voices of *resistance* to change, seemingly in contradiction to the assertion that dissents are a source of progressive change. Perhaps this dual role should not be surprising since the indeterminacy of judicial discourse in family law is itself a double-edged sword; even as we recognize the room that indeterminacy affords for changing conceptions of family and sexuality, it would be naive to assume it is all good all the time. Clearly, as we have seen in many earlier cases (and even in some contemporary ones, such as *Ex Parte H.H.* in Alabama), vague guidelines and discretion can sometimes give way to homophobic, gendered, and class bias. So too do dissents have the potential to promote both social change and stagnation. Whereas progressive dissents, such as those in *In re Interest of Z.J.H.* and *Adoption of Baby Z.*, represent the inertial pull of a paradigmatic shift in legal and social understandings of family, conservative dissents, such as those in *E.N.O. v L.M.M.* and *Matter of Dana*, represent the flipside of the same process. As sociolegal scholar Kitty Calavita has pointed out, the law can sometimes step out of sync with the currents of legal and social change, what Calavita calls a "de-constitutive" move. This makes sense because law can be "'both hegemonic and oppositional' . . . for 'law' is not of one piece."[100] The fact that Calavita contends that such de-constitutive moments are most likely to occur in unsettled cultural periods makes the argument particularly compelling in the context of a cultural and legal institution—"family"—that is so unmistakably in flux. Yet, at the same time, dissents such as that written by Justice Kaye in *Alison D.* manage to act as catalysts in the process of redefining laws to respond to the changing family form; it is notable that, although there were twenty-eight dissents arguing *against* such change, none of these was cited by later majorities. That is, although progressive and regressive dissents may be seen as bids for different futures, those bidding for a future involving *change*, or an expansion of gay and lesbian parental rights, seemed more likely to be aimed for future redemption.[101]

Sociologists Scott Phillips and Ryken Grattet have noted, "The term indeterminacy means that legal rules and concepts are inherently open to multiple and sometimes contradictory interpretations."[102] In that sense, any exploration of legal indeterminacy must take into account these contradictory interpretations, not only among but *within* the cases themselves. Dissents, then, extend family law's capacity for change—beyond what might be seen simply by virtue of its vagueness—by allowing alternative visions to plant a seed and eventually mature into new precedents. By resisting the pull of *stare decisis* and traditional formulations of family and sexuality, by sometimes resisting change propelled by the emergence of new family forms and alternative sexualities, and by arguing for a vision of law different from that which prevails at the moment, the dissent presents a sort of verbal act of rebellion. As Maurice Kelman proclaims, and the cases here show,

> The dissenter speaks in his [*sic*] own unmistakable voice, says what he thinks the law ought to be, and wields his vote in conformity to that vision. . . . He . . . shows the world that the issue remains in dispute . . . and in this way he encourages litigants to mount fresh assaults on the official position, creating new opportunities for reconsideration and hastening the "intelligence of a future day."[103]

6

Conclusion
Mastering the Double-Edged Sword

[T]he indeterminacy of particular legal norms and rights
discourses ironically contributes to their very tenacity as
traditions that resist ossification, at best, and deterioration into
an even more brutal condition of naked coercion, at worst.
— Michael McCann[1]

This book began with a story of exclusion, of a family relationship literally being judged out of existence by a set of decision-mak-
ers and mores that assumed gay male parenthood to be contrary to the
best interest of a would-be adoptive child. This Indiana man was not
alone in this respect; his fate is shared with Steven Lofton, Sharon Bottoms, and hundreds of other parents who were denied custody, visitation, or an adoption based on their homosexuality. While all but two
states have eliminated unilateral statutory rejection of gay and lesbian
adoptions, there remain few guarantees when it comes to securing full
and equal familial rights for gay men and lesbians, whether individually
or as couples, across the country. The problem is compounded when it
comes to protection for same-sex families formed outside the context of
heterosexual marriage, through surrogacy or donor insemination. Here,
as with the cases of Marla Liston, Kathleen Crandall, and others, recognition of the nonbiological parent's place in the family unit has lagged
behind the demographic realities of the gayby boom and the lived experiences of the families themselves. These decisions, too, can have devastating effects. For both Marla Liston and Kathleen Crandall, as well
as for countless others, the inability to be recognized as a parent meant

that they were barred from playing a role in their children's lives, or even from seeing them. Conversely, in the case of Robin and Sandra, the mothers in the case of *Thomas S. v Robin Y.*, the inability (or unwillingness) to understand and validate the lived realities of a two-mother family led to traumatic fear for a child who was forced into a relationship with a sperm donor she barely knew.

At the same time, the decades immediately before and after the turn of the twenty-first century saw tremendous strides in eliminating barriers to same-sex parenthood, adoption, custody, and visitation rights for LGBT parents emerging from heterosexual marriages. With the near elimination of reference to homosexuality as a disease or disorder (except for a handful of audacious antigay decisions such as Alabama Justice Moore's 2002 defamatory indictment of lesbian mothers in *Ex Parte H.H.*), it is increasingly anomalous that a parent would be denied visitation, or even shared custody, based solely on his or her sexual orientation *per se*. Greater adoption of the nexus test, increasing recognition that parental and sexual identities do not have to be mutually exclusive, and growing emphasis on the right to a parent-child relationship that benefits both parties have emerged as part and parcel of a change that also includes demographic shifts in the number and visibility of families headed by same-sex couples. These families change the set of questions asked by judges significantly, from whether custody with the heterosexual parent is better than with the homosexual parent to a new question and set of assumptions: given that this child *has* two homosexual parents and *no* heterosexual parents, what is the best arrangement for him or her? In this sense, the emergence of planned LGBT-headed families has changed the terms of the debate even for parents whose children were born in the context of a previous heterosexual relationship. At the same time, the decades of case law to which the latter parents gave rise, and the challenges they mounted to the heterosexist assumptions that previously prevailed regarding homosexuality and parental ability, have no doubt benefited those parents seeking to form families through adoption and reproductive technology during the course of the gayby boom.

Compared to the debate over same-sex marriage, the public discourse surrounding custody and adoption for gay and lesbian parents has been far less the subject of sustained attention and debate. Rarely the topic of front-page news, the development of these rights has largely flown under the political radar, despite the maneuverings of fringe religious-right groups like Focus on the Family and isolated successful movements to ban adoption, most notably Anita Bryant's 1977 "Save the Children" campaign in Florida. This relative silence is somewhat surprising, given that children—or the presumed absence of them—have loomed large in legal and political arguments over same-sex marriage. While opponents argue that marriage's procreative function is justification enough to exclude same-sex couples, close to half of all lesbians and one-quarter of all gay men have been raising their children, often without the protections of law. At the same time, obstacles to LGBT parenthood, including presumptions of unfitness, statutory regulations, and criminal prohibitions, have fallen one by one as legal advocates assert and social scientists confirm their lack of basis in fact or reason.

So, there are few guarantees of fair treatment but also fewer obstacles—how is it that both remain features of judicial decision-making in LGBT custody and adoption? Although the half century documented in this book saw tremendous change in the treatment of LGBT parents' identities and rights, and expanded definitions of what counts as a family, judicial discretion remains a constant—for better or worse. Far from moving in the direction of fixed standards and rigid determinacy (at least in the formal sense)—as have other areas of law such as criminal sentencing—family law has, if anything, become *less* fixed and *more* discretionary, with the move away from gender-specific standards for custody and toward more amorphous concepts such as "the best interest of the child" and "psychological parenthood." The analysis of gay and lesbian family court cases in the preceding chapters reveals conclusively that some meanings and rationales may have "settled" over time in these judicial narratives, but most remain indeterminate. From a sociolegal standpoint, this indeterminacy makes sense, since, as McCann notes, "human interaction is heterogeneously experienced and indeterminate in character."[2] Inevitably, judicial decisions charged with defining and regulating one of the most fundamental sites of human interaction—the family—will also reflect this indeterminacy and heterogeneity. The question becomes, then, how do we make sense of it, and what does it mean for the future of family law?

The Implications of Indeterminacy

At the start of this book I posed the problem of indeterminacy in law and its history as a critique of legal formalism. Few would argue that as an empirical phenomenon, family law does not feature the hallmark discretion that Legal Realists and Critical Legal Scholars have found in other areas of law. The ubiquitous best-interest standard ensures myriad interpretations that both support and contradict the parental rights of gay men and lesbians. Some judges have found conclusively that the stigma arising from living with a gay or lesbian parent directly undermines the best interest of a child of divorce, as in *Marlow v Marlow* and *S.E.G. v R.A.G.*, whereas others have found not only that it does *not* do so but that even to *consider* stigma is a violation of the parent's rights, as in *S.N.E. v R.L.B.* Rules mandating a significant change in circumstances or abuse of discretion by the trial judge in order to change or overturn a custody or visitation decision have been alternatively heeded or blithely discarded, depending on the judge and circumstance. A nonbiological mother's right to a relationship with her child is seen as baseless—relegated to the dissent—in *Alison D. v Virginia M.* but is redeemed with the "intelligence of a future day" in *Matter of Dana* and *V.C. v M.J.B.*

Although there are admittedly more statutory guidelines in adoption than in custody, which should provide certain judicial boundaries, even the rules that do exist have been discovered to have some flex. Jurisdictions like Ohio or Arizona, which found homosexuality entirely antithetical to the adoption of children—as in *Matter of Adoption of Charles B.*—reversed their course completely in two years' time without legislative intervention or a change in the adoption code. Different courts with equal lack of specific provision in the family code for second-parent adoptions have come to opposing conclusions about their legality. *In the Interest of Angel Lace M.* and *Adoption of C.C.G. and Z.C.G* both held that neither children nor adults had a right to a relationship protected by second-parent adoption, whereas *In re Adoption of R.B.F. and R.C.F.* found that indeed they did, and that to deny such an adoption was not only contrary to their rights but contrary to the best interest of the child. The California Supreme Court noted that second-parent adoptions have become routine in the state despite their *lack* of any legal provision or a recognized stepparent relationship (because there was no same-sex marriage prior to 2008)—and legalized them.

What explains these inconsistencies and reversals? In some instances passage of time may play a role, but certainly not always. We know of opposing decisions rendered in different courts that were contemporaneous (sometimes within a matter of days), such as those granting (or denying) surviving parental rights for a nonbiological parent after the death of the birth mother, and of other principles that wore on unchanged long after other courts, scientific data, and society in general had discounted them. One might say that differences between states account for the inconsistencies. However, this too is insufficient in explanatory breadth, since courts in neighboring states with similar political cultures have often come to very different conclusions, and in many instances the statutory language being interpreted by the judges was similar if not identical. True, the relatively recent advent of domestic partnerships, civil unions, and same-sex marriage in a handful of states has clear implications for parents and future parents in those states, particularly with regard to recognizing same-sex dual-parent families. In most of these states, however, courts had already moved toward recognizing gay and lesbian families or were well on their way to doing so, with favorable precedents in the intermediate appeals courts.

Perhaps the better question, however, is what are the implications of this incoherency for family law and for gay and lesbian parenthood, for those whose stories are told here and those to come? Why does it matter? After all, the contentions that judicial discretion abounds and that the law is indeterminate are not novel ones: legal scholars since the first half of the twentieth century have expounded on the notion that judicial decision-making is not a unilateral, logarithmic, or predictable process but rather is the product of multiple and often unpredictable contingencies, practices, strategies, and ideologies.[3] Yet what the preceding chapters show is that indeterminacy means more than "we don't know the outcome." The multiple ways in which familial and sexual identities and rights are created, shaped, negotiated, and settled in judicial decisions and dissents evince a more complex understanding of the indeterminacy of law, one that is sensitive to its nuances and its problems, as well as its creative potential.

Previous standards of family law, which specified gendered rules of custody (such as the requirement that a child of "tender years" be placed with the mother) not only afforded no room for flexibility or reinterpretation but quite obviously conformed to a narrowly defined heteronormative understanding of family—not surprisingly, since gay- and lesbian-headed families had yet to emerge on the social and legal scene in the first half of the twentieth century. Even the "primary caretaker" rule—though gender-neutral on its face—was clearly based on the traditional heterosexual family, as research shows that same-sex households tend to divide homemaking duties more equitably, making neither parent necessarily more "primary" than the other in many cases.[4] When the "best interest of the child" standard was introduced, it ushered in an era of discretion and a supposed focus on the child rather than on attributes of the parent, but heteronormative and sometimes gendered or classist presumptions about what this "best interest" was continued to prevail both in public discourse and in the courts. This bias found shelter in a custody standard that was purportedly value-neutral on its face but vague enough to encompass practically any judicial motive or path of reasoning and often used to justify elimination or restriction of custody and visitation for gay and lesbian parents. Over time, however, as demographic and cultural shifts in the social fabric were reflected in the courts, and gay and lesbian parents and families asserted and defended their existence, the very same malleability and vagueness allowed transformation and accommodation that prior, more specific custody standards could not. Even though the best-interest standard was not introduced with same-sex or other non-traditional families in mind, by omitting any specific definition of family and parenthood, it—together with the political and legal strategizing of the LGBT movement and amenability to broader interpretation in modern adoption statutes—has engendered a new set of possibilities in the legal definitions and sociolegal understandings of family, parenthood, and parental rights.

What LGBT custody and adoption cases show in multiple ways is that indeterminacy, particularly visible in the highly discretionary area of family law but certainly present in other areas of judicial decision-making as well, is a *key ingredient,* if not a necessary precondition, in the creative process of legal and social change. New definitions, rights, and identities could be created, negotiated, and reimagined in the decisions *precisely because* of the space created by the flux of the law, the "open texture" of the judicial narratives, and the fluidity of meaning attached to family and sexual orientation. Not only does such openness allow for the creation and institutionalization of new laws, rationales, and legal categories that may benefit gay and lesbian parents and would-be parents in the future, but it in turn has a profound reciprocal effect on how society decides what is a "legitimate" definition of family, parenthood, child welfare, and so on. Of course, one must also be sensitive to the power dynamics involved in judicial decision-making, and in lawmaking in general, especially when the group whose rights are at stake is, in many parts of the country, a virulently reviled minority. To be sure, the strategizing and persistence of gay and lesbian parents and their advocates are needed to drive the process, and without their success in doing so, the definitions, or lack of definitions, may be—and have in the past been—created and construed to their detriment. But their assertions of self and progress toward change are viable because of the window of opportunity afforded by the law's indeterminacy.

Evidence of this process is apparent in several realms, explored in the preceding chapters. In chapter 3, the indeterminate approach of law over the past fifty years to the identities of "parent," "legal stranger," "deviant," and "homosexual" makes room for the creative possibility of discursive compromise in the negotiation of identity. In divorces, these compromises might mean curtailing the dating behavior of *both* parents, rather than only that of gay or lesbian parents, as was previously common. In the case of breakups of same-sex parents, compromise sometimes entailed settling on quasi-parental statuses for nonbiological and nonadoptive parents, such as *de facto* parenthood, which could give a person standing to pursue a case or even visitation but does not rise to the level of equal parent. A similar process was at work in the contingent merging of previously separated and (to some people) seemingly contradictory facets of identity: homosexuality and parenthood. Predominant hegemonic gender ideology assumed lesbians and gay men would prioritize the sexual facet of their identity and not value parenthood, but the experience of the gayby boom has made clear over time that this is not the case and a "normalized" gay/lesbian parent identity has emerged in many places. Finally, these and other processes of discursive compromise and identity redefinition have led to the evolution of new parental identities for individuals not connected by blood, marriage, or even adoption in some cases. Only *after* gay parents ceased to be identified as cultural contradictions, and forged partial and contingent parentlike identities to gain standing in court, did they eventually begin to gain recognition as full parents, either through formal second-parent adoption or, in its absence, analogous statuses such as *in loco parentis* or psychological parenthood.

In chapter 4, precisely because of the indeterminacy of rights discourses and their application to different matters of law and relationships, a more complicated understanding of rights and their place in determining a child's best interest emerges, creating new possibilities for the interpretations of rights and citizenship for LGBT parents and their children. At first glance, the indeterminacy of rights seems to disserve LGBT parents more than it serves them; they are often called "selfish" if they assert their own rights as parents or as sexual minority citizens.

In addition, the increasingly frequent invocation of "children's rights," thanks to its lack of definition, has often been interpreted to mean subjugating parental rights or "protecting" children from the presumably harmful influence of their parents or would-be parents. Realizing the flaws in both of these earlier approaches, LGBT parents and their lawyers have over time been successful in exploiting the "open space" of indeterminate rights. They forged a new rights discourse that bypasses hierarchies of parents' rights or children's rights to take as its subject *relationships* in the family, rather than individuals. By redefining rights as communal rather than atomistic, they reclaim the place of rights in family law and focus attention on their bonds with their children, and on the need to protect these bonds legally.

And finally, chapter 5 shows the significance of dissenting opinions—a part of the judicial narrative that might easily be overlooked—in catalyzing future change and shows how the sedimentation of new layers and conversational processes of law are *preconditioned* by the indeterminacy of the judicial narratives to which they are responding and reacting. Majority and minority (or dissenting) opinions are wrought from the same set of facts and same body of law, and yet they come to vastly divergent conclusions. This fact in itself demonstrates law's indeterminacy in the most basic way. But the more crucial point is that the law's mutability also ultimately allows these minority opinions, in some cases, eventually to become majority opinions. It is worth noting once more that those dissents that were progressive—more open to shifting the boundaries and traditional assumptions of family law to meet the needs of LGBT families—were more likely to be redeemed eventually and become law. Whether through finding a middle ground previously overlooked or through extreme departures akin to a pendulum swing, dissents seize on the ambiguities of law to present a different path, one that has led to expanded recognition of gay and lesbian parents and families.

Making Meaning through Indeterminacy and Legal Innovation

Each of the analytical themes outlined in the preceding paragraphs, taken separately, illustrates the workings, contours, and consequences of the indeterminacy of law. Each also contributes to the growing literature supporting the theoretical vision of law and social life as mutually constitutive and interactionally involved in the processes of making meaning and "settling" of social and legal concepts. Although scholars in the tradition of Critical Legal Studies and their forebears, the Legal Realists, introduced the concept of indeterminacy and its potential for legitimizing and reifying legal hierarchies that disenfranchise less powerful individuals and groups, more-recent progressive thought has urged a reconsideration of this evaluation. After decades of dispute over the utility of legal "rights" as such and the plausibility of law as an impetus of social change, a growing group of scholars has embraced a new approach to the question of the relationship between legal and social, cultural, and personal understandings of identity, meaning, and change. Sociolegal scholars have long concerned themselves with the chicken-egg question of the relationship between social and legal change: Which comes first? Which can cause the other? This constitutive perspective, however, makes a point of not assuming a causal or unidirectional answer to this question, pointing out that the process of reciprocal diffusion is more complicated and more gradual.

Studies of "law on the ground" and ordinary citizens' legal consciousness have brought awareness of law's utility in incrementally instilling new social norms, rights, and meanings in reciprocal interaction between the "makers" and "receivers" of law. This approach is particularly à propos in the context of gay and lesbian family law, where personal and legal definitions and realities long have been at odds. So, for instance, judicial decisions certainly did not invent gay parenting, or even acknowledge it always; these parents preexisted any formal recognition by law and had to work hard with their attorneys and social movement activists to successfully assert and protect their parental identities in court. Yet, when eventually recognition began to emerge from the courts, these judicial decisions added layers of institutionalized thought about what parents look like, and the relevance (or irrelevance) of sexuality in family, to the public lexicon. This development further allowed LGBT parents to emerge from the closet and plan families of their own, again enlisting the courts to help institutionalize these new family forms. Eventually, in this back-and-forth process, new identities and rights have taken shape in a way that straddles the social and the legal, in a mutually constitutive way. The space that allows this incremental change, or even facilitates it, is in fact the very indeterminacy so bemoaned by CLS. Therefore, some rethinking of the concept of indeterminacy, and its role in constitutive meaning-making, is in order.

As a cumulative analytic whole, the themes in this book—indeterminacy and the creation of identity, rights, and dissent—form the basis of a theoretical framework that reveals the link between these two well-documented processes and visions of law. Not only does a framework emphasizing the meaning-making potential of legal language offer "a way of understanding how legal actors come to affix meaning and develop stable patterns of interpreting and rhetorically justifying legal rules" in the face of indeterminacy, but the indeterminacy and instability themselves provide a fertile ground for the creation, negotiation, and eventual sedimentation of social *and* legal definitions, processes, concepts, and identities.[5] This dynamic is seen in the negotiation of newly merged identities, the expansion and reinvention of rights, and the dialogue between competing visions of law, sexuality, "best interests," and family evident in the study of judicial dissents.

The conceptual and strategic space afforded by the recognition that some social and legal principles are not "settled," and may never be completely settled, allows for several things: a unique opportunity to witness sociolegal processes of identification, definition, and sedimentation of meaning as they happen, thus increasing our understanding of the law in action; the continued mutability and potential reinvention of social and legal institutions and constructs that seem to be best understood as more or less permanently in flux, such as family and sexuality—and the ability of the law to adapt to and follow the contours of these changes; and the creativity of legal actors in expanding on and adding to definitions of parenthood, family, child welfare, and sexuality in ways that better reflect litigants' social existence and lived reality. In essence, this space provides a canvas for the "repertoires of meaning" in legal language, which not only paint the legal picture of social constructs (such as sexuality and family), identities, and categories but also help to paint the social constructs themselves.[6] That is, the effects of this meaning-making in judicial decisions is not merely symbolic or doctrinal; the construction and sedimentation of new understandings of family and sexuality is a reciprocal process of recognition and revision, as changing social realities impel legal change, which in turn facilitates security and institutionalization. Formal legal recognition of LGBT parents and families gives the imprint of permanency and legitimacy, while the daily reality and lived existence of parents and their children provide the basis for modern standards of custody, such as psychological parenthood and, in increasing frequency, the child's best interest—however vague the term remains.

The Dynamics of Power, Resistance, and Change

Of course, such indeterminacy and freedom to invent may no doubt sometimes backfire on LGBT parents and other actors in the legal system and can also serve regressive means or result in "de-constitutive" moments, as has been seen when purported allegiance to the "best interest of the child" has meant subverting the rights of gay and lesbian parents.[7] There are more subtle risks as well. The legal contests and negotiations in which lesbian and gay parents engage to gain adoption or custody rights may also have unintended consequences for the framing of LGBT identity more generally. Proving oneself as a "fit parent" in court, for instance, may involve setting oneself apart from other gay men and lesbians, those who "flaunt" their sexuality or live with their partners. Such a gesture may win custody or adoption rights and defy stereotypes imputed to her or his person, while simultaneously marking a distinction between "good" and "deserving" lesbian and gay parents, on the one hand, and those who are "bad" or "undeserving" because of the way they choose to embody their sexual identities, on the other. The result, what has been called the "legal domestication of lesbian [and gay] existence," may reify the gendered stereotypes that are ultimately invoked to define gay and lesbian parents as problematic.[8] Thus, it is important to remember that legal ambiguity has great enabling potential but may at other times facilitate regulation and domination of the very same legal actors. But with greater access to the courts, social movement expansion and diffusion, and growing facility at strategically working the space afforded by loose definitions, LGBT parents and their attorneys have been able to rework family law and its assumptions to reflect better the growing realities of the gayby boom and to protect its members.

This success in reworking the law is evidence at least in part of another important observation: that these processes of definition and change in law are inevitably both indicative of and shaped by power dynamics and relations. This point is evident in the invocation of rights discourses to varying degrees of success, failure, cooptation, and reinvention, as shown in chapter 4; it is also evident in the negotiation of identities discussed in chapter 3, a negotiation in which preferred identities and the privileges that accompany them are sometimes attained by LGBT parents, but often as the result of discursive compromise and the privileging of certain facets of identity—sometimes to the detriment of others who are unable or unwilling to attain such compromise. The instability and multidirectionality of the law's power dynamics are also unmistakably manifest in the role of the dissent, discussed in chapter 5, at times a counterhegemonic statement and blueprint for future change and at other times a regressive resistance to social and legal change.

The variability in the manifestations and processes of power illustrated by these cases is not merely a function of temporal and social change, however. The imprint of power and resistance—both on the discursive and the material level—are in fact present throughout the stories in this book. It makes sense that power is invoked, represented, reified, and resisted in multiple settings and manners, and to widely varying degrees, throughout the judicial narratives analyzed here. After all, the connection of power to law and legal language is by no means a new revelation.[9] But its relevance to navigating the discretion of family law (or law more generally) is crucial, as the dynamics of power can determine whether this indeterminacy expands or restricts its possibilities. Chapter 4, for instance, shows how rights can be both a source of and detriment to power, depending on how they are invoked. Parents generally lose in court and are seen as selfish when they try to invoke their civil rights as members of a marginalized sexual minority, a move, ironically, meant to enhance their legal power. Power is also successfully wielded against them in the name of children's rights; but parents can harness the power of this framework when they focus on the rights attached to a parent-child bond, effectively ceding their own individual power in favor of a more relational goal. In chapter 5, the framing of the dissent as an alternative judicial narrative and an institutional act of resistance exposes the fallibility of judge-made law and the power over social life that it embodies; it also exposes the internal power struggles between opposing factions of the court for opposing visions of family law. In this sense, the dissent empowers and emboldens litigants to argue for reversal of their own case disposition or for future revision of the principle in question. Yet at the same time, the existence of the dissent adds to the legitimacy and power of judge-made law by maintaining an appearance of diligence in decision-making and evincing an openness to alternative narratives.

Power is manifest in these judicial decisions in more direct material ways as well. In chapter 3, litigants whose identities are redefined or denied by the court suffer a deficit of power in two senses: they are denied the epistemic authority and symbolic power of self-definition, and their legal identities are also redefined in ways that may literally limit their legal rights. Once a lesbian co-parent, for instance, is defined in the judicial narrative as merely a "lover" or "legal stranger," rather than "mother," she is literally defined out of contention for custody, and in many instances, she may never be allowed to see her child(ren) again. Conversely, when a court chooses to open up the definition of parenthood by allowing two parents of the same sex to adopt, or by positioning a homosexual identity and parental identity as compatible, it sways the power balance to the benefit of LGBT parents and would-be parents by allowing them the only universally recognized path to nonbiological parenthood: formal adoption. Again, the open texture of these definitions and identities, and the ways in which judges choose to interpret them, have vast power implications, both material and symbolic.

Identity and rights are not unrelated in this respect. Constructing a parent as a "legal stranger" or a lesbian as a "deviant" denies the individual of certain material and ideological rights. In this way, certain rights can be seen as constitutive of identity, and vice versa. The right of a particular person or couple to marry, for example, imputes both a potential identity—"spouse"—and a set of privileges, including child custody. The denial of this right also constitutes a denial of one's freedom to self-define and narrows the range of available identities a person may designate for him- or herself. Power, rights, and identity, then, are inextricably linked. Because these dynamics exist at both the concrete and the ideological level, and are affected by each other, the material and the symbolic effects of meaning-making and power reify each other.

Of course, the space that such indeterminacy creates for sociolegal change and assertions of power is not always a zero-sum game, because indeterminacy is not all good or all bad. Precisely because the meanings, rights, and identities here are unsettled, there is room for negotiation, cooptation, and compromise in these narratives. In chapter 3, for instance, I discussed how gay and lesbian parents, in interaction with the court, were able to locate intermediary gestures and create discursive compromises that allowed them to successfully assert certain aspects of their self-conceived identity, under certain terms. In many cases, doing so, in turn, allowed them to retain at least some custodial or visitation rights. For example, if a lesbian nonbiological mother could be identified as a *de facto* parent or even an interested party, she then could seek at least limited visitation rights to maintain contact with her child. Likewise if a gay father, for instance, was willing to suppress his gay identity and any gender-nonnormative identity markers, his parental identity might be privileged in the narrative, and he could be granted custody.

Eventually, however, these partial gains accumulated into patterns of greater—and less *conditioned*—acceptance of LGBT parents and families. With gay parenting no longer seen as a cultural contradiction or an accusation of impropriety, it has become anomalous rather than expected for LGBT biological parents to be denied custody or visitation with their children based on their sexual orientation alone. Only twice since 2000 have parents been found unsuitable for custody because of their sexual orientation *per se*. More common were cases such as *Jacoby v Jacoby*, in which justices rebutted presumptions of harm or of parenting being incompatible with "the homosexual lifestyle," offering a corrective of past decisions to this effect. And, although not legally settled to the same degree, same-sex "co-parent" has become a viable legal identity in several states, and in a handful, these nonbiological co-parents may enjoy the exact same rights and status as the biological parent. Since 2000, in fact, both divorced LGBT parents and nonbiological co-parents have won more cases than they have lost.

Similarly, compromises and negotiation facilitated by the openness of the legal language of rights helped litigants eventually reinvent rights as they apply to families. Parents were able to negotiate and in some cases successfully invoke rights discourses, provided they invoked them in the "right" way, so to speak. These parents often located an analogous conciliatory gesture, invoking rights that sustained the primacy of the family and (particularly) biological ties, rather than rights based on their status as sexual-minority citizens. Again, the result was symbolic as well as material: most often the parents who could assert such rights successfully were allowed to retain custody of their children, even while denying their own deservedness as equal *citizens*. In time, though, and as a result of these negotiations, a path has been paved to a new vision of rights that reconciles the children's interests with the parents' rights by privileging the bond between them, rather than viewing the two as opposed. Indeed, this new vision of relationship-oriented rights is well supported by recent research, which finds that children are more affected by the strength of their bond to their parents than they are by their parents' sexual orientation.[10] It is also consistent with the claim of Michael McCann that "[t]he flexibility and plurality of our rights traditions allow for adaptation to changing circumstances, for new types of claims by new groups over time, and for continued contests over the legitimacy of prevailing arrangements."[11] Thus, the process of negotiation and forward movement afforded by the open spaces of unsettled law—and sometimes by the trailblazing of a strong dissent—is a complex and multidirectional mobilization of power and resistance; ultimately, however, the creative potential of these processes is harnessed strategically to create new types of family recognition and rights.

Implications for Law, Policy and the Judicial Activism Debate

In the aftermath of the *Goodridge* marriage decision in Massachusetts, the 2004 presidential election became a breeding ground for verbal attacks on "activist judges," with the term bandied about in presidential and vice-presidential debates as the worst of the justice system's woes. This rhetoric intensified when it came time for President George W. Bush to fill two vacancies on the Supreme Court created by the death of Chief Justice William Rehnquist and the retirement of Justice Sandra Day O'Connor. President Bush and Vice President Cheney railed against the evils of judicial activism, using as examples the *Goodridge* decision and the Supreme Court's 1857 antiabolition *Dred Scott v Sandford* ruling, respectively. Of course, in the strictest sense, neither of these decisions accurately falls under the rubric of "judicial activism" as such; both had clear bases in the Constitution as it stood at their time (the Thirteenth Amendment, abolishing slavery, had not yet been ratified in the latter case). But the accuracy of the statements is almost beside the point; as journalist Dahlia Lithwick notes, "The words [activist judges] have become so loaded—so fraught with non-meaning—that no one ever stops to question them. . . . Running a political campaign on the promise of neutralizing 'activist judges' is the worst form of cynicism."[12] The "activist judge" has become the bogeyman *du jour* for politicians (mostly on the right, but also across the political spectrum), a ready scapegoat for, essentially, legal developments they disagree with, such as same-sex marriage. But even if we agreed that it is present, is judicial activism really such a bad thing?

Legal scholars will tell you that the Bill of Rights is an intentionally vague document, although how much interpretation this vagueness is meant to yield is a subject of ongoing debate between strict and liberal constructionists. Most specific rights that we now enjoy, then, are the product of "activist judges" who broadly construed the Constitution to apply to a new group or situation. The right to privacy is one obvious example. Its later application to the right to abortion in *Roe v Wade* is another. George W. Bush's very presidency came courtesy of an act of judicial activism in *Bush v Gore*, in which the Supreme Court entered the "political thicket" and found a basis to stop the manual recount of Florida's ballots within the Fourteenth Amendment's Equal Protection Clause, by making the novel assertion that the inability to ensure that all counties would recount in the same way was a violation of equal protection.[13]

Broad construction is no less vital to judicial interpretation of family law statutes and case law. From choosing one's marriage partner to the creation of new categories of crime, legal innovation affects all areas of life and is by no means unusual in the United States. Moreover, as political scientist Thomas Keck has noted, judicial activism is no longer the province of liberal courts, having been a hallmark of the politically conservative and long-serving Rehnquist Court.[14] To suggest that judicial activism has no place in American law, then, is not only historically inaccurate but short-sighted, regardless of one's position on the political spectrum.

For a minority group that did not even have a name at the time the Constitution and most family codes were written, the ability to innovate is particularly important, and even necessary to ensure the protection of legal rights. Notwithstanding the disputed accuracy of the critique of judicial activism, it is not surprising, therefore, that the most recent political skirmish over judicial activism was spurred by a gay family rights case. Much of the debate over gay rights and so-called family values has concerned the extent to which gay and lesbian relationships and families are perceived as changing the "traditional" definition of family and marriage, and whether these new definitions deserve the imprimatur of law. Both sides of the debate, of course, realize the stakes of such an institutionalized redefinition.

Again, however, a distinction must be made between the empirical and the normative; in other words, the question "*has* the definition of family changed from what is often considered traditional?" is different from "*should* the definition of family be changed?" Among family scholars and historians, there is little empirical dispute as to the oft-shifting definition of family over the course of centuries (not just since the gayby boom). In fact, the term *family* can be traced to its Latin roots in the Roman Empire, where the definition was much more expansive than how modern Americans define the "traditional family," as it included all slaves and servants, as well as relatives by blood or marriage.[15] This was also at a time when marriage was more a political and financial arrangement than a romantic one, and when most families could not afford to raise their own children. In the early United States, African Americans were barred from forming what would now be considered the "traditional" family because slaves were not allowed to marry or have custody of their own children. Today's concept of the "traditional family" itself, consisting of a two-parent nuclear family and rooted in the 1950s, was in fact a stark departure from earlier, more expansive conceptions of family (what would today be called "extended family") from the early twentieth century. Sociologist Judith Stacey notes that the *Oxford English Dictionary* lists *eleven* definitions of *family,* only one of which consists only of two parents and their children.[16] Thus, the expansion of today's family forms is not so much a reinvention but the most recent iteration in a long history of shifting boundaries. One may or may not agree that this is a good thing. But it seems reasonable that the law should have the flexibility to respond to these changes in ways that reflect and protect the identities and bonds of the families that *do* exist, as opposed to what a judge feels *should* exist. The temptation to restrictively police the boundaries of family law by maintaining rigid rules about members' legal identities and rights according to what the "average" family looks like *now* will only serve to damage the family of tomorrow—or those that fall within the margins today.

At the same time, much has been made—and rightly so—of the dangers of unchecked discretion and the need to manage it strategically. A number of cases demonstrate that there is no guarantee, for example, that a judge will interpret a vague adoption statute to apply to both members of a same-sex couple; and in a precedent-setting appellate decision, an unwillingness to do so will adversely affect not only the couple in question but other would-be parents in the future. Abstract debates over statutory interpretation and judicial activism do little to assist parents or attorneys in navigating family law and its indeterminacy. What does it mean, then, to strategize around and "work" the indeterminacy of family law?

The development of case law and judicial narratives chronicled in this book reveal a number of useful patterns and developments. One is the emergence of a gay/lesbian parent identity that does not assume the two are mutually exclusive. Judges have become increasingly less likely to adopt a *per se* finding of unfitness based on a parent's sexual orientation or to treat a same-sex relationship as fodder for gossip or criticism. Although overt homophobia is far from gone—and is still all too present in some particularly conservative jurisdictions—the overwhelming trend supports parents being open about their sexual orientation and significant relationships, rather than treating them as something to hide or fear disclosing in court. By treating the relationship as a fact of life—not any more or less relevant to child custody and visitation than a heterosexual divorced parent's new relationship—and by emphasizing one's commitment to effective parenting simultaneously, it may well be rendered a legal nonissue. This strategy of openness also helps to "challenge the apartheid of the closet" by countering the suggestion that a "good" LGBT parent must be closeted or avoid so-called flaunting.[17] Today's LGBT parents also benefit from a wealth of social scientific evidence demonstrating their ability to parent effectively, which helps to eliminate any perceived barriers between their parental and sexual identities as well. At the same time, using this data to show that gay parents do not "turn" their children gay is an ideological compromise and risk that may advance an individual claim but could ultimately be destructive to LGBT identity more globally—both parents and youth—as it suggests that there is something inherently bad about homosexuality that would be a harm to the child.

A second clear trajectory emerging from these cases is an increased recognition of planned same-sex families. Legal recognition of these relationships—in particular the relationship between the nonbiological parent and the child—is still far from ubiquitous, but it is also arguably the fastest changing element of modern family law. Gay and lesbian couples that live in states where second-parent adoption is available by case law or statute, or where they can marry or enter a civil union, are at an obvious advantage, as adoption is by far the safest method for legally securing the parent-child relationship. As of 2008, however, only fourteen states and the District of Columbia had such laws.[18] But it is still possible to assert a parental identity and gain visitation rights as a *de facto* parent, minimally, if this option is not available. Several courts have begun to embrace the "psychological parent" concept, which privileges the epistemic reality of the child by focusing on the nature of the relationship and the child's dependence on the would-be parent, rather than focusing on their biological or adoptive ties. Where a more institutionalized form is not available, nonbiological parents may craft an identity as such by prioritizing and emphasizing the markers of parental identity (as opposed to sexual or other identity facets) in relation to the child—attachment, commitment, and support—in efforts to be found *in loco parentis*, or at least a *de facto* parent.

In the same vein, despite significant jurisprudential support in some quarters for applying equal protection and other constitutional principles to gay and lesbian custody and adoption, approaches such as these that emphasize individual rights rather than children and family connections are bound to be viewed antagonistically by judges. The future of rights claims in the family law context—for not just gay and lesbian but any parents or would-be parents—is a concept of rights that emphasizes relationships rather than individuals. Even a focus on the child's rights can backfire by treating the child as an autonomous rights-bearer in need of protection *from* parents or would-be parents; in the case of a non-biological parent seeking connection to the child, there is the additional hurdle of even being allowed to assert the rights of a child whom the court does not view as yours. Reenvisioning rights as communal rather than autonomous, and treating the *relationship* between two or more people as the unit of analysis, rather than the individual members of the family, avoids the pitfalls of both the sometimes dangerous "children's rights" paradigm *and* the oft-rejected parents' rights approach.

One cannot discuss the future of LGBT family law without addressing its connection to the debate over same-sex marriage. Clearly, protecting the bonds and legal obligations between parents and children is one argument in favor of legal same-sex marriage, and those states that do recognize such partnerships (whether they call it marriage, civil union, or domestic partnership) are more likely to allow second-parent adoptions and custody or visitation rights for nonbiological parents, whether these rights existed prior to the partnership laws or whether they came in tandem. The obvious conclusion is that any legal policy trajectory that aims to help solidify LGBT parent-child relationships and families would also include legal same-sex marriage.

However, one need not look beyond the LGBT rights community to find disagreement with this proposition. The queer critique of marriage as both an institution and a goal of the gay rights movement was temporarily muted in the avalanche of news coverage following *Goodridge v Massachusetts* as well as *In re Marriage Cases* in California, but it remains a significant voice. Two of the leading figures in LGBT family law, Nancy Polikoff and Paula Ettelbrick, have in fact been quite critical of same-sex marriage as a goal of the gay rights movement and as a path to liberation for LGBT individuals and families.[19] They and others argue that basing other rights for same-sex couples and families, such as second-parent adoption or visitation, on marriage will contract, rather than expand, the range of legal options. In interviews, some attorneys felt strongly that the pursuit of LGBT parenting rights should therefore ideally be unattached to either it or analogous institutions such as civil unions. The concern is that making the two co-determinative diminishes parenting rights for those who are not drawn to marriage or similar state-sanctioned relationship recognition. Enough feminist and queer skepticism of the institution of marriage remains that the attaching of parenting rights to marriage could be a significant hindrance for some people, who quite reasonably do not want their parenting rights to be affected by their ideological or practical opposition to marriage.[20] Therefore, an ideal trajectory for LGBT family law would be to pursue custody and adoption rights independent of marriage or other formal relationship recognition as much as possible, for two reasons: first, because this would best suit the needs of all families, including those in which the parents choose not to marry; and second, because parental rights—for whatever reason—are less of a lightning rod for public controversy than is same-sex marriage, and they can be secured through piecemeal litigation (as seen in this book) as well as legislation, making them more strategically viable on their own. At the same time, in those jurisdictions where lawmakers or courts have already decided that parental rights are contingent on same-sex relationship recognition, it makes sense to continue to protect and expand these rights to benefit the greatest number of LGBT families.

Finally, dissenting opinions in past cases—even from other jurisdictions—are a powerful source of progressive ideas to be mined by parents, advocates, and judges. It is no longer disputed that today's minority opinion may well be tomorrow's majority. Because justices do sometime consider developments in public opinion or social science that were noted or predicted in previous dissents, it is well worth investigating the basis of prior forward-looking minority opinions. Particularly in cases of first impression—in which the court is considering a new family right or formation for the first time—even dissents in other states may be a useful source of material and ideas. Except in cases directly challenging a specific unique facet of a state adoption statute, enough of a "national community" exists in custody law to argue that justices are no more or less bound by other majority decisions than they are by dissents and that both are sources of argument that may well prove compelling to a new set of ears. At the very least, understanding the law as a dialogue that unfolds over time rather than as a static or linear phenomenon encourages legal actors to know the other half of the conversation and to gain a fuller sense of the body of legal thought and its trajectory. The pace of growth in LGBT family recognition in the twenty-first century has been so dramatic that this perspective, provided by dissents and applied to future cases, is increasingly not only helpful but in fact *crucial*. As Thomas Keck notes, "the particular sequence by which competing norms become entrenched within constitutional discourse has a substantial effect on subsequent events"; no doubt, the same is true in family law discourse.[21]

Broader Legal Implications of Indeterminacy

Family law, both because of its notorious discretion and its inescapably personal and culturally contingent subject matter, is a particularly apt legal setting in which to study the relationship between the indeterminacy of law and the processes of legal and social change in definitions of behavior, rights, and identities. However, these processes are at work elsewhere as well, in other arenas of judicial decision-making and law. Indeed, the framework developed here could be applied to analyze a number of areas of social life and social change that have come under the law's domain. Sociologists Valerie Jenness and Ryken Grattet, for instance, have artfully shown how a vague human condition—hate and violent prejudice—became a new category of criminal behavior—hate crime—and how this new concept and the meanings attached to it developed in law.[22] Thus, while generally criminal law has moved in the direction of less judicial discretion, the emergence of new categories of crime allows for some degree of indeterminacy and space to make meaning through legal language and action.[23]

Similarly, the sociolegal positioning of drug use—which is particularly variable by type of drug—has been the subject of significant flux and shifts in meaning in the United States in the past hundred years, and even over the course of decades. Paradoxically, whereas family lawmakers responded to bias in earlier status-specific guidelines' by moving in the direction of *less* determinacy (by dropping gender-specific guidelines), drug lawmakers responded to similar pressures produced by racist enforcement by moving in the opposite direction: determinate sentencing.[24] Like that of "homosexual," "drug user" has been an identity alternatively marked by criminal, medical, and moral discourses in law as well as in social life and popular vernacular. Although the "drug user" identity and activity may not mirror that of homosexuality or LGBT parenting in that the former is presumably volitional and potentially physically harmful, many of the same processes may be at work: the negotiation of complex and contested identities marked by discourses of morality, psychology, and criminality; the invocation of a rights paradigm (particularly pertaining to the right to privacy) that is not entirely accepted or even completely articulated; and the discursive space for change that is afforded by its temporally shifting status and fate in law (even in the face of determinate sentencing laws enacted since the 1980s) and its close connection to other realms of social life, including personal well-being and self-determination.

The campaign to legalize medical marijuana has already embraced this potential in some states by successfully redefining users' identities as "patients" and the ability to use marijuana as a *right* to medical treatment. The fact that this redefinition has not been more widely successful is due no doubt to the overly determinate character of current drug law; one need look no further than New York's Rockefeller laws to see how such rigidity can devolve into "ossification" at best and totalitarianism at worst.[25] Although the indeterminate sentencing of an earlier era was certainly not a panacea for equal enforcement of drug laws, today's determinate sentencing schemes have only served to legitimize and mask racism and classism. An obvious example is the famous Anti-Drug Abuse Act of 1986, which instituted a 100-to-1 ratio for the amount of powder versus crack cocaine needed to trigger an automatic five-year sentence, and the extreme disproportionate impact it has had on African American and poor drug offenders as compared to middle-class or Caucasian offenders who are more likely to use powder cocaine.[26] As in family law, then, it is important to manage discretion and indeterminacy effectively with smart strategizing by legal actors and advocates and guard against the dangers of a "radical" or unconstrained indeterminacy.[27]

Gay Rights and Family Law in International Perspective

An important caveat of this study is its locality in the United States, a distinct (though increasingly not unique) legal atmosphere that relies on both case law and statutory law. This is particularly true in family law, since adoption tends to be regulated by statute, whereas custody and visitation are more likely products of judge-made law. The two also intersect in important ways, when, for instance, judges are asked to interpret adoption statutes and custody standards broadly to fit the best interest of the child. Indeed, some of the most important innovations in modern family law, such as second-parent adoption, have been borne of the power of appellate judges to interpret and adapt existing statutes to serve the needs of nontraditional families and, in doing so, to create new legal categories. The indeterminacy and capacity for reinvention revealed at the heart of this study, then, may in fact be unique to those legal systems in which judicial interpretation is relied on—or at least possible—in family law matters.

At the same time, with many countries in Europe and elsewhere beginning to recognize same-sex partnerships to a greater extent nationally than in the United States, family law is clearly in a state of flux abroad, as it is domestically. Future studies would do well, then, to contrast the judicial narratives analyzed here with legal language related to gay and lesbian parenting in other countries such as the Netherlands, Canada, Norway, Spain, Belgium, and South Africa, where same-sex marriage is now legal, as well as in England, France, Germany, and many of the Scandinavian countries, where there is nationwide legal domestic partnership. Legal scholars have noted the ambivalence of many European and Commonwealth nations toward granting adoption rights to gay and lesbian individuals and couples, despite an apparent openness to recognizing same-sex domestic partnerships—almost a reversal of the pattern in the United States. The Netherlands, the first country in the world to legalize same-sex marriage, allowed registered partnerships as early as 1998, but it did not allow gay and lesbian couples to adopt children until 2000 (and it continues to ban intercountry adoption for same-sex couples). Denmark was the first country to allow registered partnerships, as early as 1989, but it did not allow adoption or custody rights until much later, a pattern followed by other European countries that subsequently introduced domestic partnership. In Belgium, where 75 percent of the population is Roman Catholic, same-sex marriage was legalized in 2003, but it did not include the right to adopt children until 2006. In Sweden, same-sex registered partnerships have been recognized since the 1990s, yet lesbians (and even single heterosexual women) are barred from accessing reproductive technology to have their own children (the same is true in Italy). Germany has allowed "life partnerships" for same-sex couples since 2001. These partnerships include the right to adopt a partner's biological children (via second-parent adoption) but do *not* include the right for couples to adopt jointly. France, similarly, offers relationship recognition but not parental rights.

Conversely, in countries such as Great Britain, Canada, and the United States, parenting rights have tended to precede marriage or partnership rights. Although Great Britain began offering civil unions in 2005, it had legalized adoption rights for same-sex couples in 2002. In both Canada and the United States, parenting rights had been on the rise, in various parts of the two countries, for several years before 2002. Perhaps surprisingly, then, LGBT *parenting* rights have the longest history in the United States, the one country among these three that is the furthest from any nationwide legalization of same-sex marriage or even domestic partnership. Some observers have argued that European countries are less averse to legalizing same-sex marriage because they are less likely to blur religious and legal lines than is the United States. However, this fails to explain why those countries have lagged behind the United States in institutionalizing LGBT parental rights. Employing a similar constitutive interpretive framework to analyze approaches to custody and adoption in other countries, particularly those with some degree of partnership recognition, would elucidate the culturally contingent dimensions of legal meaning-making and social change in a way that this study is unable to do.

Concluding Remarks: The Future of LGBT Family Law

One need look no further than the vast changes in LGBT family law in the early twenty-first century, documented in this book, to realize how futile an enterprise it would be to try to predict the future. Though there are many scholars and activists qualified to venture educated guesses, no amount of legal strategizing or sociological theorizing can forecast with any degree of certainty what major changes lie ahead in the world of gay and lesbian rights or the evolving family form. It would be easy to assume that LGBT parental rights will continue on the ascent evident in recent developments, but there is also the possibility of backlash. An instructive parallel can again be drawn to same-sex marriage, which has taken a far from linear path of unprecedented advances, followed by major setbacks; indeed, many a worthwhile scholarly study of the marriage movement was superseded when Massachusetts legalized same-sex marriage in the *Goodridge* case; and post-*Goodridge* predictions of proliferating same-sex marriage rights, by both proponents and opponents, were either temporarily put to rest or given pause by defeats that followed in the states of New York and Washington, as well as in a slew of constitutional or statutory marriage bans in other states before California became the second state to legalize same-sex marriage in May 2008. Thus, with few exceptions, anyone beginning a study of the possibility of same-sex marriage in America (or even internationally) in 2002 had an entirely different legal and political landscape with which to grapple in six short years' time.

Likewise, this has become a far different book than it would have been were it completed in 1999, when I began my research. The tragic story that introduced this book—of a child left in foster care and exposed to abuse in lieu of being placed with a gay adoptive parent—has become an anomaly in most corners of the country, rather than an unspoken but all-too-common extension of antigay bias.[28] The vast changes that took place or culminated after the new millennium—including the legalization and expansion of civil unions and domestic partnerships, the elimination of sodomy laws that implicitly defined gay parents' existence as criminal and justified adoption bans, the establishment and proliferation of legally recognized parental identities for nonbiological parents, and the further institutionalization of second-parent adoption—forced me to reconsider my earlier conclusions about the position of LGBT parents in American family law and the role of indeterminacy, as embodied most commonly in the "best interest of the child" standard.[29] Although interpretation of the best-interest standard remains problematic—in many cases being used as subterfuge to deny parents rights and contact with their children in the name of "protecting" the children's best interest or rights as separate from their parents—the indeterminacy and mutability that it embodies has yielded greater strides in recognition of nontraditional families in the new millennium than even I would have predicted. Nowhere is this shift more apparent, arguably, than in California, where a series of rulings between 2002 and 2008 expanded LGBT family rights and recognition—in particular the rights of nonbiological co-parents and second-adopters—in ways almost unimaginable a decade before. The California courts have seized on the recognition that same-sex families exist in practice regardless of formal legal definitions and that the relative imprecision of definition in our family codes and court standards allows legal recognition to adapt to meet the needs of these families as they come to the fore.

What remains unknown is to what new developments and types of families the social, medical, and legal worlds will next give rise, and how the needs and definitions of these families will follow or differ from those currently recognized in law. Few people could have imagined fifty years ago—or even less—the ability of reproductive science to create *two* biological mothers (one gestational, one genetic) or the social and political conditions necessary for a massive gayby boom to surface and become part of the cultural fabric of the nation without widespread public outcry. It would be naive to think that this gayby boom—or any recent trend in family, law, and gay rights, for that matter—is the endpoint of the social trajectory of family in the United States. Surely developments beyond the horizon will necessitate yet another reconsideration of what we linguistically and legally consider to be a family, as has been the case for generations. Fortunately, the law is equipped for such a task; as legal scholar Peter Goodrich notes, law is a discourse that is "inevitably answerable or responsible, like any other discourse, for its place and role within the ethical, political, and sexual commitments of its times."[30] But the law is necessarily reactive; if judges are to continue to make case law that responds meaningfully to social and sexual change, and not slip into regression, the process must be driven by parents, activists, and legal professionals who use their intelligent strategizing and understanding of the law's indeterminacy to harness its creative and progressive potential and shape its outcomes.

Likewise, the processes of invention, negotiation, revision, and sedimentation over the past six decades, documented and analyzed in this book, certainly did not come to a close when the data collection did. With each new layer of law, the process of sedimentation continues, but these new layers have the capacity to bring new meanings, rhetoric, and frameworks that may disrupt and reconfigure the existing layers of meaning and law. Tomorrow's "brave new families" may reveal something unknown or unconsidered about today's most progressive social and legal understandings of parenthood, family, and sexuality.[31] While some legal rights and identities may coalesce and congeal over time, others are constantly reconfigured and renegotiated. Both of these processes are illustrated here; both are evocative, creative, and significant, and both are part and parcel of a literature of law that is at once incoherent and meaningful.

Appendix 1
Case Names and Citations

Case Name	Citation	Year
Commonwealth ex rel. Bachman v Bradley	171 Pa.Super.587, 91 A.2d 379	1952
Immerman v Immerman	176 Cal.App.2d 122	1959
Evans v Evans	185 Cal.App.2d 566	1960
Commonwealth ex rel. Ashfield v Cortes	210 Pa. Super. 515, 234 A.2d 47	1967
Nadler v Superior Court In and For Sacramento County	255 Cal.App.2d 523	1967
People v Brown	49 Mich.App. 358, 212 N.W.2d 55	1973
A.v A.	15 Or.App. 353, 514 P.2d 358	.1973
Christian v Randall	33 Colo. App. 129	1973
In the Matter of J.S. & C.	129 N.J.Super.486, 324 A.2d 90	1974
Anagnostopoulos v Anagnostopoulos	22 Ill.App.3d 479, 317 N.E.2d 681	1974
Chaffin v Frye	45 Cal.App.3d 39	1975
Roberts v Roberts	25 N.C.App. 198, 212 S.E.2d 410	1975
Matter of Doe	88 N.M. 505, 542 P.2d 1195	1975
In re Jane B.	85 Misc.2d 515 N.Y.S.2d 848	1976
DiStefano v DiStefano	51 A.D.2d 885, 380 N.Y.S.2d 394	1976
Towend v Towend	1976 Ohio App. LEXIS 6193	1976
In the Matter of J.S. and C.	142 N.J. Super. 499, 362 A.2d 54	1976
Buck v Buck	238 Ga. 540, 233 S.E.2d 792	1977
DiStefano v DiStefano	60 A.D.2d 976, 401 N.Y.S.2d 636	1978
Adams v Adams	357 So.2d 881	1978
Cook v Cobb	245 S.E.2d 612	1978
Scarlett v Scarlett	257 Pa.Super. 468, 390 A.2d 1331	1978
Neal v White	362 So.2d 1148	1978
Schuster v Schuster	90 Wash.2d 626, 585 P.2d 130	1978
In re Marriage of Teepe	271 N.W.2d 626, 585 P.2d 130	1978
Gay v Gay	149 Ga.App. 173, 253 S.E.2d 846	1979
M.P.v S.P.	169 N.J.Super. 425	1979

Case Name	Citation	Year
Newsome v Newsome	42 N.C.App. 416, 256 S.E.2d 849	1979
Matter of Marriage of Ashling	42 Or.App. 47, 599 P.2d 475	1979
Woodruff v Woodruff	44 N.C.App. 350, 260 S.E.2d 775	1979
Hall v Hall	95 Mich.App. 614	1980
Kallas v Kallas	614 P.2d 641	1980
S. v S.	608 S.W.2d 64	1980
N.K.M. v L.E.M.	606 S.W.2d 179	1980
Bezio v Patenaude	381 Mass. 563, 410 N.E.2d 1207	1980
Gerald D. v Peggy R.	1980 WL 20452	1980
Irish v Irish	102 Mich.App. 75	1980
In re Ragas	393 So.2d 925	1981
Jilek v Chatman	613 S.W.2d 558	1981
D.H. v J.H.	418 N.E.2d 286	1981
Matter of Adrianson	105 Mich.App. 300	1981
In Interest of Jones	286 Pa.Super. 574, 429 A.2d 671	1981
In Interest of Dalton	98 Ill.App.3d 902	1981
In re Breisch	290 Pa.Super. 404, 434 A.2d 815	1981
Doe v Doe	660 F.2d 101	1981
Dailey v Dailey	635 S.W.2d 391	1981
Doe v Doe	222 Va. 736, 284 S.E.2d 799	1981
Jacobson v Jacobson	314 N.W.2d 78	1981
Cisek v. Cisek	59 A.L.R. 4th 1170	1982
	(7th App. Dist. Ohio July 20, 1982)	
M.J.P. v J.G.P.	640 P.2d 966, 1982 OK 13	1982
Sweet v White	104 Ill.App.3d 738	1982
In Interest of T.L.H.	630 S.W.2d 441	1982
L.v D.	630 S.W.2d 240	1982
Greening v Newman	6 Ark.App. 261, 640 S.W.2d 463	1982
J.L.P.(H.) v D.J.P.	643 S.W.2d 865	1982
Doe v Doe	16 Mass.App.Ct. 499	1983
Matter of Marriage of Cabalquinto	100 Wash.2d 325, 669 P.2d 886	1983
Wolff v Wolff	349 N.W.2d 656	1984
Guinan v Guinan	02 A.D.2d 963, 477 N.Y.S.2d 830	1984
Zaller v Zaller	1984 WL 7417	1984
Peyton v Peyton	457 So.2d 321	1984
Karin T. v Michael T.	127 Misc.2d 14, 484 N.Y.S.2d 780	1985
Roe v Roe	228 Va. 722, 324 S.E.2d 691	1985
Gottlieb v Gottlieb	108 A.D.2d 120	1985
S.N.E. v R.L.B.	699 P.2d 875	1985
Roberts v Roberts	22 Ohio App.3d 127	1985
Constant A. v Paul C.A.	344 Pa.Super. 49, 496 A.2d 1	1985

Case Name	*Citation*	*Year*
T.C.H. v K.M.H.	693 S.W.2d 802	1985
Bark v Bark	479 So.2d 42	1985
Bennett v O'Rourke	1985 WL 3464	1985
In Interest of McElheney	705 S.W.2d 161	1985
Brownell v Brownell	1985 WL 17450	1985
Daly v. Daly	715 P.2d 56 (Nev. 1986)	1986
Matter of Marriage of Cabalquinto	43 Wash.App. 518, 718 P.2d 7	1986
Pascarella v Pascarella	335 Pa.Super. 5, 512 A.2d 715	1986
Matter of Appeal in Pima County Juvenile Action	151 Ariz.335, 727 P.2d 830	1986
M.A.B. v R.B.	134 Misc.2d 317	1986
Strohman v Williams	291 S.C. 376, 353 S.E.2d 704	1987
Conkel v Conkel	31 Ohio App.3d 169	1987
Wolf v Wolf	1987 WL 11132	1987
Adoption of J.M.G.	226 Mont. 525, 736 P.2d 967	1987
Thigpen v Carpenter	21 Ark.App. 194, 730 S.W.2d 510	1987
S.E.G. v R.A.G.	735 S.W.2d 164 USLW 2131	1987
Jane W. v John W.	137 Misc.2d 24, 519 N.Y.S.2d 603	1987
G.A. v D.A.	745 S.W.2d 726	1987
In re Marriage of Birdsall	197 Cal.App.3d 1024	1988
Charpentier v Charpentier	206 Conn. 150, 536 A.2d 948	1988
S.L.H. v. D.B.H.	745 S.W.2d 848	1988
Black v Black	1988 WL 22823	1988
Collins v Collins	1988 WL 20173	1988
Stewart v Stewart	521 N.E.2d 956, 56 USLW 2646	1988
In Interest of C.M.M.	757 S.W.2d 601	1988
Henry v Henry	296 S.C. 285, 372 S.E.2d 104	1988
In the Matter of Adoption of Charles B.	1988 WL 119937 (Ohio App. 5 Dist.)	1988
State ex rel. Human Services Department	764 P.2d 1327	1988
Doe v Roe	139 Misc.2d 209, 526 N.Y.S.2d 718	1988
Mohrman v Mohrman	57 Ohio App.3d 33	1989
J.P. v P.W.	772 S. W.2d 786	1989
Beauregard v Suiter	1989 WL 117275	1989
T.C.H. v K.M.H.	784 S.W.2d 281	1989
In re Marriage of Walsh	451 N.W.2d 492	1990
Alison D. v Virginia M.	155 A.D.2d 11, 552 N.Y.S.2d 321	1990
In re Adoption of Charles B.	50 Ohio St.3d 88, 552 N.E.2d 884	1990
Patricia M. Boucher v David E. Boucher	1990 WL 751138	1990
Glover v Glover	66 Ohio App.3d 724	1990
Lundin v Lundin	563 So.2d 1273	1990
In re Interest of Z.J.H.	157 Wis.2d 431, 459 N.W.2d 602	1990

Case Name	*Citation*	*Year*
McGinnis v McGinnis	567 So.2d 390	1990
Curiale v Reagan	22 Cal.App.3d 1597	1990
White v Thompson	569 So.2d 1181	1990
In Interest of J.L.O.	197 Ga.App. 596, 398 S.E.2d 853	1990
Hodson v Moore	464 N.W.2d 699	1990
In re Marriage of Williams	205 Ill.App.3d 613	1990
In re Marriage of Fahy	208 Ill.App.3d 677	1991
Nancy S. v Michele G.	228 Cal.App.3d 831	1991
Alison D. v Virginia M.	77 N.Y.2d 651, 572 N.E.2d 27	1991
Kulla v McNulty	472 N.W.2d 175	1991
In re Interest of Z.J.H.	162 Wis.2d 1002, 471 N.W.2d 202	1991
In re Michael M.	1991 WL 126460 (Conn.Super.)	1991
Barron v Barron	406 Pa.Super. 401, 594 A.2d 682	1991
Stuart v. New Hampshire, Division for Children and Youth Services	134 N.H. 702	1991
In re Marriage of Diehl	221 Ill.App.3d 410	1991
In re J.A.	601 A.2d 69	1991
In re Brian R.	2 Cal. App. 4th 904	1991
Chicoine v Chicoine	479 N.W.2d 891, 60 USLW 2528	1992
A.C. v C.B.	113 N.M. 581, 829 P.2d 660	1992
Matter of Adoption of Evan	153 Misc.2d 844	1992
Nickerson v Nickerson	158 Vt. 85, 605 A.2d 1331	1992
Kelly v Klein	827 S.W.2d 609	1992
Pennington v. Pennington	596 N.E. 2d 305	1992
In Interest of M.D.S.	837 S.W.2d 338	1992
Sheppard v Hood	605 So.2d 708	1992
T.G.S. v D.L.S.	608 So.2d 743	1992
Marjorie G. v Stephan G.	156 Misc.2d 198	1992
Blew v Verta	420 Pa.Super. 528, 617 A.2d 31	1992
Thomas S. v Robin Y.	157 Misc.2d 858	1993
Collins v Collins	1993 WL 177159	1993
Matter of Commitment of J.N.	158 Misc.2d 97, 601 N.Y.S.2d 215	1993
Adoptions of B.L.V.B. and E.L.V.B.	160 Vt. 368, 628 A.2d 1271	1993
In re Marriage of Wiarda	505 N.W.2d 506	1993
Johnson v Schlotman	502 N.W.2d 831	1993
H.J.B. v P.W.	628 So.2d 753	1993
Matter of Adoption of Child by J.M.G.	267 N.J.Super. 622, 632 A.2d 550	1993
In re Hirenia C.	18 Cal. App. 4th 504	1993
Adoption of Tammy	416 Mass. 205, 619 N.E.2d 315	1993
In re Marriage of D.F.D.	261 Mont. 186, 862 P.2d 368	1993

Case Name	Citation	Year
State of Florida v. James W. Cox and Rodney M. Jackman	627 So.2d 1210	1993
Large v Large	1993 WL 498127	1993
Pleasant v Pleasant	256 Ill.App.3d 742	1993
Flowers v Flowers	1993 WL 542086	1993
Matter of Adoption of Caitlin/ Matter of Adoption of Adam	163 Misc.2d 999, 622 N.Y.S.2d 835	1994
Matter of Adoption of Jessica N.	202 A.D.2d 320	1994
In re Marriage of Salmon	519 N.W.2d 94	1994
Leckie and Voohries	128 Or.App. 289, 875 P.2d 521	1994
In Interest of Angel Lace M.	184 Wis.2d 492, 516 N.W.2d 678	1994
Bottoms v Bottoms	18 Va.App. 481, 444 S.E.2d 276	1994
Matter of R.L.S.	1994 OK CIV APP 102	1994
Tucker v Tucker	881 P.2d 948	1994
Matthews v Weinberg	645 So.2d 487	1994
North v North	102 Md.App. a, 648 A.2d 1025	1994
Matter of Adoption of Anonymous	209 A.D.2d 960	1994
Paul C. v Tracy C.	209 A.D.2d 955 N.Y.S.2d 159	1994
Thomas S. v Robin Y.	209 A.D.2d 298	1994
Teegarden v Teegarden	642 N.E.2d 1007	1994
Matter of Camilla	163 Misc.2d 272	1994
Van Driel v Van Driel	525 N.W.2d 37	1994
P.L.W. v T.R.W.	890 S.W.2d 688	1994
In re Marriage of Martins	269 Ill.App.3d 380	1995
D.B. v R.B.	279 N.J.Super. 405	1995
Phillips v Phillips	1995 WL 115426	1995
In re Marriage of Cupples	531 N.W.2d 656	1995
Matter of Dana	209 A.D.2d 8, 624 N.Y.S.2d 634	1995
Bottoms v Bottoms	249 Va. 410, 457 S.E.2d 102	1995
Cox v Florida Department of Health and Rehabilitative Services	656 So.2d 902	1995
Music v Rachford	654 So.2d 1234	1995
Hembree v Hembree	660 So.2d 1342	1995
In re Custody of H.S.H.-K.	193 Wis.2d 649, 533 N.W.2d 419	1995
In re M.M.D.	662 A.2d 837, 64 USLW 2079	1995
Larson v Larson	50 Ark.App. 158, 902 S.W.2d 254	1995
Fox v Fox	904 P.2d 66, 1995 OK 87	1995
Petition of K.M.	274 Ill. App. 3d 189	1995
Matter of Parsons	914 S.W.2d 889	1995
In re T.J.	666 A.2d 1	1995

Case Name	*Citation*	*Year*
McGuffin v Overton	214 Mich.App. 95	1995
Matter of Guardianship of Astonn H.	167 Misc.2d 840	1995
In the Matter of Adoption of Two Children by H.N.R.	285 N.J. Super. 1	1995
In the Matter of Jacob/ In the Matter of Dana	86 N.Y.2d 651, 660 N.E.2d 397	1995
Scott v Scott	665 So.2d 760	1995
Hertzler v Hertzler	908 P.2d 946	1995
J.A.L. v E.P.H.	1995 WL 1316001 (Pa.Com.Pl), 31 Phila.Co.Rptr. 528	1995
In re Marriage of McKay v McKay	1996 WL 12658	1996
Tucker v Tucker	910 P.2d 1209	1996
In Interest of R.E.W.	220 Ga.App. 861, 471 S.E.2d 6	1996
In re Adoption of Baby Z.	45 Conn.Supp. 33, 699 A.2d 1065	1996
Matter of T.L.	1996 WL 393521	1996
Matter of Adoption of T.K.J.	931 P.2d 488, 65 USLW 2043	1996
In re R.E.W.	267 Ga. 62, 472 S.E.2d 295	1996
Maradie v Maradie	680 So.2d 538	1996
Matter of Christine G.	229 A.D.2d 540; 644 N.Y.S.2d 1016	1996
Ward v Ward	1996 WL 491692	1996
J.A.L. v E.P.H.	453 Pa.Super. 78, 682 A.2d 1314	1996
Pulliam v Smith	124 N.C.App. 144, 476 S.E.2d 446	1996
In re Marriage of R.S.	286 Ill.App.3d 1046	1996
In re Marriage of Wicklund	84 Wash. App. 763, 932 P.2d 652	1996
R.W. v D.W.W.	717 So.2d 790	1997
Bowen v Bowen	688 So.2d 1374, 62 A.L.R.5th 891	1997
Titchenal v Dexter	166 Vt. 373, 693 A.2d 682	1997
J.L.S. v D.K.S.	943 S. W.2d 766	1997
Barnae v Barnae	123 N.M. 583, 943 P.2d 1036	1997
Adoption of Galen	425 Mass. 201, 680 N.Y.S.2d 916	1997
Inscoe v Inscoe	121 Ohio App.3d 396	1997
In re Price v Price	1997 WL 338588 (Tenn.App.)	1997
Fowler v Arbuckle and Tjoren	949 S.W.2d 442	1997
Liston v Pyles	1997 WL 467327	1997
Packard v Packard	697 So.2d 1292	1997
J.B.F. v J.M.F.	730 So.2d 1186	1997
Hassenstab v Hassenstab	6 Neb.App. 13, 570 N.W.2d 368	1997
Boswell v Boswell	118 Md.App. 1, 701 A.2d 1153	1997
West v Superior Court	59 Cal.App.4th 302	1997
Delong v Delong	1998 WL 15536	1998
T.K.T. v F.P.T.	716 So.2d 1235	1998

Case Name	Citation	Year
Ex parte D.W.W.	717 So.2d 793	1998
R.W. v D.W.W.	717 So.2d 799	1998
Knotts v Knotts	693 N.E.2d 962	1998
Piatt v Piatt	27 Va.App. 426, 499 S.E.2d 567	1998
In Matter of Linda A.H. v Diane T.O.	243 A.D.2d 24, 673 N.Y.S.2d 989	1998
K.T.W.P. v D.R.W.	721 So.2d 699	1998
Ex parte J.M.F.	730 So.2d 1190	1998
Pulliam v Smith	348 N.C. 616, 501 S.E.2d 898	1998
J.A.D. v F.J.D.	978 S.W.2d 704	1998
J.B.F. v J.M.F.	730 So.2d 1197	1998
Dorn v Dorn	724 so.2d 554	1998
Marlow v Marlow	702 N.E.2d 733	1998
In re Adoption of Jane Doe	130 Ohio App.3d 288, 719 N.E.2d 1071	1998
Boswell v Boswell	352 Md. 204, 721 A.2d 662	1998
In re Adoption of Baby Z.	247 Conn. 474 A.2d 1035	1999
Weigand v Houghton	730 So.2d 581	1999
V.C. v M.J.B.	319 N.J.Super. 103, 725 A.2d 13	1999
Kathleen C. v Lisa W.	71 Cal. App. 4th 524	1999
Pryor v Pryor	709 N.E.2d 374	1999
Kazmierazak v Query	736 So.2d 106	1999
Bottoms v Bottoms	1999 Va. App. LEXIS 402	1999
E.N.O. v L.M.M.	429 Mass. 824, 711 N.E.2d 886	1999
In re C.M.A.	1999 WL 507853	1999
In re De La Pena	1999 WL 553829	1999
Pryor v Pryor	714 N.E.2d 743	1999
D.L. v R.B.L.	1999 WL 553770	1999
Pamela J. v. Santiago J.	1999 WL 1456949	1999
In re Thompson	1999 WL 787517	1999
Laspina-Williams v Laspina-Williams	1999 WL 989432 (Conn. Super.)	1999
Eldridge v Eldridge	1999 WL 994099 (Tenn. Ct. App.)	1999
In re Matter of Visitation with C.B.L. v H.L.	1999 WL 1204780 (Ill.App. 1 Dist.)	1999
In the Matter of B.P. and A.P.	995 P.2d 982 (Mont. 2000)	2000
V.C. v. M.J.B.	163 N.J. 200, A.2d 539 2000 N.J. LEXIS 359,	2000
S.F. v. M.D.	132 Md. App. 99	2000
LaChapelle v. Mitten	607 N.W.2d 151	2000
Jacoby v Jacoby	763 So.2d 410	2000
In the matter of J.C. v C.T.	184 Misc.2d 935, 711 N.Y.S.2d 295	2000
T.B. v L.R.M.	753 A.2d 873	2000
Gestl v. Frederick	133 Md. App. 216 754 A.2d 1087	2000

Case Name	Citation	Year
Rubano v DiCenzo	759 A.2d 959	2000
In re Adoption of M.J.S.	44 S.W.3d 41	2000
Guardianship of Olivia J. v Jennifer J.	84 Cal. App.4th 1146	2000
In re Adoption of R.B.F. and R.C.F.	762 A.2d 739	2000
In re Adoption of C.C.G. and Z.C.G.	762 A.2d 724, 2000 PA Super. 338	2000
In re Bonfield (1st)	2001 Ohio App. LEXIS 548	2001
In the Matter of Fouty	2001 WL 227672 (Ohio App. 5 Dist. Mar. 7 2001)	2001
S.B. v. L.W.	793 So. 2d 656	2001
A.F. v D.L.P.	339 N.J.Super. 312	2001
Eldridge v Eldridge	42 S.W.3d 82	2001
In the Interest of Hart	806 A.2d 1179	2001
Lofton v Kearney	157 F.Supp.2d 1372 (S.D. Fl. 2001)	2001
In re Marriage of Dorworth	33 P.3d 1260 (Colo. App. 2001)	2001
Sharon S. v Superior Court	93 Cal.App.4th 218	2001
State of Washington on behalf of D.R.M.	109 Wn. App. 182, 34 P.3d 887	2001
T.B. v L.R.M.	567 Pa. 222, 786 A.2d 913	2001
Tripp v. Hinckley	290 A.D.2d 767, 736 N.Y.S.2d 506	2002
Sinclair v. Sinclair	804 So. 2d 589, 2002 Fla. App.	2002
Ex parte H.H.	830 So. 2d 21	2002
In re Adoption of Luke	263 Neb. 365, 640 N.W.2d 374	2002
In re Jones	2002 Ohio 2279	2002
(Muffley) Downey v. Muffley	767 N.E.2d 1014	2002
Janis C. v Christine T.	294 A.D.2d 496	2002
Thomas v. Thomas	203 Ariz. 34, 49 P.3d 306	2002
Lacey v Lacey	822 So.2d 1132	2002
In re Adoption of R.B.F. and R.C.F.	569 Pa. 269, 803 A.2d 1195	2002
Fulk v Fulk	827 So.2d 736	2002
Lavoie v. MacIntyre	2002 Conn. Super. LEXIS 3825	2002
In re Bonfield	97 Ohio St.3d 387, 780 N.E.2d 241	2002
L.S.K. v H.A.N	813 A.2d 872	2002
Strome v. Strome	60 P.3d 1158 (Or. 2003)	2003
In re Adoption of M.M.G.C., H.H.C., and K.E.A.C.	785 N.E.2d 267	2003
Taylor v. Taylor	353 Ark. 69, 110 S.W.3d 731	2003
Sharon S v Superior Court of San Diego	31 Cal.4th 417, 73 P.3d 554	2003
Davis v. Kania	48 Conn. Supp. 141, 836 A.2d 480	2003
In re Adoption of A.W., J.W., and M.W.	343 Ill. App. 3d 396, 796 N.E.2d 729	2003
Damron v Damron	670 N.W.2d 871	2003
Lofton v Secretary of Department of Children and Family Services	358 F.3d 804	2004

Case Name	Citation	Year
Sharon S. v Superior Court of San Diego County	2004 WL 304340	2004
C.M. v. C.H.	789 N.Y.S.2d 393	2004
Matter of Adoption of Carolyn B., Nancy E.H., and Sheila M.S.	6 A.D.3d 67, 774 N.Y.S.2d 227	2004
In the Matter of the Adoption of Infant K.S.P. and Infant J.P.	804 N.E.2d 1253	2004
Hogue v. Hogue	147 S.W.3d 245 (Tenn. Ct. App. 2004)	2004
C.E.W. v. D.E.W.	2004 ME 43, 845 A.2d 1146	2004
In re Parentage of L.B.	121 Wn.App. 460, 89 P.3d 271	2004
K.M. v. E.G.	118 Cal. App. 4th 477	2004
Elisa B. v Emily B.	118 Cal. App. 4th 966, 97 P.3d 72	2004
Adoption of Joshua S.	2004 Cal. App. Unpub. LEXIS 5534	2004
Kristine H. v. Lisa R.	120 Cal. App. 4th 143	2004
In the Interest of E.L.M.C.	100 P.3d 546	2004
Lofton v Secretary of Department of Children and Family Services	377 F.3d 1275, 2004 U.S. App. LEXIS 15056	2004
Kantaras v. Kantaras	884 So. 2d 155	2004
S.A.S. v. E.M.S.	2004 Del. Fam. Ct. LEXIS 188	2004
In re Parentage of A.B.	818 N.E.2d 126	2004
Davis v. Davis	2004 Ohio 6500, 2004 Ohio App. LEXIS 5972	2004
L.A.M. v. B.M.	2004 Ala. Civ. App. LEXIS 917	2004

Appendix 2

Interview Questions for Attorneys

I. Questions regarding professional background, how you got
    involved in this sort of litigation/advocacy:
    1. Brief history of involvement in custody litigation and
        organizational involvement (at Lambda, elsewhere?)
    2. Nature of involvement as an attorney and as activist/advocate
        (how roles differ)?
II. General questions regarding custody cases involving gay/lesbian
    parents:
    1. What tend to be the most important focal points for you to
        drive home in litigating these cases? And how do you think
        they are received generally by judges? What are the range of
        responses?
    2. Given that these cases force judges to "think outside of the
        box" and their often traditional notions of family, relationships,
        civil rights, etc., to what extent do you think judges have the
        ability to redefine what family is? And what rights are, what
        harm and morality are?
    3. How does the fact that the trier of fact in family law is a judge
        instead of a jury change your job in these cases?
    4. The "best interest of the child" standard purposefully allows
        discretion to the judge—family court is infamous even for
        allowing such wide discretion to judges. How does this facet of
        family court—the vast discretion and relative lack of judicial
        constraints—affect your role as an attorney?
    5. How have you experienced this discretion on the part of the
        judges in cases you tried involving gay/lesbian parents? How
        has it manifested?
    6. How often do you feel that judges have abused their discretion

in these cases? Relied too much on their own version of morality or "family values"? Examples?

7. With regard to the use of expert testimony—what types do you tend to cite in your amicus briefs or use on the stand? What is the most effective? Were there any cases that were notable for the way that judges dealt with expert testimony (interpretation, ignoring)? What were the circumstances?

III. Questions regarding specific cases that you have been involved with:

1. In each case, please explain your involvement and your impressions. What were the most salient issues? What stood out about the case that one would not know just by reading the recorded (appellate decision)? Why did they succeed?

   a. *In re CMW* (1999, IL)

   b. *Inscoe v Inscoe* (1997, OH)

   c. *In re Marriage of R.S.* (1996, IL)

   d. Others that stand out or went on to the appellate courts? Abuses of discretion?

IV. References to others, judges, litigants

Appendix 3
Interview Questions for Judges

I.   Professional background:
  1.   How long have you been (or were you) on the family law bench?
  2.   Did you practice family law before being elected (or appointed) to the bench?
II. General questions regarding custody cases involving gay/lesbian parents:
  1.   For divorce cases (heterosexual marriage ends when one party comes out as gay or lesbian, and there is an ensuing custody/visitation case): Have you seen this type of case? What were the major issues? How did you rule? (or, if you have not seen this type of case, what types of issues do you think it would raise)? What types of issues are generally raised by each side and for you (or other family court judges)?
  2.   For lesbian co-parent cases (when a pair of lesbians splits up after one had a child through artificial insemination): Have you seen this type of case? What were the major issues? How did you rule? What types of issues are generally raised by each side and for you (or other family court judges) that are different from those raised by cases involving traditional heterosexual families?
  3.   For second-parent adoption cases (where the same-sex life partner of the biological or officially adoptive parent would like to formally adopt the child as well): Have you seen this type of case? What were the major issues? How did you rule? If you have never seen this type of case, would you allow such an adoption? Why or why not? If adoption is not feasible, what would you suggest to a second parent who would like to

formalize or protect his/her relationship with a child that is not biologically related?

4. With regard to expert witness testimony (clinical psychologists, social workers, experts in child development or in sexual orientation)—how do you evaluate its relevance and validity? When do you allow it? How do you deal with competing claims from opposing experts (for example, an expert on one side claims that sexual orientation is likely to be transmitted from parent to child, while an opposing expert refutes that claim)?

5. How do statements and research reports from expert groups, such as the recent one from the American Academy of Pediatrics (or statements from the American Psychiatric Association), affect your decision-making, if at all? Do these have an impact on your thinking about the best interest of child?

6. The "best interest of the child" standard purposefully allows discretion to the judge—how do you interpret your role, and how far do you extend that discretion? Do you rely on any particular set of standards to determine best interest? What do you think constitutes an abuse of discretion?

7. Statutory considerations: How do you weigh best interest of the child against statutory law (for example, if a lesbian co-parent wants to adopt a child and the adoption statutes does not specifically allow for two parents of the same gender)? What issues are best left for legislature?

8. How do you determine what constitutes harm to a child? How do you deal with claims of stigma affecting a child?

9. How do you interpret and weigh rights (rights of parent vs. rights of child)? What do you do when a conflict arises between the two? Or between these rights and statutes? Do you think constitutional claims based on due process or equal protection are valid in the family law arena?

III. Hypothetical case situations (in each, what types of problems would this case pose for you? What are the most salient issues for you? How would you handle this case?):

1. Joan and Paula (two lesbians) were in a committed marriage-like relationship for 10 years. They decided together to have a child, and Joan was artificially inseminated and carried the child to term. After the child was born, the two shared equally

the responsibility of raising the child (Ann) and providing financially for her. Ann calls both Joan and Paula "mommy." When Ann was 6 years old, Joan and Paula broke up and moved into separate homes. They are unable to resolve on their own the issue of who should have primary custody of Ann. Joan tells Paula she is not the real (or legal) mother, and therefore has no right to visitation or custody; Paula tells Joan that she is indeed Ann's mother and deserves shared custody, or at least liberal visitation. They eventually end up in family court to resolve the issue.

2. Bob and Jan are married for 15 years before Bob comes to the realization that he is gay, and has been repressing it his entire life. They file for divorce based on this realization, they sell their house, and both parents move to new homes in different parts of town. Their two children, Jenny and Tom, like both parents equally but would prefer to live with Tom during the week because they prefer his neighborhood, where Tom has begun to make friends with other gay and lesbian parents and their children. Jan thinks Bob has been a good father in the past, but fears that spending too much time alone with Bob or with his new friends will adversely affect the kids' gender development or sexual orientation, and that they will be stigmatized in their community if they live with a gay father. Also, she is a devout Christian and believes that homosexuality is immoral. So far, both children are well-adjusted and healthy, but Jan fears future harm, so she asks the judge to give her primary custody and limit Bob's visitation to daytime hours only, and around no other adults. Bob wants primary custody during the week, and weekend custody for Jan.

IV. Any other thoughts or comments? Suggest other names?

Appendix 4

Interview Questions for Parents

I. Tell me your story in a nutshell—events leading up to court case:
   1. Decision to have child, division of responsibility
   2. Were you confident going in that the law (going to court) would secure your parental rights?
   3. What has happened since the Court of Appeals decision?
II. How does it affect you to have this court say that you are not a parent?
   1. How does it make you feel?
   2. How has the decision changed your identity, if at all?
   3. Do you think people in your community identify you as no longer a parent since the decision?
   4. Did they identify you as a parent before? Are they supportive of you?
III. Do you think the decision was based at all on the fact that you are a lesbian?
   1. If so, how?
   2. Do you have any indications that the judge or justices had antigay leanings?
IV. Did you or the attorneys introduce expert testimony or briefs to support your position? What did it consist of? How do you think the judges received it?
V. Talk about the court's ability to define what a family is and what a parent is:
   1. Should they be able to do this?
   2. What should their role be?
   3. What would you like people (lawmakers and judges) to learn from your experience?

Appendix 5
List of Interviews

Interview Number	Position	Date	Location
1	Judge	3/7/02	Southern California
2	Judge	12/12/01	Southern California
3	Judge	12/11/01	Southern California
4	Judge	2/4/02	Southern California
5	Judge	2/28/02	Illinois
6	Judge	1/24/02	Northern California
7	Attorney	1/24/02	Northern California
8	Judge	3/18/02	Northern California
9	Attorney	3/18/02	Northern California
10	Judge	3/18/02	Northern California
11	Judge	5/1/02	Illinois
12	Judge	4/16/02	Southern California
13	Judge	3/21/02	Southern California
14	Judge	5/15/02	Northern California
15	Judge	4/18/02	Southern California
16	Judge	5/16/02	Southern California
17	Judge	4/22/02	Southern California
18	Judge	4/29/02	Southern California
19	Judge	4/22/02	Southern California
20	Judge	6/7/02	Southern California
21	Attorney	1/23/02	Northern California
22	Attorney	1/23/02	Northern California
23	Attorney	1/28/02	New York
24	Attorney	3/5/02 & 4/10/02	New York
25	Attorney	2/21/02	Illinois
26	Attorney	3/13/02	Washington, D.C.
27	Litigant	2/28/02	Ohio
28	Litigant	3/19/02	Northern California

Interview Number	Position	Date	Location
29	Attorney	4/29/02	Illinois
30	Attorney	5/24/02	New York
31	Attorney	5/15/02 & 5/20/02	Tennessee
32	Attorney	4/26/02	Northern California
33	Litigant	6/17/02	Tennessee
34	Litigant	7/24/02	Tennessee
35	Litigant	6/24/02	New York
36	Litigant	6/24/02	New York

Notes

NOTES TO CHAPTER I

1. *In re Parentage of A.B.*, 818 N.E.2d 126 (2004).

2. *Ex Parte H.H.* 830 So.2d 21, 26 (2002).

3. *Lawrence v Texas*, 539 U.S. 558 (2003); *Lofton v Florida*, 543 U.S. 1081 (2005).

4. Interview #29, transcript page 4.

5. *McGuffin v Overton*, 542 N.W.2d 288 (1995); *Matter of Guardianship of Astonn H.*, 635 N.Y.S.2d 418 (1995). Although these cases were heard in different states (Michigan and New York, respectively), there were no specific independent differences in the settled law in each state that would account for the different outcomes.

6. Critical legal scholar Mark Tushnet has defined indeterminacy this way: "a proposition of law (or legal proposition) is indeterminate if the materials of legal analysis—the accepted sources of law and the accepted methods of working with those sources such as deduction and analogy—are insufficient to resolve the question, 'Is this proposition or its denial a correct statement of the law?'" In other words, indeterminacy refers to the inability to predict a rational path that the law will take, based on the set of rules and circumstances present. Mark Tushnet, "Defending the Indeterminacy Thesis," *Quinnipiac Law Review* 16 (1996): 339, 341.

7. Indeed, recent studies have confirmed that this is so. In his study of federal judges' demographic attributes and their votes in LGBT rights cases, political scientist Daniel Pinello found significant differences by race, gender, religion, and age, as well as support for the notion that the majority of judges deciding these cases are of traditional majority demographic categories (Caucasian, male, age fifty and over). See Daniel Pinello, *Gay Rights and American Law* (Cambridge: Cambridge University Press, 2003).

8. *Lochner v New York*, 198 U.S. 45 (1905); *Muller v Oregon*, 208 U.S. 412 (1908).

9. Stephan Landsman and Richard F. Rakos, "A Preliminary Inquiry into the Effect of Potentially Biasing Information on Judges and Jurors in Civil Litigation," *Behavioral Sciences and the Law* 12 (1994): 113–126.

10. Sheila D. Ards, William A. Darity Jr., and Samuel L. Myers Jr., "'If It Shall Seem Just and Proper': The Effect of Race and Morals on Alimony and Child Support Appeals in the District of Columbia, 1950–1980," *Journal of Family History* 23, no. 4 (1998): 441–475.

11. See, for example, Frances Olsen, "The Sex of Law," in *The Politics of Law: A Progressive Critique,* 3rd ed., ed. David Kairys (New York: Basic Books, 1998).

12. Katharine Bartlett, "Feminist Legal Methods," in *Feminist Legal Theory: Foundations,* ed. D. Kelly Weisberg (Philadelphia: Temple University Press, 1993), 553.

13. Stephen Parker, "The Best Interests of the Child: Principles and Problems," in *The Best Interests of the Child: Reconciling Culture and Human Rights,* ed. Philip Alston (Oxford, UK: Clarendon, 1994), 35. Other works that have critiqued the best-interest standard as excessively vague are Andrea Charlow, "Awarding Custody: The Best Interests of the Child and Other Fictions," in *Child, Parent, and State: Law and Policy,* ed. S. Randall Humm, Beate Anna Ort, Martin Mazen Anbari, Wendy S. Lader, and William Scott Biel (Philadelphia: Temple University Press, 1994); and Martin Guggenheim, "The Best Interest of the Child: Much Ado about Nothing?" in Humm et al., *Child, Parent, and State.*

14. Kathryn L. Mercer, "A Content Analysis of Judicial Decision-Making— How Judges Use the Primary Caretaker Standard to Make a Custody Determination," *William and Mary Journal of Women and the Law* 5 (1998): 1–149, 67.

15. Timothy E. Lin, "Social Norms and Judicial Decisionmaking: Examining the Role of Narratives in Same-Sex Adoption Cases," *Columbia Law Review* 99 (1999): 739–794.

16. See *M.A.B. v R.B.,* 510 N.Y.S.2d 960 (1986).

17. This presumption, commonly called the *"per se"* standard, is discussed in more detail in chapter 2.

18. C. Herman Pritchett, *The Roosevelt Court: A Study in Judicial Politics and Values, 1937–1947* (Chicago: Quadrangle Books, 1969), 47.

19. James Tully, *Strange Multiplicity: Constitutionalism in an Age of Diversity* (New York: Cambridge University Press, 1995), 103–104.

20. See Michael McCann, *Rights at Work: Pay Equity Reform and the Politics of Legal Mobilization* (Chicago: University of Chicago Press, 1994), 285.

21. Ibid.

22. Tushnet, "Defending the Indeterminacy Thesis," 340.

23. Interview #24, transcript page 8.

24. The use of quotation marks around the term "judicial activism" is deliberate, for two reasons. First, different people and different disciplines have varying definitions of the term and varying opinions about whether it applies only to constitutional interpretation, for instance, or to statutory construction or to simply not adhering strictly to prior precedents. Second, it is far from

given that one person's evaluation of a piece of decision-making as "activist"—whether based on constitutional law, statutory law, or case law—would be evaluated as "activist" by others. The term has evolved into a catch phrase of sorts for any judicial act that one finds politically objectionable. Given this often glib use, therefore, it is important to take use of the term with a grain of salt. For the purposes of this book, I use "activist" to refer to decisions that broadly construe either prior case law, constitutional principles, or statutes to strike out on a path that does not adhere strictly to past principles of family law—whether one thinks of that as a good thing or a bad thing. For more on judicial activism, see Thomas M. Keck, *The Most Activist Supreme Court in History: The Road to Modern Judicial Conservatism* (Chicago: University of Chicago Press, 2004).

25. No such cases appeared earlier than 1952 in the United States, though it is possible that parents whose orientation or behavior would identify them as homosexual or bisexual today—but were not identified as such in the published judicial decision—were involved in appellate cases earlier than 1952. A more detailed description of the universe of cases included in this study can be found in appendix 1.

26. I sifted through the cases to exclude only those in which child custody, adoption, or visitation is not at stake or in which at least one of the parties is not (allegedly) homosexual, bisexual, or transsexual/transgender. Examples of cases excluded at this step include those in which the word "homosexual" is used only in the context of an insult by one party to the other or in which the word only appears in the context of a citation of another case as precedent. In addition, my initial search revealed a number of cases in which the opposing litigant or judges claimed that a parent was homosexual or bisexual, but the parent denied it. See *Grant v Grant*, WL 80951 (Ohio App. 6 Dist. 1989) and *Rowsey v Rowsey*, 329 S.E.2d 57 (1985). These cases were excluded from the analysis for this reason, except when there was substantial discussion of the matter in the decision and the court found (or assumed) the parent to be gay in the face of his or her denial. See *Guinan v Guinan*, 02 A.D.2d 963 (1984); *D.L. v R.B.L.*, 741 So.2d 417 (1999). In the latter situations, even though the parent denied homosexuality, this facet of the parents' identity was still a substantial part of the court's reasoning. Indeed, those cases in which the sexual orientation of the parent was contested as a finding in court were valuable components of my analysis in chapter 3 of the imposition of identity in law.

27. These include the current and previous directors of NCLR, the founder of NCLR, the current and three previous legal directors of Lambda, the current director of the Lambda Midwest office, and noted author and attorney Nancy Polikoff, among others.

28. In many cases, the full names of the litigants were concealed in the public record, because of the private nature of the cases. This is why it would have been difficult, if not impossible in some cases, for me to pursue interviews with

the litigants without the assistance of the attorneys. In addition, some of the litigants whose names I had obtained had moved since the trial, and therefore I was not able to locate them.

29. Those interviewees that did not allow me to tape-record did allow me to take written notes and spoke slowly so that I could capture their original words. In addition, one interviewee, by her own request, was interviewed by email. See list of interviews in appendix 5; interviews cited in the text are referred to according to the number of the interview as listed in the appendix.

30. Jean Overcash, "Narrative Research: A Review of Methodology and Relevance to Clinical Practice," *Critical Review of Oncology and Hematology* 48 (2003): 179, 180.

31. The exception here is adoption cases; adoption statutes do differ depending on the state—particularly between those few states (such as Florida) that have an explicit ban against gay and lesbian adoption and the rest that do not. This variation is discussed in chapter 2, and where state-specific adoption rules are relevant in the analysis, they are noted throughout the book.

32. *In re R.E.W.*, 471 S.E.2d 6 (1996); *Bottoms v Bottoms*, 457 S.E.2d 102 (1996).

33. Maurice Kelman, "The Forked Path of Dissent," *Supreme Court Review* (1985): 227–298, 248.

NOTES TO CHAPTER 2

1. *In re Parentage of A.B.*, 818 N.E.2d 126, 131 (2004).

2. See Kath Weston, *Families We Choose: Lesbians, Gays, Kinship* (New York: Columbia University Press, 1991); John D'Emilio, *Sexual Politics, Sexual Communities: The Making of a Homosexual Minority in the United States, 1940–1970*, 2nd ed. (Chicago: University of Chicago Press, 1998).

3. The term "families of choice" is borrowed from Weston, *Families We Choose*.

4. Carol Stack, *All Our Kin: Strategies for Survival in a Black Community* (New York: Harper & Row, 1974).

5. Stephanie Coontz, *The Way We Never Were: American Families and the Nostalgia Trap* (New York: Basic Books, 1992).

6. For more in-depth discussions of the rise of reproductive technology used by gay and lesbian families and its legal implications, see Kate Kendell and Robin Haaland, *Lesbians Choosing Motherhood: Legal Implications of Alternative Insemination and Reproductive Technology*, 3rd ed. (San Francisco: National Center for Lesbian Rights, 1996).

7. Jeanne Howard, *Expanding Resources for Children: Is Adoption by Gays and Lesbians Part of the Answer for Boys and Girls Who Need Homes?* (New York: Evan B. Donaldson Adoption Institute, 2006).

8. See ibid.

9. Elizabeth Say and Mark Kowalewski, *Gays, Lesbians and Family Values* (Cleveland: Pilgrim, 1998).

10. Weston, *Families We Choose*, 22.

11. Judith Stacey, *In the Name of the Family: Rethinking Family Values in the Postmodern Age* (Boston: Beacon, 1996), 7.

12. These first cases are documented, respectively, in Laura Benkov, *Reinventing the Family: The Emerging Story of Lesbian and Gay Parents* (New York: Crown, 1994), and Nancy Polikoff, "Raising Children: Lesbian and Gay Parents Face the Public and the Courts," in *Creating Change: Sexuality, Public Policy, and Civil Rights*, ed. John D'Emilio, William Turner, and Urvashi Vaid (New York: St. Martin's, 2000).

13. *Alison D. v Virginia M.*, 77 N.Y.2d 651 (1990); *Curiale v Reagan*, 22 Cal.App.3d 1597 (1990).

14. Interview #24, transcript page 27.

15. *Griswold v Connecticut*, 381 U.S. 479 (1965).

16. *Eisenstadt v Baird*, 405 U.S. 438 (1972); *Roe v Wade*, 410 U.S. 113 (1973).

17. *Lawrence v Texas*, 539 U.S. 558 (2003); *Romer v Evans*, 517 U.S. 620 (1996).

18. *Lawrence*, 539 U.S. at 509.

19. In discussing the likely implications for gay family rights in the wake of *Lawrence*, law professor Martin Gardner notes as much and quotes the dissent: "This case does not involve the issue of homosexual marriage only if one entertains the belief that principle and logic have nothing to do with the decisions of this court. Many will hope that, as the Court comfortingly assures us, this is so." See Martin R. Gardner, "Adoption by Homosexuals in the Wake of *Lawrence v Texas*," *Journal of Law & Family Studies* 6 (2004): 19, 42.

20. *Goodridge v Department of Public Health*, 798 N.E.2d 941 (2003).

21. See Polikoff, "Raising Children."

22. As of 2008, states with civil union or domestic partnership laws affording rights akin to marriage included Vermont, Connecticut, New Jersey, California, New Hampshire, and Oregon.

23. *Baehr v Lewin*, 852 P.2d 44 (1993); this case was later renamed *Baehr v Miike*, 910 P.2d 112 (1996).

24. "Family values," as a moral paradigm, are often considered by conservatives to be incompatible with homosexuality. See Robert Knight, "How Domestic Partnerships and 'Gay Marriage' Threaten the Family," *Insight* (Family Research Council) (1994): 1–10. Say and Kowalewski, however, show that the same pattern of morals and values can be found in gay and lesbian families. See Say and Kowalewski, *Gays, Lesbians, and Family Values*; also see Stacey, *In the Name of the Family*. In chapter 3, I show how LGBT parents' sexual and

parental identities are rendered compatible, albeit often conditionally, in the judicial narratives. I also discuss the ways in which the parents' sexual identities are marked normatively, as appropriate versus not.

25. Interview #4, transcript page 15.

26. Whether sexual practice *should* be considered the defining attribute of the LGBT community is, of course, a highly debatable issue. See Patricia Cain, *Rainbow Rights: The Role of Lawyers and Courts in the Lesbian and Gay Civil Rights Movement* (Boulder, CO: Westview, 2000); Janet Halley, "The Construction of Heterosexuality," in *Fear of a Queer Planet: Queer Politics and Social Theory*, ed. Michael Warner (Minneapolis: University of Minnesota Press, 1997). This issue is revisited in chapter 3.

27. See Martha Fineman, *The Neutered Mother, the Sexual Family, and Other Twentieth Century Tragedies* (New York: Routledge, 1995).

28. This hypothetical title is borrowed from Maureen Sullivan, "Rozzie and Harriet? Gender and Family Patterns of Lesbian Coparents," *Gender and Society* 10 (1996): 747–767.

29. Even this decision by the APA, however, yielded a certain degree of indeterminacy and confusion in the eyes of some judges as to the mental state of homosexuals. For example, in the case of *In the Matter of J.S. & C.* (1974), the judges cited this recent change and the surrounding controversy, declaring a "lack of understanding and controversy which surrounds homosexuality" as a significant factor in limiting the gay father's visitation rights. *In the Matter of J.S. & C.*, 324 A.2d 90, 97 (1974).

30. For more on the history of family rights advocacy in the LGBT movement, see Polikoff, "Raising Children."

31. A more in-depth examination of these rights claims appears in chapter 4.

32. Interview #2, transcript page 10.

33. For a more lengthy discussion of the decision by the APA to delete homosexuality from the DSM, see Ronald Bayer, *Homosexuality and American Psychiatry: The Politics of Diagnosis* (Princeton, NJ: Princeton University Press, 1987).

34. Two of the best-known researchers who have examined these question and provided the data that support the proposition that gay men and lesbians do not differ significantly from their heterosexual counterparts are psychologists Richard Green and Charlotte Patterson. See Richard Green, Jane Barclay Mandel, Mary E. Hotvedt, James Gray, and Laurel Smith, "Lesbian Mothers and Their Children: A Comparison with Solo Parent Heterosexual Mothers and Their Children," *Archives of Sexual Behavior* 15, no. 2 (1986): 167–183; Charlotte Patterson, "Lesbian Mothers, Gay Fathers, and Their Children," in *Lesbian, Gay, and Bisexual Identities over the Lifespan: Psychological Perspectives*, ed. Anthony D'Augelli and Charlotte Patterson (New York: Oxford University Press, 1995).

35. See Michael Wald, "Adults' Sexual Orientation and State Determinations Regarding Placement of Children," *Family Law Quarterly* 40 (2006): 381.

36. These points are supported, respectively, by Jerry Bigner and R. Brooke Jacobsen, "Parenting Behaviors of Homosexual and Heterosexual Fathers," *Journal of Homosexuality* 18 (1989): 173–186; and Carol Jenny, Thomas A. Roesler, and Kimberly L. Poyer, "Are Children at Risk for Sexual Abuse by Homosexuals?" *Pediatrics* 94, no. 1 (1994): 41.

37. Stacey and Biblarz, in their much-cited meta-analysis revealing and recasting the specifics of these developmental studies, found emerging in the empirical literature the following differences among offspring of gay/lesbian parents: a decreased "level of aggressiveness and domineering disposition" among boys; increased level of affection, responsiveness, and concern for younger children among all children; increase in self-reported popularity among girls; increase in children who have gay or lesbian friends or would consider having a gay or lesbian relationship; and an increase in children's ability to discuss sexual development with their parents while growing up. See Judith Stacey and Timothy J. Biblarz, "(How) Does Sexual Orientation of Parents Matter?" *American Sociological Review* 66, no. 2 (2001): 159–183.

38. Still, judges are expected to look closely at mediations and negotiations involving child custody and visitation, out of a similar concern for children's well-being.

39. There are no juries in family or dependency court, so the trier of fact in all cases is the judge.

40. The notorious vagueness of the "best interest of the child" standard as it applies to custody more generally is discussed by Stephen Parker in "The Best Interests of the Child: Principles and Problems," in *The Best Interests of the Child: Reconciling Culture and Human Rights*, ed. Philip Alston (Oxford, UK: Clarendon, 1994).

41. In some states, the maternal presumption of "tender years" extended to female children of any age.

42. See Alba Conte, *Sexual Orientation and Legal Rights, Volume 1*, (New York: Aspen, 2000), 661. The critique of the "best interest" standard was launched mainly by the work of Joseph Goldstein, Anna Freud, and Albert Solnit in their landmark book, *Beyond the Best Interest of the Child* (New York: Free Press, 1973).

43. Given the extant gender dynamics of the home and the workplace during this time, the "primary caretaker" rule generally kept custody with mothers. Moreover, the "tender years" doctrine continued to be a consideration in some states through the 1980s; see *Bah v Bah*, 668 S.W.2d 663 (1983). For a more detailed history of changing child custody standards, see Michael Grossberg, *Governing the Hearth: Law and the Family in Nineteenth-Century America* (Chapel Hill: University of North Carolina Press, 1985); and Mary Ann Mason

and Ann Quirk, "Are Mothers Losing Custody? Read My Lips: Trends in Judicial Decision-Making in Custody Disputes—1920, 1960, and 1995," *Family Law Quarterly* 31, no. 2 (1997): 215–236.

44. Other considerations include "the interaction and interrelationship of the child with his parent or parents, his siblings and any other person who may significantly affect the child's best interest, . . . the physical violence or threat of physical violence by the child's potential custodian . . . whether directed against the child or directed against another person, . . . the willingness and ability of each parent to facilitate and encourage a close and continuing relationship between the other parent and the child, . . . and . . . whether one of the parents is a sex offender." Uniform Marriage and Divorce Act § 402, 45.

45. *Bah*, 668 S.W.2d at 666.

46. This principle of biological parents' rights was affirmed in *Troxel v Granville*, 527 U.S. 1069 (1999), and its predecessors, Meyer v. Nebraska, 262 U.S. 390 (1923), and *Pierce* v. *Society of Sisters*, 268 U.S. 510 (1925).

47. See, for example, *Ward v Ward*, 675 So.2d 941 (1996).

48. *Troxel*, 527 U.S. 1069.

49. See Nancy D. Polikoff, "The Impact of *Troxel v Granville* on Lesbian and Gay Parents," *Rutgers Law Journal* 32, no. 3 (2001): 825–855.

50. At one time additional requirements of eligibility applied to children—they were only suitable for adoption if they were not "defective" (i.e., disabled)—but these restrictions were largely abandoned by the end of the twentieth century. See Naomi Cahn and Joan Hollinger, eds., *Families by Law: An Adoption Reader* (New York: New York University Press, 2004).

51. The legislatures of California, Connecticut, Colorado, and Vermont have legalized second-parent adoption by statute. Case law supports second-parent adoptions in California, Illinois, Indiana, Massachusetts, New York, New Jersey, Pennsylvania, and the District of Columbia; and trial courts have allowed them in Alabama, Alaska, Delaware, Hawaii, Iowa, Louisiana, Maryland, Michigan, Minnesota, Nevada, New Mexico, Oregon, Rhode Island, Texas, and Washington. See National Gay and Lesbian Task Force, "Second-Parent Adoption in the U.S.," www.thetaskforce.org.

52. For more on the history and advent of legal adoption in the United States, see Grossberg, *Governing the Hearth*.

53. 42 U.S.C. § 1996 (as amended in 1996); see also Joan Heifetz Hollinger, "The What and Why of the Multiethnic Placement Act (MEPA)," in *Families by Law: An Adoption Reader*, ed. Naomi Cahn and Joan Hollinger (New York: New York University Press, 2004).

54. *Johnson v Calvert*, 851 P.2d 776, 776 (1993).

55. Florida prohibits any and all adoptions by gay and lesbian individuals *or* couples and is the only state to do so; Mississippi prohibits adoption by same-sex couples, but not necessarily individuals who are gay or lesbian. See

National Gay and Lesbian Task Force, *Report: Adoption Laws in the United States* (2006).

56. See Barbara Bennett Woodhouse, "Hatching the Egg: A Child-Centered Perspective on Children's Rights," *Cardozo Law Review* 14 (1993): 1747–1806.

57. See *Michael H. v Gerald D.*, 491 U.S. 110 (1989). The fact that a similar recognition has not been extended to women who hold a child out as their own has been the subject of some criticism from both feminist and queer legal scholars.

58. See *West v Superior Court*, 59 Cal.App.4th 302 (1997).

59. *Adoptions of B.L.V.B. and E.L.V.B.*, 628 A.2d 1271 (1993). The first second-parent adoption by a lesbian co-parent was approved by a low-level appeals court in New York in 1992 (*Matter of Adoption of Evan*, 583 N.Y.S.2d 997 (1992)); however, it did not rely on any of the legal theories delineated here.

60. *J.A.L. v E.P.H.*, 682 A.2d 1314 (1996).

61. *V.C. v M.J.B.*, 748 A.2d 539, 551 (2000).

62. *In the Interest of E.L.M.C.*, 100 P.3d 546 (2004).

63. *Nadler v Superior Court in and for Sacramento County*, 255 Cal.App.2d 523 (1967).

64. This test was established in *Nadler* in response to the presumption of the trial court that evidence of mother Ellen Doreen Nadler's lesbianism was sufficient *per se* to require that she not have custody of her children. Since its inception, the use of the nexus test has become quite common, although by no means universal: 21 percent of the decisions (sixty-five cases) invoked the nexus test in determining harm, and an additional 4 percent (fourteen cases) discussed it but did not use it; 20 percent of the decisions (sixty-four cases) used the *per se* standard to determine harm, and an additional 14 percent (forty-three cases) discussed or weighed its merits but did not use it. For more on the nexus test versus the *per se* standard, see Benkov, *Reinventing the Family*.

65. See, for example, Joe Rollins, *AIDS and the Sexuality of Law: Ironic Jurisprudence* (New York: Palgrave Macmillan, 2004).

66. This phrase is from William Eskridge, *Gaylaw: Challenging the Apartheid of the Closet* (Cambridge, MA: Harvard University Press, 1999).

67. See Adrienne Rich, *Compulsory Heterosexuality and Lesbian Existence* (Denver: Antelope, 1982); Jeffrey Weeks, *Invented Moralities: Sexual Values in an Age of Uncertainty* (Cambridge, UK: Polity, 1995).

68. See, for example, *Cook v Cobb*, 245 S.E.2d 612 (1978).

69. See *In Interest of Dalton*, 424 N.E.2d 1226 (1981).

70. *Kantaras v Kantaras*, 884 So. 2d 155, 159 (2004).

71. See Alfred C. Kinsey, Wardell B. Pomeroy, and Clyde E. Martin, *Sexual Behavior in the Human Male* (Philadelphia: Saunders, 1948).

72. See Anne Fausto-Sterling, "The Five Sexes," *Sciences* 33, no. 2 (1993): 20.

73. See Kinsey, Pomeroy, and Martin, *Sexual Behavior in the Human Male*.

NOTES TO CHAPTER 3

1. *In the Matter of Adoption of Charles B.*, WL 119937 (1988).
2. *Matter of Adoption of Camilla*, 620 N.Y.S.2d 897 (1994).
3. *Alison D. v Virginia M.*, 155 A.D.2d 11 (1990).
4. See, for example, Howard Becker, *Outsiders: Studies in the Sociology of Deviance* (London: Free Press of Glencoe, 1963); John Braithwaite, *Crime, Shame, and Reintegration* (New York: Cambridge University Press, 1989).
5. Edwin Lemert, *Social Pathology: A Systematic Approach to the Theory of Sociopathic Behavior* (New York: McGraw-Hill, 1951).
6. Braithwaite, *Crime, Shame, and Reintegration.*
7. Examples include limitations on women's working hours, women's ability to own property, and wives' ability to be free from sexual assault from their husbands. See *Muller v Oregon*, 208 U.S. 412 (1908).
8. Wendy Espeland, "Legally Mediated Identity: The National Environmental Policy Act and the Bureaucratic Construction of Interests," *Law & Society Review* 28, no. 5 (1994): 1149–1178.
9. Ibid., 1150.
10. This scenario, for example, would apply to gay or lesbian individuals wishing to adopt a child for whom they have been a foster parent or to a non-biological mother whose partner underwent donor insemination in order for the couple to have a child.
11. Barbara Yngvesson discusses this notion—in particular in relation to motherhood—in her article "Negotiating Motherhood: Identity and Difference in 'Open' Adoptions," *Law & Society Review* 31, no. 1 (1997): 31–80.
12. *Thomas S. v Robin Y.*, 599 N.Y.S.2d 377 (1993).
13. This decision was subsequently overturned in a higher appellate court, in *Thomas S. v Robin Y.*, 618 N.Y.S.2d 356 (1994). In a postscript to the appellate decision, the two mothers appealed to the highest court in New York, the Court of Appeals, which issued a stay on the order of filiation granted by the lower appeals court, and Thomas S. eventually gave up the suit, after being diagnosed with AIDS.
14. Interview #35, transcript page 2.
15. In materials provided by Robin Y. and Sandy R.
16. Interview #1, transcript page 9.
17. See Gary Kinsman, *The Regulation of Desire: Homo and Hetero Sexualities*, 2nd ed. (Montreal: Black Rose Books, 1996); the reference to "men" only in this context is deliberate, as the Wolfenden Report specifically dealt with male homosexual conduct.
18. For more on the medicalization of homosexuality, see Bayer, *Homosexuality and American Psychiatry.*

19. *Hertzler v Hertzler*, 908 P.2d 946 (1995).

20. *J.P. v P.W.*, 772 S.W.2d 786 (1989).

21. Interview #24, transcript page 5.

22. *Bennett v O'Rourke*, WL 3464, 8 (1985).

23. See Patterson, "Lesbian Mothers, Gay Fathers, and Their Children."

24. Stacey and Biblarz provide a comprehensive meta-analysis of the varied data, which show these differences and their relative advantages. See Stacey and Biblarz, "(How) Does the Sexual Orientation of Parents Matter?"

25. *S.N.E. v R.L.B.*, 99 P.2d 875 (1985).

26. *Conkel v Conkel*, 509 N.E.2d 983, 986 (1987).

27. Interview #2, transcript page 1.

28. Interview #4, transcript page 4.

29. *Eldridge v Eldridge*, WL 994099 (1999); this ruling was modified on appeal in 2001 but still was premised on Julie Eldridge not sleeping in the same room as her live-in partner. Another narrative implicit in the discussion of whether gay or lesbian parents may affect the sexual orientation of their children is whether such a hypothetical outcome should even be considered harmful or have a bearing on the best interest of the child. As a former Lambda legal director remarked, "that was a screwed up question to have to ask in the first place, like, assume for the moment being raised by a gay parent makes you very, very likely to be gay, who cares?" (interview #30, transcript page 2; for more on this, see Stacey and Biblarz, "(How) Does the Sexual Orientation of Parents Matter?").

30. See Bruce MacDougall, *Queer Judgments: Homosexuality, Expression, and the Courts in Canada* (Toronto: University of Toronto Press, 2000), 17.

31. See Heinrich Hartog, *Man and Wife in America: A History* (Cambridge, MA: Harvard University Press, 2000).

32. It is no accident that bisexuality does not appear as an option in these cases. Even when a litigant self-identified as bisexual, she or he was thought of and treated as homosexual, thus rendering the possibility of bisexual identity invisible (for more on "bisexual erasure," see Kenji Yoshino, "The Epistemic Contract of Bisexual Erasure," *Stanford Law Review* 52, no. 2 (2000): 353–561). For this reason, the litigants whose cases are discussed in this book are most often referred to as either homosexual, gay, or lesbian.

33. *Guinan v Guinan*, 102 A.D.2d 963 (1984).

34. *D.L. v R.B.L.*, 741 So.2d 417 (1999).

35. *In re Mara*, 3 Misc.2d 174 (1956).

36. *Taylor v Taylor*, 110 S.W.3d 731 (2003).

37. Interestingly, the references to deviance did not decrease after the APA declassified homosexuality as a psychiatric disease in 1973. The most significant drop in these references occurred only in the past decade, since the mid-1990s.

38. For further discussion, see MacDougall, *Queer Judgments*.

39. *A. v A.*, 514 P.2d 358 (1973).

40. For examples of such work, see Kinsman, *The Regulation of Desire*; Marianne T. O'Toole, "Gay Parenting: Myths and Realities," *Pace Law Review* 9 (1989): 129–164.

41. *N.K.M. v L.E.M.*, 606 S.W.2d 179 (1980).

42. *In re Jane B.*, 380 N.Y.S.2d 848 (1976).

43. *State ex rel. Human Services Department*, 764 P.2d 1327 (1988).

44. *Chicoine v Chicoine*, 479 N.W.2d 891 (1992).

45. *Ex Parte H.H.*, 830 So.2d 21 (2002).

46. *Ex Parte H.H.*, 830 So.2d at 13.

47. For more on the evaluation of expert testimony in these cases, see Kimberly D. Richman, "Judging Science: The Court as Arbiter of Social Scientific Knowledge and Expertise in LGBT Parents' Child Custody and Adoption Cases," *Studies in Law, Politics, and Society* 35 (2005): 3–28.

48. *J.L.P.(H.) v D.J.P.*, 643 S.W.2d 865 (1982).

49. Interview #34, transcript page 2.

50. For more on the notion of law "settling" over time, see Scott Phillips and Ryken Grattet, "Judicial Rhetoric, Meaning-Making, and the Institutionalism of Hate Crime Law," *Law & Society Review* 34, no. 3 (2000): 567–606.

51. The term "partner" is used anachronistically here. Before the 1990s, one would far more likely fall into the category of "lover" or "roommate" in the parlance of the law. Any reference to one's same-sex partner in less sexualized or, alternatively, more familial terms would be met with either disbelief or, in some cases, accusations of delusion. For a more lengthy discussion of terminology used to describe same-sex partnerships, see Peter Nardi, "Friends, Lovers, and Families: The Impact of AIDS on Gay and Lesbian Relationships," in *In Changing Times: Gay Men and Lesbians Encounter HIV/AIDS*, ed. Martin Levine, Peter Nardi, and John Gagnon (Chicago: University of Chicago Press, 1997).

52. *Wolff v Wolff*, 349 N.W.2d 656 (1984).

53. Interview #8, transcript page 1.

54. *Immerman v Immerman*, 176 Cal.App.2d 122 (1959).

55. *Henry v Henry*, 372 S.E.2d 104 (1988).

56. Interview #23, transcript page 14.

57. This refers to the distinction between the *per se* standard and the nexus test, discussed in chapter 2.

58. Interview #4, transcript page 6.

59. *Scott v Scott*, 665 So.2d 760, 764 (1995).

60. *Collins v Collins*, WL 20173 (1988).

61. Yngvesson, "Negotiating Motherhood."

62. Interview #3, transcript page 7.

63. These statistics apply mainly to lesbian couples, one of whom had a child by donor insemination (or in a smaller number of cases, one of whom legally

adopted a child). Only one of the cases involved two gay men, one of whom was the biological father; and only two cases involved a second-parent adoption by a gay male couple.

64. *McGuffin v Overton*, 542 N.W.2d 288 (1995); *Matter of Guardianship of Astonn H.*, 635 N.Y.S.2d 418 (1995).

65. It is also important to note that no significant difference in statutory law existed between New York and Michigan to account for the difference in outcomes.

66. *In re Custody of H.S.H.-K.*, 533 N.W.2d 419 (1995); in addition, the child carried both mothers' surnames and was referenced in court with the last name "Holtzman-Knott."

67. *In re Adoption of Baby Z.*, 699 A.2d 1065 (1996); this case was later overturned on appeal, and the adoption was denied by the Connecticut Supreme Court in 1999. See *In re Adoption of Baby Z.*, 724 A.2d 1035 (1999).

68. *Liston v Pyles*, WL 467327 (1997); interview #27, transcript page 3.

69. Interview #26, transcript page 17. At the time of the interview, only Vermont offered same-sex domestic partnerships at the state level. Later, California, New Jersey, Connecticut, Oregon, and Maine were added to this list. In 2003, Massachusetts legalized same-sex marriage, followed by California in 2008 (after each state had already separately legalized second-parent adoption).

70. Interview #5, transcript page 5. This interview took place before same-sex marriage was legalized in California in May 2008. See *In re Marriage Cases*, 2008 Cal. LEXIS 5247.

71. Interview #5, transcript page 14.

72. Interview #6, transcript page 3.

73. Interview #7, transcript page 2.

74. Interview #24, transcript page 17.

75. *West v Superior Court*, 59 Cal.App.4th 302 (1997).

76. Interview #21, transcript page 13.

77. *Kathleen C. v Lisa W.*, 71 Cal.App.4th 524 (1999).

78. Oklahoma was a notable exception at the time these cases were decided, as the only state that would not recognize legally valid adoptions by gay/lesbian couples performed in a different state. This statute was overturned by a federal judge in 2006 in the case of *Finstuen v Edmonson*, but an appeal of the decision is now under review at the 10th Circuit U.S. Court of Appeals.

79. In the case of *Adoptions of B.L.V.B. and E.L.V.B.*, 628 A.2d 1271 (1993), the ruling did afford parental rights to a nonbiological parent based on an analogy to the stepparent exception rule.

80. Interview #4, transcript page 2; this procedure was subsequently legalized in California, after this interview took place, in the case of *Sharon S. v Superior Court*, 73 P.3d 554 (2003).

81. *In the Interest of Angel Lace M.*, 516 N.W.2d 678 (1994).

82. Interview #4, transcript page 3. This interview took place before the legalization of marriage in California in May 2008.

83. There were no cases involving a biological father versus his male partner prior to 2000.

84. *J.A.L. v E.P.H.*, 682 A.2d 1314 (1996).

85. Interview #27, transcript page 11.

86. Interview #9, transcript page 2.

87. *Matter of Adoption of Camilla*, 620 N.Y.S.2d at 280.

88. *In re Parentage of A.B.*, 818 N.E.2d 126, 131 (2004).

89. *Sharon S. v Superior Court*, 93 Cal.App.4th 218 (2001); this case is also widely known as *Sharon S. v Annette F.*

90. *Sharon S. v Superior Court,* 31 Cal.4th 417, 437 (2003).

91. In 2001, the California legislature passed Assembly Bill 25, which legalized same-sex domestic partnerships that, in turn, allowed registered domestic partners to adopt each others' biological children. The precedent in *Sharon S.* was nevertheless novel in that it did not limit the practice to *registered* domestic partners, as the statute did.

92. *K.M. v E.G.*, 118 Cal. App. 4th 477 (2004); *K.M. v E.G.*, 37 Cal.4th 130 (2005).

93. *Elisa B. v Emily B.*, 37 Cal. 4th 108 (2005). Interestingly, however, the court's rationale rested on the framing of the nonbiological mother as fulfilling an absent father's role: "The child was deprived of the right to have a traditional father to take care of the financial needs of the child. Respondent chose to step into those shoes and assume the role and responsibility of the 'other' parent." Ibid. at 115. Thus, the court, while expanding the legal conception of parenthood to include lesbian families, still relied on a very traditional heteronormative model of family. It is also interesting to note that this case arose not by the volition of the nonbiological mother, Elisa B., but by the county from which her partner was receiving public assistance, in order to compel Elisa to pay child support.

94. *Karin T. v Michael T.*, 484 N.Y.S.2d 780, 780 (1985).

95. In only one other case, up to that point, was a transsexual or transvestite parent successful in gaining or retaining custody. In *Christian v Randall*, 33 Colo. App. 129 (1973), a divorce case involving a mother who underwent sex-reassignment surgery *after* the divorce, the Colorado Court of Appeals reversed a decision rescinding custody from her. This decision was distinct from both *Kantaras* and *Karin T.* in that the sex change occurred after the marriage, therefore not calling into question the legitimacy of the marriage. It was also anomalous as a victory among other cases involving postdivorce sex changes, such as *Daly v Daly*, 715 P.2d 56 (1986), in Nevada and *Cisek v Cisek,* 59 A.L.R. 4th 1170 (1982), in Ohio.

96. *Matter of Adoption of Evan*, 583 N.Y.S.2d 997 (1992).

97. *Daly,* 715 P.2d 56.

98. See *Kantaras,* 884 So. 2d 155; Michael Kantaras, whose sex change occurred before his marriage and was known of by Linda, later regained shared custody of the children through an out-of-court settlement reached with his former wife through mediation by television celebrity Dr. Phil.

99. Additional case materials were provided by Kathleen herself, who testified at trial that the children called both Lisa and her by their first names often but were equally likely to call either of them "Mom." She also introduced evidence that the children's schools recognized her as the girls' mother and that the children were claimed as dependents on her taxes.

100. *In re Price v Price,* WL 338588, 7 (1997).

101. Interview #21, transcript page 10.

102. An ironic twist to this narrative was seen in the case of *Collins v Collins,* in which the mother, Beverly Collins, revealed in an interview that she "was chastised in court by his [her ex-husband's] lawyer for not showing love and affection in front of [her daughter]," while at the same time being accused by her husband and the judge of exhibiting inappropriate lesbian behavior in front of her daughter. Interview #34, transcript page 1.

103. See, for example, the work of Wendy Brown, "Rights and Identity in Late Modernity: Revisiting the 'Jewish Question,'" in *Identities, Politics, and Rights,* ed. Austin Sarat and Thomas Kearns (Ann Arbor: University of Michigan Press, 1995).

104. *S.N.E. v R.L.B.,* 99 P.2d 875, 879 (1985).

105. *Matter of Adoption of Child by J.M.G.,* 632 A.2d 550, 553 (1993).

106. Interview #26, transcript page 6.

107. Interview #26, transcript page 16.

108. Interview #24, transcript page 27.

109. Interview #23, transcript page 13. For more on this case, see Jon and Michael Galluccio's autobiographical account, *An American Family* (New York: St. Martin's, 2001).

110. *Dailey v Dailey,* 635 S.W.2d 391, 391 (1981).

111. *M.A.B. v R.B.,* 510 N.Y.S.2d 960, 963 (1986).

112. *Bowers v Hardwick,* 106 S.Ct. 2841, 2850 (1986).

113. See Halley, "The Construction of Heterosexuality."

114. *Watkins v United States Army,* 847 F.2d 1329 (1988).

115. Halley, "The Construction of Heterosexuality," 91.

116. Interview #24, transcript page 9.

117. *Jacobson v Jacobson,* 314 N.W.2d 78 (1981).

118. Interview #3, transcript page 4.

119. Interview #5, transcript page 13. Interestingly, judges deciding the case of *Hogue v Hogue* in Tennessee took issue with such references to the parents' gay "lifestyle," noting, "'Lifestyle' is certainly not a specific term. Moreover,

adding the word gay or another adjective does little if anything to enhance the specificity of the term or a description of the acts. For example, prohibiting a parent from exposing a child to his or her 'heterosexual' lifestyle or 'stoic' lifestyle . . . affords little if any guidance to the court." See *Hogue v Hogue*, 147 S.W.3d 245, 252 (2004).

120. This organization is now called the National Gay and Lesbian Task Force, or NGLTF.

121. *In the Matter of J.S. & C.*, 324 A.2d at 95.

122. *Marlow v Marlow*, 702 N.E.2d 733 (1998).

123. *Commonwealth ex rel. Ashfield v Cortes*, 234 A.2d 47, 48 (1967); In an interesting side note, the grandmother who made this claim had come to pursue the custody case from England, where same-sex sodomy had already been decriminalized for a decade.

124. *In re Marriage of Dorworth*, 33 P.3d 1260, 1261 (2001).

125. *Eldridge v Eldridge*, 42 S.W.3d 82, 86 (2001).

126. *Newsome v Newsome*, 256 S.E.2d 849 (1979).

127. *Ward v Ward*, 675 So.2d 941 (1996).

128. The term "passing" is most often used, as in Goffman's original use and Calavita's more recent work on Chinese immigration, to describe a process of "duping" others—particularly moral and legal authorities or gatekeepers—for the purpose of hiding one's marginalized identity. In these custody cases, passing occurs without duping—that is, the law knows of the parents' marginalized sexual identity and encourages them to conceal it and act otherwise. See Erving Goffman, *Stigma: Notes on the Management of a Spoiled Identity* (Englewood Cliffs, NJ: Prentice-Hall, 1963); Kitty Calavita, "The Paradoxes of Race, Class, Identity, and 'Passing': Enforcing the Chinese Exclusion Acts, 1882–1910," *Law & Social Inquiry* 25, no. 1 (2000): 1–40.

129. The concept of "master status" is taken from Goffman, *Stigma*; Interestingly, longitudinal studies of lesbian identity over the lifespan have found exactly the opposite to be true of lesbians who become mothers, that often the identity of "mother" tends to eclipse the more politicized lesbian identity that they may have embraced earlier in life. See Arlene Stein, *Sex and Sensibility: Stories of a Lesbian Generation* (Berkeley: University of California Press, 1997).

130. Interview #33, transcript page 1.

131. Interview #8, transcript page 9.

132. *Roe v Roe*, 324 S.E.2d 691, 694 (1985).

133. *Hall v Hall*, 291 N.W.2d 143, 144 (1980)

134. *Bottoms v Bottoms*, 457 S.E.2d 102, 107 (1995).

135. *Towend v Towend*, Ohio App. LEXIS 6193, 17 (1976).

136. *In Interest of R.E.W.*, 471 S.E.2d 6.

137. Interview #25, transcript page 8.

138. *Matter of Appeal in Pima County Juvenile Action*, 727 P.2d 830, 835 (1986); although this decision has never been explicitly overturned, even in the wake of *Lawrence v Texas*, judges have since allowed gay and lesbian parents to adopt in Arizona.

139. Florida's law, a result of Anita Bryant's "Save the Children" crusade in the 1970s, has been (thus far) also unsuccessfully challenged in media campaigns involving celebrities such as Rosie O'Donnell. It is the only law as of this writing that explicitly bans adoptions by any and all homosexual individuals.

140. *Lofton v Secretary of Department of Children and Family Services*, 358 F.3d 804, 819 (2004).

141. *State ex. rel. Human Services Department*, 764 P.2d 1327 (1988).

142. *In the Matter of Adoption of Charles B.*, WL 119937, 2.

143. See, respectively, the work of Niaz Kasravi, "Women Renegotiating Islamic Identities: A Study of the Iranian-American Diaspora" (Ph.D. diss., University of California, Irvine, 2001); Jack Katz, *Seductions of Crime: Moral and Sensual Attractions of Doing Evil* (New York: Basic Books, 1988); and David R. Simon, *Elite Deviance* (Boston: Allyn and Bacon, 1999).

144. Stacey, *In the Name of the Family*, 139.

NOTES TO CHAPTER 4

1. Stuart Scheingold, *The Politics of Rights: Lawyers, Public Policy, and Political Change* (New Haven, CT: Yale University Press, 1974).

2. See Mary Ann Glendon, *Rights Talk: The Impoverishment of Political Discourse* (New York: Free Press, 1991).

3. For sociolegal discussions of the "rights revolution," see Glendon, *Rights Talk*; and Mark Tushnet, "An Essay on Rights," *Texas Law Review* 62, no. 8 (1984): 1363.

4. See Peter Westen, "The Rueful Rhetoric of Rights," *UCLA Law Review*, 33 (1986): 977.

5. See, for example, McCann, *Rights at Work*.

6. Stuart Scheingold, "Constitutional Rights and Social Change," in *Judging the Constitution*, ed. Michael W. McCann and Gerald L. Houseman (Glenview, IL: Scott, Foresman/Little, Brown, 1989), 76. This indeterminacy has been implicated in the Critical Legal Studies (CLS) and post-CLS rights critiques; not only are rights unstable across specific contexts (and in some cases, as apparent in this study, within a single context), but they produce no reliable consequences. For a fuller discussion of this critique, see Tushnet, "An Essay on Rights."

7. See Polikoff, "The Impact of *Troxel v Granville*," 827. This article examines in detail the range of implications of *Troxel* for LGBT parents and families.

8. See Glendon, *Rights Talk*, 60.

9. *Bowers,* 106 S.Ct. 2841.

10. For more on this critique of rights, see Glendon, *Rights Talk*.

11. *Stanley v Illinois*, 405 U.S. 645 (1972); the concept of "fundamental rights," as opposed to other rights, is discussed by Milton R. Konvitz in *Fundamental Rights: History of a Constitutional Doctrine* (New Brunswick, NJ: Transaction/Rutgers University Press, 2001).

12. Interview #5, transcript page 8.

13. Interview #21, transcript page 9.

14. *In the Matter of J.S. & C.,* 324 A.2d at 92.

15. Ibid. at 93.

16. *R. W. v D. W. W.,* 717 So.2d 793, 796 (1998).

17. *Strome v Strome*, 60 P.3d 1158, 1162 (2003).

18. See Henry Sumner Maine, *Ancient Law* (London: Dent & Sons, 1917).

19. Ibid., 99.

20. Importantly, as noted in chapter 2, depending on where they live, most nonbiological parents in such families are not legally allowed to adopt the child formally through a second-parent adoption. This means that parents who are not biologically related may have no formal legal link to the child. If, however, an adoption has been completed, it would be very rare that such a nonbiological parent would be denied parental rights absent a showing of abuse or neglect.

21. Interview #4, transcript page 1; this comment was made prior to the establishment of parental rights for nonbiological parents by the California Supreme Court in 2005.

22. *Liston,* WL 467327 at 8.

23. Interview #27, transcript page 11.

24. Interview #35, transcript page 6; this comment was made by a lesbian mother whose daughter had been the subject of a paternity claim by her sperm donor.

25. *In the Matter of T.L.,* WL 39351 (Mo.Cir.) (1996).

26. *In re Thompson*, 11 S.W.3d 913, 915 (1999).

27. In several works, Goldberg-Hiller demonstrates this possibility with evidence from the opposition's reaction to the debate in Hawaii about same-sex marriage. He shows that the opposition's strategy was to use the LGBT activists' invocation of civil rights *against* them, conjuring up images of the race-based 1960s civil rights movement and its African American participants as the "true" and "rightful" recipients of civil rights. See Jonathan Goldberg-Hiller, "'Making a Mockery of Marriage': Domestic Partnership and Equal Rights in Hawaii," in *Law and Sexuality: The Global Arena*, ed. Carl Stychin and Didi Herman (Minneapolis: University of Minnesota Press, 2001); Jonathan Goldberg-Hiller, *The Limits to Union: Same-Sex Marriage and the Politics of Civil Rights* (Ann Arbor: University of Michigan Press, 2002); Jonathan Goldberg-Hiller and Neal Milner, "Rights as Excess: Understanding the Politics of Special Rights," *Law & Social Inquiry* 28, no. 4 (2003): 1075.

28. *Kazmierazak v Query,* 736 So.2d 106, 109, 107, 110 (1999).

29. Interview #5, transcript page 9.

30. See Jeffrey Dudas, "On the Cultural Limits of American Rights Practice: Treaty Rights, Progressive Politics, and Equality's Enduring Call," paper presented at the annual meeting of the Law and Society Association, Vancouver, 2002.

31. Interview #7, transcript page 2.

32. Interview #13, transcript page 5.

33. See *LaChapelle v Mitten,* 607 N.W.2d 151 (2000).

34. *In the Interest of Angel Lace M.,* 516 N.W.2d at 686.

35. *Adoption of C.C.G. and Z.C.G.,* 762 A.2d 724, 727 (2000).

36. *In re Adoption of R.B.F. and R.C.F.,* 803 A.2d 1195 (2002).

37. *Towend v Towend,* Ohio App. LEXIS 6193 (1976); *In re Marriage of Diehl,* 582 N.E.2d 281 (1991).

38. *In re Marriage of Diehl,* 582 N.E.2d at 292.

39. *Marlow,* 702 N.E.2d 733; an almost identical argument was made by gay fathers in the earlier cases of *J.L.P.(H.) v D.J.P.* in 1982 and *In the Matter of J.S. & C.* in 1974 and was likewise rejected. In a later case, *J.A.D. v F.J.D.* in 1998, a lesbian mother argued that the trial court had erred in denying her custodial rights and restricting her visitation based on her sexual orientation, because "the state cannot discriminate against a parent and violate a parent's constitutional rights on the basis of homosexuality." Because she did not specify which portion of the Constitution she was appealing to, or what specific rights had been violated, however, these arguments were found to be without merit. See *J.A.D. v F.J.D.,* 978 S.W.2d 336, 338 (1998).

40. *Weigand v Houghton,* 730 So.2d 581 (1999).

41. *Hogue,* 147 S.W.3d at 246.

42. For more on the treatment of gay rights as "special rights," see Goldberg-Hiller and Milner, "Rights as Excess."

43. *Thigpen v Carpenter,* 730 S.W.2d 510, 513 (1987); *In re Marriage of Diehl,* 582 N.E.2d at 289.

44. *In re Jane B.,* 380 N.Y.S.2d 848 (1976).

45. Interview #11, transcript page 3. Notably, such restrictions were not applied to parents who remarried, which of course created a *de facto* presumption against gay and lesbian parents, since same-sex marriage was legal nowhere in the United States at the time.

46. *Thigpen,* 730 S.W.2d at 513.

47. Cain, *Rainbow Rights.*

48. Interview #9, transcript page 8.

49. Interview #21, transcript page 9.

50. Interview #32, transcript page 10.

51. See Jeni Loftus, "America's Liberation in Attitudes toward Homosexuality, 1973–1988," *American Sociological Review* 66, no. 5 (2001): 762.

52. Interview #8, transcript page 10.

53. Interview #26, transcript page 28.

54. See *Palmore v Sidotti*, 466 U.S. 429 (1984).

55. *Marlow*, 702 N.E.2d at 737.

56. *S.E.G. v R.A.G.*, 735 S.W.2d 164, 166 (1987).

57. Interview #26, transcript page 8.

58. Interview #1, transcript page 10.

59. *L. v D.*, 630 S.W.2d 240, 243 (1982).

60. *Ex Parte H.H.*, 830 So.2d at 26.

61. *Constant A. v Paul C.A.*, 344 Pa.Super. 49, 55 (1985).

62. This decision's contention that "consensual sodomy cannot be made criminal" was based on precedent that was later nullified by the U.S. Supreme Court in *Bowers v Hardwick*. *In re Jane B.*, 380 N.Y.S.2d at 857.

63. *In the Matter of T.L.*, WL 39351 at 4.

64. *Jacoby v Jacoby*, 763 So.2d 410, 413 (2000).

65. *In re Marriage of Dorworth*, 33 P.3d at 1262.

66. *Damron v Damron*, 670 N.W.2d 871, 875 (2003).

67. Ibid. at 875.

68. The *Eldridge* case was later overturned in part, allowing the mother not full custody but less-restricted visitation, including overnight visitation in the presence of Julie Eldridge's domestic partner. See *Eldridge v Eldridge*, 42 S.W.3d 82 (2001).

69. See Eskridge, *Gaylaw*.

70. For more on this framework of children's rights, see Martha Fineman, "The Politics of Custody and Gender: Child Advocacy and the Transformation of Custody Decision Making in the USA," in *Child Custody and the Politics of Gender*, ed. Carol Smart and Selma Sevenhuijsen (London: Routledge, 1989).

71. See Lawrence H. Tribe, *American Constitutional Law*, 2nd ed. (Mineola, NY: Foundation Press, 1998), 1416; Glendon, *Rights Talk*, 123.

72. Interview #3, transcript page 12.

73. Interview #9, transcript page 10.

74. Interview #17, transcript page 11.

75. Interview #9, transcript page 10.

76. *In re Jane B.*, 380 N.Y.S.2d at 859.

77. *Collins*, WL 20173 at 9.

78. Interview #34, transcript page 1.

79. Interview #29, transcript page 8; *Pleasant v Pleasant*, 628 N.E.2d 633 (1993).

80. *In re Adoption of Baby Z.*, 699 A.2d at 1067.

81. *S.E.G.*, 735 S.W.2d at 166.

82. *Marlow*, 702 N.E.2d at 737.

83. Interview #5, transcript page 22.

84. Interview #1, transcript page 10.
85. *Conkel,* 509 N.E.2d at 987.
86. *Liston,* WL 467327 at 22.
87. Interview #27, transcript page 11.
88. *Matter of Adoption of T.J.K.,* 931 P.2d 488, 494 (1996).
89. Interview #17, transcript page 3.
90. *Conkel,* 509 N.E.2d at 985.
91. Interview #3, transcript page 12.
92. *Weigand,* 730 So.2d at 587.
93. Interview #23, transcript page 9.
94. *In re Custody of H.S.H.-K.,* 533 N.W.2d at 435. This was a stark reversal of Wisconsin's earlier precedent denying the right to second-parent adoption by a nonbiological mother in *In the Interest of Angel Lace M.* in 1994.
95. Interview #8, transcript page 4.
96. *Sharon S.,* 73 P.3d at 569.
97. *In the Matter of Adoption of K.S.P. and J.P.,* 804 N.E.2d 1253, 1253 (2004).
98. The schools of thought most closely associated with the call to expose the limitations of rights as popularly conceived in American jurisprudence are those of Critical Legal Studies (CLS), feminist jurisprudence, Critical Race Theory, and more recently, queer theory. Scholars in these traditions, such as Mark Tushnet, point out that the common reliance on rights can be problematic, noting specifically the indeterminacy of their consequences. See Tushnet, "An Essay on Rights," 1364. Similar critiques are asserted in the field of feminist jurisprudence; see, for example, Janet Rifkin, "Toward a Theory of Law and Patriarchy," *Harvard Women's Law Journal* 3 (1980): 83; and Frances Olsen, "Statutory Rape: A Feminist Critique of Rights Analysis," *Texas Law Review* 63 (1984): 387.
99. For scholarly work applying the sociolegal insights of Maine to gay and lesbian rights, see Goldberg-Hiller, "Making a Mockery of Marriage"; and Eskridge, *Gaylaw.*
100. Interview #23, transcript page 6.
101. Interview #21, transcript page 10.
102. Interview #13, transcript page 3.
103. *Schuster v Schuster* and *Isaacson v Isaacson,* 585 P.2d 130, 132 (1978).
104. *E.N.O. v L.M.M.,* 429 Mass. 824, 833 (1999); the fact that the same rationale was used to deny custody to lesbian mothers in the Washington cases and to defend a lesbian co-parent's visitation in *E.N.O.* is indicative not only of a wide range of discretion in interpretation of a relatively undefined set of rights but also of the space afforded by this discretion to respond creatively to increasingly diverse and inchoate family forms.
105. Interview #9, transcript page 8.
106. Interview #27, transcript page 7.

107. Interview #8, transcript page 8.

108. *J.L.P.(H.)*, 643 S.W.2d at 867. The court also rejected the request by Lambda to submit an *amicus curiae* brief.

109. Interview #5, transcript page 20.

110. Interview #21, transcript page 3.

111. Interview #22, transcript page 3.

112. Interview #26, transcript page 28.

113. *Cook*, 245 S.E.2d at 615.

114. *T.C.H. v K.M.H.*, 784 S.W.2d 281, 285 (1989).

115. *Thomas S.*, 618 N.Y.S.2d at 362. In New York, unlike in most other states, the Court of Appeals is the highest court, akin to most states' supreme court.

116. Interview #35, transcript page 5.

117. Interview #27, transcript page 13.

118. Interview #32, transcript page 5.

119. Interview #6, transcript page 7.

120. *Boswell v Boswell*, 721 A.2d 662, 669 (1998).

121. *Rubano v DiCenzo*, 759 A.2d 959, 976 (2000).

122. *In the Interest of E.L.M.C.*, 100 P.3d 546, 562(2004).

123. *In re Parentage of L.B.*, 89 P.3d 271, 286 (2004).

124. *Lawrence*, 539 U.S. at 578.

125. See, for example, Westen, "The Rueful Rhetoric of Rights."

126. Helena Silverstein, "In the Matter of Anonymous, A Minor: Fetal Representation in Hearings to Waive Parental Consent for Abortion," *Cornell Journal of Law and Public Policy* 11 (2001): 69.

127. See McCann, *Rights at Work*, 297; "The flexibility and plurality of our rights traditions allow for adaptation over time, and for continued contests over the legitimacy of prevailing arrangements."

128. Ibid., 299.

129. *In re Bonfield*, 780 N.E.2d 241 (2002).

130. Eskridge, *Gaylaw*, 284; see also Neil S. Binder, "Taking Relationships Seriously: Children, Autonomy, and the Right to a Relationship," *New York University Law Review* 69 (1994): 1150.

131. *In the Matter of Adoption of K.S.P. and J.P.*, 804 N.E.2d at 1257.

132. *Kristine H. v Lisa R.*, 120 Cal.App.4th 143 (2004).

133. This description is borrowed from Scheingold, *The Politics of Rights*, 30: "legal rules are never without a certain range of ambiguity or open texture."

134. *Elisa B. v Emily B.*, 37 Cal.4th 108 (2005); *Kristine H. v Lisa R.*, 37 Cal.4th 156 (2005); *K.M. v E.G.*, 37 Cal.4th 130 (2005).

135. Even though second-parent adoption was formally legalized in California two years after the child's birth, and before the couple broke up, Lisa did not pursue such an adoption because the couple believed that the parenting contract they signed before the child's birth sufficiently established her as a parent.

NOTES TO CHAPTER 5

1. Preface to *Justice Musmanno Dissents* (Indianapolis, IN: Bobbs-Merrill, 1956).

2. Charles Evan Hughes, *The Supreme Court of the United States, Its Foundation, Methods and Achievements: An Interpretation* (Garden City, NY: Garden City Publishing, 1936), 68.

3. See, for example, David R. Papke and Kathleen H. McManus, "Narrative Jurisprudence: Narrative and the Appellate Opinion," *Legal Studies Forum* 23 (1999): 449; Mona Lynch, "Pedophiles and Cyber-predators as Contaminating Forces: The Language of Disgust, Pollution, and Boundary Invasions in Federal Debates on Sex Offender Legislation," *Law & Social Inquiry* 27 (2002): 529; Laura Beth Nielsen, *License to Harass: Law, Hierarchy, and Offensive Public Speech* (Princeton, NJ: Princeton University Press, 2004).

4. These terms are borrowed from Patricia Ewick and Susan Silbey, "Subversive Stories and Hegemonic Tales: Toward a Sociology of Narrative," *Law & Society Review* 29 (1995): 197.

5. In her book *Same-Sex Marriage: The Cultural Politics of Love and Law* (Cambridge: Cambridge University Press, 2006), for example, Kathleen Hull examines the practice of same-sex commitment ceremonies as a way to enact legality in its absence.

6. This chapter's analysis is based mainly on the seventy-six judicial decisions from 1975 to 2004 that contained dissents, as no published dissents were found in cases before 1975.

7. The role of dissents in LGBT family law is even less surprising given the more general trend away from consensus and toward more dissents, a trend apparent in studies of the Supreme Court. See Lee Epstein and Jack Knight, *The Choices Justices Make* (Washington, DC: CQ Press, 1998).

8. This analogy is borrowed from Lawrence Douglas, "Constitutional Discourse and Its Discontents: An Essay on the Rhetoric of Judicial Review," in *The Rhetoric of Law*, ed. Austin Sarat and Thomas Kearns (Ann Arbor: University of Michigan Press, 1994).

9. *In re R.E.W.*, 472 S.E.2d 295 (1996); in this case, the dissenting justice objected to the majority's removal of certain visitation restrictions that had been placed on the gay father by the trial court. This judge argued vehemently that the sodomy law existent at that time in Georgia forbade such a ruling, and proclaimed, "Hopefully, another case soon will present this court with the opportunity to overrule this erroneous precedent." Ibid. at 297. Before this could happen, however, Georgia's sodomy law was overturned in 1998.

10. *Nickerson v Nickerson*, 605 A.2d 1331 (1992).

11. Despite the failure in this case, the State of Connecticut subsequently adopted an explicit policy of legally recognizing second-parent adoptions.

12. Interview #24, transcript page 13.

13. Interview #24, transcript page 14.

14. *Hertzler,* 908 P.2d at 954–956.

15. *Weigand,* 730 So.2d at 588–589.

16. *S.B. v L.W.,* 793 So.2d 656, 664 (2001).

17. *Strome,* 60 P.3d at 1169.

18. Cass R. Sunstein, "Ginsburg's Dissent May Yet Prevail," *Los Angeles Times,* April 20, 2007, A31.

19. Charles Curtis, *Lions under the Throne* (Boston: Houghton Mifflin, 1947), 74–75.

20. See, for example, William J. Brennan, "In Defense of Dissents," *Hastings Law Journal* 37, no. 3 (1986): 427–438.

21. Interview #24, transcript page 14.

22. *Matter of Marriage of Cabalquinto,* 669 P.2d 886, 890 (1983).

23. *Matter of Marriage of Cabalquinto,* 718 P.2d 7 (1986).

24. *Matter of Adoption of Charles B.,* WL 119937 (Ohio App. 5 Dist.) (1988); *Matter of Adoption of Charles B.,* 552 N.E.2d 884 (1990).

25. *Matter of Adoption of Charles B.,* WL 119937 at 18–19.

26. *In re Adoption of R.B.F. and R.C.F.,* 762 A.2d 739, 748 (2000).

27. It is interesting to note, however, that the second dissent in this case pointed out the fact that the Courts of Common Pleas in Pennsylvania had already issued over one hundred such adoptions in at least fourteen counties; these adoptions were subsequently suspended between the time that the dissent was written and when the supreme court overturned the superior court decision. The supreme court then formally reintroduced and institutionalized the process in *In re Adoption of R.B.F. and R.C.F.* in 2002.

28. Quoted in Henry J. Abraham, *The Judicial Process: An Introductory Analysis of the Courts of the United States, England, and France,* 7th ed. (New York: Oxford University Press, 1998), 221.

29. Interview #24, transcript page 13.

30. *In re Interest of Z.J.H.,* 471 N.W.2d 202 (1991).

31. See Peter Simmons, "The Use and Abuse of Dissenting Opinions," *Louisiana Law Review* 16 (1956): 497, 498.

32. *In re Interest of Z.J.H.,* 471 N.W.2d at 215.

33. *Cox v Williams,* 177 Wis.2d 433 (1993).

34. *J.P. v P.W.,* 772 S.W.2d at 795.

35. *Delong v Delong,* WL 15536, 25 (1998).

36. *J.P. v P.W.,* 772 S.W.2d at 795.

37. See Alan Barth, *Prophets with Honor: Great Dissents and Great Dissenters in the Supreme Court* (New York: Knopf, 1974).

38. For more discussion of Judge Judith Kaye as a "prophet with honor," see Vincent M. Bonventre, "New York's Chief Judge Kaye: Her Separate Opin-

ions Bode Well for Renewed State Constitutionalism at the Court of Appeals," *Temple Law Review* 67 (1994): 1163.

39. *Alison D. v Virginia M.*, 572 N.E.2d 27, 32 (1991). See also *In re Custody of H.S.H.-K.* in Wisconsin and *V.C. v M.J.B.* in New Jersey, which both used a rationale almost identical to that espoused by Kaye's dissent to justify a ruling in favor of visitation rights for the nonbiological mothers in both cases.

40. Interview #24, transcript page 13.

41. *Matter of Dana*, 209 A.D.2d 8 (1995). See also *V.C.*, 725 A.2d 13; *Matter of Adoption of Caitlyn*, 622 N.Y.S.2d 835 (1994); *Matter of Jacob*, 86 N.Y.2d 651 (1995), with which *Matter of Dana* was combined on appeal; *In the Matter of J.C. v C.T.*, 711 N.Y.S.2d 295 (2000).

42. See Stanley H. Fuld, "The Voices of Dissent," *Columbia Law Review* 62 (1962): 923, 928.

43. *Matter of Appeal in Pima County Juvenile Action*, 727 P.2d at 840.

44. Because of the intricacies and inconsistencies that arise by virtue of the United States' hybrid civil-law/common-law tradition, and because of the indeterminacy of family law and the great degree of discretion granted to family law judges, the discrepancy between this ruling and the adoption statute allows for no clear course for future rulings. Although no other analogous case has since been heard in Arizona's appellate courts, it is entirely possible that different trial judges in different jurisdictions in Arizona decide the issue in differing ways, depending on their deference to either the court of appeals decision or the statute, as well as on their own predilections and the individual circumstances of the case. Adoptions by gay and lesbian parents have since happened in Arizona, but it is not known how many or through what specific legal mechanism.

45. *Thomas v Thomas*, 49 P.3d 306 (2002).

46. See Ruth Bader Ginsberg, "Remarks on Writing Separately," *Washington Law Review* 65 (1990): 133–150, 139.

47. Interview #26, transcript page 9.

48. Interview #9, transcript page 10.

49. Interview #35, transcript page 12.

50. Interview #35, transcript page 7.

51. Frank X. Altimari, "The Practice of Dissenting in the Second Circuit," *Brooklyn Law Review* 59, no. 2 (1993): 275–284, 277.

52. *Chicoine*, 479 N.W.2d at 897.

53. *E.N.O.*, 429 Mass. at 835.

54. *Matter of Dana*, 660 N.E.2d 397, 409 (1995).

55. As discussed in chapter 2, the standard for review in family law, "abuse of discretion," is widely open to interpretation. Generally, the consensus is that, because custody cases are so fact intensive, and because of the trial court's role as fact finder, there should be a presumption against overturning the trial decision unless there is clear and substantial error or injustice.

56. *Eldridge*, 1999 WL 994099 (Teen. Ct. App.) at 3.

57. *Adoption of Tammy*, 619 N.E.2d 315, 322 (1993).

58. *V.C.*, 725 A.2d at 26. Interestingly, a second dissent was filed in this case, arguing that the nonbiological parent should be given not just visitation but full joint-custody rights. This dissenting justice relied on the reasoning that, "[w]hile it would be appropriate for the Legislature to address the issues raised by this case, these children cannot wait. It is the function of the courts to address those interstitial areas where no statute literally controls. . . . When social mores change, governing statutes must be interpreted to allow for those changes in a manner that does not frustrate the purposes behind their enactment." Ibid. at 21.

59. *In re Custody of H.S.H.-K.*, 533 N.W.2d at 442.

60. Ibid. at 448.

61. *In the Interest of Angel Lace M.*, 516 N.W.2d at 687.

62. Ibid. at 693.

63. *In re Adoption of Baby Z.*, 724 A.2d at 1065.

64. Ibid. at 1060.

65. Ibid. at 1081.

66. *Rubano*, 759 A.2d at 967.

67. Ibid. at 967.

68. Ibid. at 967.

69. Ibid. at 972.

70. *Lofton v Secretary of Department of Children and Family Services*, 377 F.3d 1275, 1296 (2004).

71. *Matter of Adoption of Charles B.*, WL 119937 at 7.

72. *In re Adoption of Luke*, 640 N.W.2d 374, 389 (2002).

73. Ibid. at 388.

74. *T.B. v L.R.M.*, 786 A.2d 913 (2001).

75. See Douglas, "Constitutional Discourse and Its Discontents," 258.

76. Hugo Black, quoted in Edward C. Voss, "Dissent: Sign of a Healthy Court," *Arizona State Law Journal* 24, no. 2 (1992): 643–676, 654.

77. *Ex Parte D.W.W.*, 717 So.2d 793, 797 (1998).

78. Ibid. at 798.

79. *White v Thompson*, 569 So.2d 1181, 1186 (1990).

80. *Titchenal v Dexter*, 693 A.2d 682, 693 (1997).

81. *Weigand*, 730 So.2d at 588.

82. Ibid. at 591.

83. *Matter of Dana*, 660 N.E.2d at 413.

84. *Sharon S.*, 73 P.3d at 575.

85. Ibid. at 576.

86. *Chicoine*, 479 N.W.2d at 896.

87. *Sharon S.*, 73 P.3d at 586.

88. Quoted in Abraham, *The Judicial Process*, 224.

89. *Adoption of Tammy*, 619 N.E.2d at 320.

90. *Hassenstab v Hassenstab*, 570 N.W.2d 368, 375 (1997).

91. *Schuster*, 585 P.2d at 135.

92. *Chicoine*, 479 N.W.2d at 897.

93. *J.B.F. v J.M.F.*, 730 So.2d 1186 (1997).

94. *Weigand*, 730 So.2d at 593.

95. *Matter of Marriage of Cabalquinto*, 669 P.2d at 889.

96. *Alison D.*, 572 N.E.2d at 30.

97. *In the Interest of Angel Lace M.*, 516 N.W.2d at 690.

98. *V.C.*, 725 A.2d at 28.

99. For more on this function of dissents, see Altimari, "The Practice of Dissenting in the Second Circuit."

100. Kitty Calavita, "Blue Jeans, Rape, and the 'De-Constitutive' Power of Law," *Law & Society Review* 35, no. 1 (2001): 89–116, 109.

101. This is consistent with the findings of Richard Primus, who argues that those arguing in favor of the "underdog" or less powerful group tend to be more likely to become "canonical," or "redeemed" dissents, later turned into law. Richard Primus, "Canon, Anti-Canon, and Judicial Dissent," *Duke Law Journal* 48 (1998): 243, 276.

102. Phillips and Grattet, "Judicial Rhetoric, Meaning-Making, and the Institutionalism of Hate Crime Law," 596.

103. See Kelman, "The Forked Path of Dissent," 254.

NOTES TO CHAPTER 6

1. McCann, *Rights at Work*, 299.

2. Ibid., 15.

3. For example, Lee Epstein and Jack Knight's strategic account of judicial decision-making allows for the notion that judges are ultimately goal oriented but claims that their decision-making behavior is strategic, not based simply on attitudes and desires. See Epstein and Knight, *The Choices Justices Make*. Somewhat to the contrary, Lawrence Baum argues that judges are indeed motivated by legal policy concerns but that their goals may not be completely altruistic. See Lawrence Baum, "The Judicial Gatekeeping Function: A General Analysis," in *American Court Systems: Readings in Judicial Process and Behavior*, ed. Sheldon Goldman and Austin Sarat (San Francisco: Freeman, 1978).

4. See Susan E. Dalton and Denise D. Bielby, "'That's Our Kind of Constellation': Lesbian Mothers Negotiate Institutionalized Understandings of Gender within the Family," *Gender & Society*, 14, no. 1 (2000): 36–61.

5. See Phillips and Grattet, "Judicial Rhetoric, Meaning-Making, and the Institutionalism of Hate Crime Law," 596.

6. The term "repertoire of meaning" is based on the work of Ann Swidler, "Culture in Action: Symbols and Strategies," *American Sociological Review* 51 (1986): 273–286.

7. The notion of "de-constitutive" moments is borrowed from Calavita, "Blue Jeans, Rape, and the 'De-Constitutive' Power of Law."

8. See Ruthann Robson, "Mother: The Legal Domestication of Lesbian Existence," in *Mothers in Law: Feminist Theory and the Legal Regulation of Motherhood*, ed. Martha Fineman and Isabel Karpin (New York: Columbia University Press, 1995).

9. Legal theorist Peter Goodrich is only one of many to assert that "the concept of legal discourse [is] pre-eminently the discourse of power." See Peter Goodrich, *Legal Discourse: Studies in Linguistics, Rhetoric and Legal Analysis* (London: Macmillan, 1987), 88. See also John M. Conley and William M. O'Barr, *Just Words: Law, Language, and Power* (Chicago: University of Chicago Press, 1998); and Michel Foucault, *Power/Knowledge: Selected Interviews and Other Writings, 1972–1977* (New York: Pantheon Books, 1980). Specific to gay rights, see MacDougall, *Queer Judgments*.

10. See Charlotte Patterson, "Children of Lesbian and Gay Parents," *Current Directions in Psychological Science* 15, no. 5 (2006): 241–244.

11. See McCann, *Rights at Work*, 299.

12. See Dahlia Lithwick, "The Myth of Activist Judges," *Los Angeles Times*, October 12, 2004, B13.

13. See Thomas Keck, "Activism and Restraint on the Rehnquist Court: Timing, Sequence, and Conjecture in Constitutional Development," *Polity* 35, no. 1 (2002): 121–152.

14. See Keck, *The Most Activist Supreme Court in History*.

15. For a more complete history of the family, see Stacey, *In the Name of the Family*. A history of the role of marriage in the United States can be found in Nancy Cott, *Public Vows: A History of Marriage and the Nation* (Cambridge, MA: Harvard University Press, 2000).

16. See Stacey, *In the Name of the Family*.

17. See Eskridge, *Gaylaw*.

18. In California, Connecticut, Vermont, Illinois, Indiana, Massachusetts, New York, New Jersey, Pennsylvania, Colorado, Delaware, and the District of Columbia second-parent adoption is legal by case law or statute; in New Hampshire, Oregon, and Maine, civil unions are available and include the right to adopt as a "stepparent," even though this right does not exist independently.

19. See Paula L. Ettelbrick, "Since When Is Marriage a Path to Liberation?" *OUT/LOOK National Gay and Lesbian Quarterly* 8–12 (1989); and Nancy Polikoff, "We Will Get What We Ask For: Why Legalizing Gay and Lesbian Marriage Will Not 'Dismantle the Structure of Gender in Every Marriage,'" *Virginia Law Review* 79 (1993): 1535.

20. For some people, this opposition is political or ideological in nature; that is, they believe marriage is a patriarchal institution or that same-sex marriage is an attempt to "ape" heterosexual relationships. For others, the fact that same-sex marriage and civil unions are recognized only at the state level and not at the federal level imposes significant financial and other logistical problems and leaves them better suited to remaining unmarried (or "un-unioned"). For example, a couple that enters a civil union in Vermont can put one partner on the other's medical plan through an employer, but the dependent partner will be taxed by the federal government for this benefit, a tax expense that is not imposed on married couples and can be a significant burden.

21. See Keck, "Activism and Restraint on the Rehnquist Court," 130.

22. Valerie Jenness and Ryken Grattet, *Making Hate a Crime: From Social Movement to Law Enforcement* (New York: Russell Sage Foundation, 2001).

23. See generally Phillips and Grattet, "Judicial Rhetoric, Meaning-Making, and the Institutionalism of Hate Crime Law."

24. It is also important to note the different decision-making mechanisms of family law and criminal law: whereas most drug offenders have a right to a trial by jury, in family court the judge is the sole trier of fact. This difference may affect the types of rationales that are most likely to be successful in redefining drug users and use. Drug law has also been largely statutorily driven, though it is equally subject to revision by appellate opinion.

25. See McCann, *Rights at Work*; and Tully, *Strange Multiplicity*.

26. This disproportionate impact is because crack is a less expensive form of cocaine, which is more likely to be used by inner-city minority offenders with less financial means. According to a study by the U.S. Sentencing Commission, 84.7 percent of federal crack offenders are African American, and only 5.6 percent are Caucasian. The result has been that African Americans are fourteen times more likely to be sentenced to a federal prison term for cocaine use than whites, despite the facially neutral determinate sentencing scheme and despite Caucasian users of cocaine outnumbering their African American counterparts. See Debra Saunders, "Heavy Time for Drug Lightweights," *San Francisco Chronicle,* July 10, 2007, C11.

27. For further discussion about the difference between a radical, unconstrained indeterminacy, advocated by some Critical Legal Scholars, and a more "bounded" approach, see Michael McCann and Gerald Houseman, *Judging the Constitution: Critical Essays on Judicial Lawmaking* (Glenview, IL: Scott Foresman, 1989).

28. An obvious exception is Florida, where the state's sweeping ban on LGBT adoption has no doubt led to similarly tragic outcomes for an unknown number of would-be adopted children forced to remain in foster care.

29. In earlier works I took issue with the indeterminacy of the "best interest of the child" standard and of family law more generally because of its ability to

obscure and justify rights violations and incursions into LGBT parents' ability to gain and retain custody of their children and autonomy over their own self-definition as parents. See Kimberly D. Richman, "Lovers, Legal Strangers, and Parents: Negotiating Parental and Sexual Identity in Family Law," *Law & Society Review* 36, no. 2 (2002): 285–324; Kimberly D. Richman, "(When) Are Rights Wrong? Rights Discourses and Indeterminacy in Gay and Lesbian Parents' Custody Cases," *Law & Social Inquiry* 30, no. 1 (2005): 137–176; Richman, "Judging Science."

30. See Goodrich, *Legal Discourse,* 159.

31. The term "brave new families" is borrowed from the title of Judith Stacey's 1998 book, *Brave New Families: Stories of Domestic Upheaval in Late-Twentieth-Century America* (New York: Basic Books, 1998).

References

Abraham, Henry J. (1998) *The Judicial Process: An Introductory Analysis of the Courts of the United States, England, and France,* 7th ed. New York: Oxford University Press.

Altimari, Frank X. (1993) "The Practice of Dissenting in the Second Circuit," 59(2) *Brooklyn Law Review* 275.

Ards, Sheila D., William A. Darity Jr., and Samuel L. Myers Jr. (1998) "'If It Shall Seem Just and Proper': The Effect of Race and Morals on Alimony and Child Support Appeals in the District of Columbia, 1950–1980," 23(4) *Journal of Family History* 441.

Barth, Alan (1974) *Prophets with Honor: Great Dissents and Great Dissenters in the Supreme Court.* New York: Knopf.

Baum, Lawrence (1987) "The Judicial Gatekeeping Function: A General Analysis." In *American Court Systems: Readings in Judicial Process and Behavior.* Ed. Sheldon Goldman and Austin Sarat. San Francisco: Freeman.

Bartlett, Katharine (1993) "Feminist Legal Methods." In *Feminist Legal Theory: Foundations.* Ed. D. Kelly Weisberg. Philadelphia: Temple University Press.

Bayer, Ronald (1987) *Homosexuality and American Psychiatry: The Politics of Diagnosis.* Princeton, NJ: Princeton University Press.

Becker, Howard (1963) *Outsiders: Studies in the Sociology of Deviance.* London: Free Press of Glencoe.

Benkov, Laura (1994) *Reinventing the Family: The Emerging Story of Lesbian and Gay Parents.* New York: Crown.

Bigner, Jerry J., and R. Brooke Jacobsen (1989) "Parenting Behaviors of Homosexual and Heterosexual Fathers," 18 *Journal of Homosexuality* 173.

Binder, Neil S. (1994) "Taking Relationships Seriously: Children, Autonomy, and the Right to a Relationship," 69 *New York University Law Review* 1150.

Bonventre, Vincent M. (1994) "New York's Chief Judge Kaye: Her Separate Opinions Bode Well for Renewed State Constitutionalism at the Court of Appeals," 67 *Temple Law Review* 1163.

Braithwaite, John (1989) *Crime, Shame, and Reintegration.* New York: Cambridge University Press.

Brennan, William J. (1986) "In Defense of Dissents," 37(3) *Hastings Law Journal* 427.

Brown, Wendy (1995) "Rights and Identity in Late Modernity: Revisiting the 'Jewish Question.'" In *Identities, Politics, and Rights*. Ed. Austin Sarat and Thomas Kearns. Ann Arbor: University of Michigan Press.

Cahn, Naomi, and Joan Hollinger, eds. (2004) *Families by Law: An Adoption Reader*. New York: New York University Press.

Cain, Patricia A. (2000) *Rainbow Rights: The Role of Lawyers and Courts in the Lesbian and Gay Civil Rights Movement*. Boulder, CO: Westview.

Calavita, Kitty (2000) "The Paradoxes of Race, Class, Identity, and 'Passing': Enforcing the Chinese Exclusion Acts, 1882–1910," 25(1) *Law & Social Inquiry* 1.

Calavita, Kitty (2001) "Blue Jeans, Rape, and the 'De-Constitutive' Power of Law," 35(1) *Law & Society Review* 89.

Charlow, Andrea (1994) "Awarding Custody: The Best Interests of the Child and Other Fictions." In *Child, Parent, and State: Law and Policy*. Ed. S. Randall Humm, Beate Anna Ort, Martin Mazen Anbari, Wendy S. Lader, and William Scott Biel. Philadelphia: Temple University Press.

Conley, John M., and William M. O'Barr (1998) *Just Words: Law, Language, and Power*. Chicago: University of Chicago Press.

Conte, Alba (2000) *Sexual Orientation and Legal Rights, Volume 1*. New York: Aspen.

Coontz, Stephanie (1992) *The Way We Never Were: American Families and the Nostalgia Trap*. New York: Basic Books.

Cott, Nancy (2000) *Public Vows: A History of Marriage and the Nation*. Cambridge, MA: Harvard University Press.

Curtis, Charles (1947) *Lions under the Throne*. Boston: Houghton Mifflin.

Dalton, Susan E., and Denise D. Bielby (2000) "'That's Our Kind of Constellation': Lesbian Mothers Negotiate Institutionalized Understandings of Gender within the Family," 14(1) *Gender & Society* 36.

D'Emilio, John (1998) *Sexual Politics, Sexual Communities: The Making of a Homosexual Minority in the United States, 1940–1970*, 2nd ed. Chicago: University of Chicago Press.

Douglas, Lawrence (1994) "Constitutional Discourse and Its Discontents: An Essay on the Rhetoric of Judicial Review." In *The Rhetoric of Law*. Ed. Austin Sarat and Thomas Kearns. Ann Arbor: University of Michigan Press.

Dudas, Jeffrey (2002) "On the Cultural Limits of American Rights Practice: Treaty Rights, Progressive Politics, and Equality's Enduring Call." Paper presented at the annual meeting of the Law and Society Association, Vancouver.

Epstein, Lee, and Jack Knight (1998) *The Choices Justices Make*. Washington, DC: CQ Press.

Eskridge, William N. (1999) *Gaylaw: Challenging the Apartheid of the Closet.* Cambridge, MA: Harvard University Press.

Espeland, Wendy (1994) "Legally Mediated Identity: The National Environmental Policy Act and the Bureaucratic Construction of Interests," 28(5) *Law & Society Review* 1149.

Ettelbrick, Paula L. (1989) "Since When Is Marriage a Path to Liberation?" 8–12 *OUT/LOOK National Gay and Lesbian Quarterly.*

Ewick, Patricia, and Susan Silbey (1995) "Subversive Stories and Hegemonic Tales: Toward a Sociology of Narrative," 29 *Law & Society Review* 197.

Falk, Patricia (1989) "Lesbian Mothers: Psychosocial Assumptions in Family Law," 44(6) *American Psychologist* 941.

Fausto-Sterling, Anne (1993) "The Five Sexes," 33(2) *Sciences* 20.

Fineman, Martha L. (1989) "The Politics of Custody and Gender: Child Advocacy and the Transformation of Custody Decision Making in the USA." In *Child Custody and the Politics of Gender.* Ed. Carol Smart and Selma Sevenhuijsen. London: Routledge.

Fineman, Martha L. (1995) *The Neutered Mother, the Sexual Family, and Other Twentieth Century Tragedies.* New York: Routledge.

Foucault, Michel (1980) *Power/Knowledge: Selected Interviews and Other Writings, 1972–1977.* New York: Pantheon Books.

Fuld, Stanley H. (1962) "The Voices of Dissent," 62 *Columbia Law Review* 923.

Galluccio, Jon, and Michael Galluccio (2001) *An American Family.* New York: St. Martin's.

Gardner, Martin R. (2004) "Adoption by Homosexuals in the Wake of *Lawrence v Texas,*" 6 *Journal of Law & Family Studies* 19.

Ginsburg, Ruth Bader (1990) "Remarks on Writing Separately," 65 *Washington Law Review* 133.

Glendon, Mary Ann (1991) *Rights Talk: The Impoverishment of Political Discourse.* New York: Free Press.

Goffman, Erving (1963) *Stigma: Notes on the Management of a Spoiled Identity.* Englewood Cliffs, NJ: Prentice-Hall.

Goldberg-Hiller, Jonathan (2001) "'Making a Mockery of Marriage': Domestic Partnership and Equal Rights in Hawaii." In *Law and Sexuality: The Global Arena.* Ed. Carl Stychin and Didi Herman. Minneapolis: University of Minnesota Press.

Goldberg-Hiller, Jonathan (2002) *The Limits to Union: Same-Sex Marriage and the Politics of Civil Rights.* Ann Arbor: University of Michigan Press.

Goldberg-Hiller, Jonathan, and Neal Milner (2003) "Rights as Excess: Understanding the Politics of Special Rights," 28(4) *Law & Social Inquiry* 1075.

Goldstein, Joseph, Anna Freud, and Albert Solnit (1973) *Beyond the Best Interest of the Child.* New York: Free Press.

Green, Richard, Jane Barclay Mandel, Mary E. Hotvedt, James Gray, and Laurel Smith (1986) "Lesbian Mothers and Their Children: A Comparison with Solo Parent Heterosexual Mothers and Their Children," 15(2) *Archives of Sexual Behavior* 167.

Grossberg, Michael (1985) *Governing the Hearth: Law and the Family in Nineteenth-Century America.* Chapel Hill: University of North Carolina Press.

Guggenheim, Martin (1994) "The Best Interest of the Child: Much Ado about Nothing?" In *Child, Parent, and State: Law and Policy.* Ed. S. Randall Humm, Beate Anna Ort, Martin Mazen Anbari, Wendy S. Lader, and William Scott Biel. Philadelphia: Temple University Press.

Halley, Janet (1997) "The Construction of Heterosexuality." In *Fear of a Queer Planet: Queer Politics and Social Theory.* Ed. Michael Warner. Minneapolis: University of Minnesota Press.

Hartog, Heinrich (2000) *Man and Wife in America: A History.* Cambridge, MA: Harvard University Press.

Hollinger, Joan Heifetz (2004) "The What and Why of the Multiethnic Placement Act (MEPA)." In *Families by Law: An Adoption Reader.* Ed. Naomi Cahn and Joan Hollinger. New York: New York University Press.

Howard, Jeanne (2006) *Expanding Resources for Children: Is Adoption by Gays and Lesbians Part of the Answer for Boys and Girls Who Need Homes?* New York: Evan B. Donaldson Adoption Institute.

Hughes, Charles Evan (1936) *The Supreme Court of the United States, Its Foundation, Methods and Achievements: An Interpretation.* Garden City, NY: Garden City Publishing.

Hull, Kathleen (2006) *Same-Sex Marriage: The Cultural Politics of Love and Law.* Cambridge: Cambridge University Press.

Jenness, Valerie, and Ryken Grattet (2001) *Making Hate a Crime: From Social Movement to Law Enforcement.* New York: Russell Sage Foundation.

Jenny, Carol, Thomas A. Roesler, and Kimberly L. Poyer (1994) "Are Children at Risk for Sexual Abuse by Homosexuals?" 94(1) *Pediatrics* 41.

Kasravi, Niaz (2001) "Women Renegotiating Islamic Identities: A Study of the Iranian-American Diaspora." Ph.D. dissertation, Department of Criminology, Law and Society, University of California, Irvine.

Katz, Jack (1988) *Seductions of Crime: Moral and Sensual Attractions of Doing Evil.* New York: Basic Books.

Keck, Thomas (2002) "Activism and Restraint on the Rehnquist Court: Timing, Sequence, and Conjecture in Constitutional Development," 35(1) *Polity* 121.

Keck, Thomas (2004) *The Most Activist Supreme Court in History: The Road to Modern Judicial Conservatism.* Chicago: University of Chicago Press.

Kelman, Maurice (1985) "The Forked Path of Dissent." *Supreme Court Review* 227.

Kendell, Kate, and Robin Haaland (1996) *Lesbians Choosing Motherhood: Legal Implications of Alternative Insemination and Reproductive Technology,* 3rd ed. San Francisco: National Center for Lesbian Rights.

Kinsey, Alfred C., Wardell B. Pomeroy, and Clyde E. Martin (1948) *Sexual Behavior in the Human Male.* Philadelphia: Saunders.

Kinsman, Gary (1996) *The Regulation of Desire: Homo and Hetero Sexualities,* 2nd ed. Montreal: Black Rose Books.

Knight, Robert H. (1994) "How Domestic Partnerships and 'Gay Marriage' Threaten the Family," *Insight* (Family Research Council) 1.

Konvitz, Milton R. (2001) *Fundamental Rights: History of a Constitutional Doctrine.* New Brunswick, NJ: Transaction/Rutgers University Press.

Landsman, Stephan, and Richard F. Rakos (1994) "A Preliminary Inquiry into the Effect of Potentially Biasing Information on Judges and Jurors in Civil Litigation," 12 *Behavioral Sciences and the Law* 113.

Lemert, Edwin M. (1951) *Social Pathology: A Systematic Approach to the Theory of Sociopathic Behavior.* New York: McGraw-Hill.

Lin, Timothy E. (1999) "Social Norms and Judicial Decisionmaking: Examining the Role of Narratives in Same-Sex Adoption Cases," 99 *Columbia Law Review* 739.

Lithwick, Dahlia (2004) "The Myth of Activist Judges," *Los Angeles Times,* October 12, B13.

Loftus, Jeni (2001) "America's Liberation in Attitudes toward Homosexuality, 1973–1988," 66(5) *American Sociological Review* 762.

Lynch, Mona (2002) "Pedophiles and Cyber-predators as Contaminating Forces: The Language of Disgust, Pollution, and Boundary Invasions in Federal Debates on Sex Offender Legislation," 27 *Law & Social Inquiry* 529.

MacDougall, Bruce (2000) *Queer Judgments: Homosexuality, Expression, and the Courts in Canada.* Toronto: University of Toronto Press.

Maine, Sir Henry Sumner (1917) *Ancient Law.* London: Dent & Sons.

Mason, Mary Ann, and Ann Quirk (1997) "Are Mothers Losing Custody? Read My Lips: Trends in Judicial Decision-Making in Custody Disputes—1920, 1960, and 1995," 31(2) *Family Law Quarterly* 215.

McCann, Michael (1994) *Rights at Work: Pay Equity Reform and the Politics of Legal Mobilization.* Chicago: University of Chicago Press.

McCann, Michael and Gerald Houseman (1989) *Judging the Constitution: Critical Essays on Judicial Lawmaking.* Glenview, Illinois: Scott, Foresman and Company.

Mercer, Kathryn L. (1998) "A Content Analysis of Judicial Decision-Making— How Judges Use the Primary Caretaker Standard to Make a Custody Determination," 5 *William and Mary Journal of Women and the Law* 1.

Milner, Neal, and Jonathan Goldberg-Hiller (2002) "Special Rights Claims as a Momentary Advantage: Native Hawaiian Autonomy, U.S. Law, and

International Politics." Paper presented at the annual meeting of the Law and Society Association, Vancouver.

Nardi, Peter (1997) "Friends, Lovers, and Families: The Impact of AIDS on Gay and Lesbian Relationships." In *In Changing Times: Gay Men and Lesbians Encounter HIV/AIDS*. Ed. Martin Levine, Peter Nardi, and John Gagnon. Chicago: University of Chicago Press.

Nardi, Peter (1999) *Gay Men's Friendships: Invincible Communities*. Chicago: University of Chicago Press.

National Gay and Lesbian Task Force (NGLTF) (2007) "Second-Parent Adoption in the U.S." www.thetaskforce.org.

National Gay and Lesbian Task Force (NGLTF) (2006) *Report: Adoption Laws in the United States*. National Gay and Lesbian Task Force.

Nielsen, Laura Beth (2004) *License to Harass: Law, Hierarchy, and Offensive Public Speech*. Princeton, NJ: Princeton University Press.

Olsen, Frances (1984) "Statutory Rape: A Feminist Critique of Rights Analysis," 63 *Texas Law Review* 387.

Olsen, Frances (1998) "The Sex of Law." In *The Politics of Law: A Progressive Critique*, 3rd ed. Ed. David Kairys. New York: Basic Books.

O'Toole, Marianne T. (1989) "Gay Parenting: Myths and Realities," 9 *Pace Law Review* 129.

Overcash, Jean (2003) "Narrative Research: A Review of Methodology and Relevance to Clinical Practice," 48 *Critical Review of Oncology and Hematology* 179.

Papke, David R., and Kathleen H. McManus (1999) "Narrative Jurisprudence: Narrative and the Appellate Opinion," 23 *Legal Studies Forum* 449.

Parker, Stephen (1994) "The Best Interests of the Child: Principles and Problems." In *The Best Interests of the Child: Reconciling Culture and Human Rights*. Ed. Philip Alston. Oxford, UK: Clarendon.

Patterson, Charlotte (1995) "Lesbian Mothers, Gay Fathers, and Their Children." In *Lesbian, Gay, and Bisexual Identities over the Lifespan: Psychological Perspectives*. Ed. Anthony D'Augelli and Charlotte Patterson. New York: Oxford University Press.

Patterson, Charlotte (2006) "Children of Lesbian and Gay Parents," 15(5) *Current Directions in Psychological Science* 241.

Phillips, Scott, and Ryken Grattet (2000) "Judicial Rhetoric, Meaning-Making, and the Institutionalism of Hate Crime Law," 34(3) *Law & Society Review* 567.

Pinello, Daniel (2003) *Gay Rights and American Law*. Cambridge: Cambridge University Press.

Polikoff, Nancy D. (1990) "This Child Does Have Two Mothers: Redefining Parenthood to Meet the Needs of Children in Lesbian-Mother and Other Nontraditional Families," 78 *Georgetown Law Journal* 459.

Polikoff, Nancy D. (1993) "We Will Get What We Ask For: Why Legalizing Gay and Lesbian Marriage Will Not 'Dismantle the Structure of Gender in Every Marriage,'" 79 *Virginia Law Review* 1535.

Polikoff, Nancy D. (2000) "Raising Children: Lesbian and Gay Parents Face the Public and the Courts." In *Creating Change: Sexuality, Public Policy, and Civil Rights*. Ed. John D'Emilio, William Turner, and Urvashi Vaid. New York: St. Martin's.

Polikoff, Nancy D. (2001) "The Impact of *Troxel v Granville* on Lesbian and Gay Parents," 32(3) *Rutgers Law Journal* 825.

Pound, Roscoe (1956) Preface to *Justice Musmanno Dissents*. Indianapolis, IN: Bobbs-Merrill.

Primus, Richard (1998) "Canon, Anti-Canon, and Judicial Dissent," 48 *Duke Law Journal* 243.

Pritchett, C. Herman (1969) *The Roosevelt Court: A Study in Judicial Politics and Values, 1937–1947*. Chicago: Quadrangle Books.

Rich, Adrienne (1982) *Compulsory Heterosexuality and Lesbian Existence*. Denver: Antelope.

Richman, Kimberly D. (2002) "Lovers, Legal Strangers, and Parents: Negotiating Parental and Sexual Identity in Family Law," 36(2) *Law & Society Review* 285.

Richman, Kimberly D. (2005) "(When) Are Rights Wrong? Rights Discourses and Indeterminacy in Gay and Lesbian Parents' Custody Cases," 30(1) *Law & Social Inquiry* 137.

Richman, Kimberly D. (2005) "Judging Science: The Court as Arbiter of Social Scientific Knowledge and Expertise in LGBT Parents' Child Custody and Adoption Cases," 35 *Studies in Law, Politics, and Society* 3.

Rifkin, Janet (1980) "Toward a Theory of Law and Patriarchy," 3 *Harvard Women's Law Journal* 83.

Robson, Ruthann (1995) "Mother: The Legal Domestication of Lesbian Existence." In *Mothers in Law: Feminist Theory and the Legal Regulation of Motherhood*. Ed. Martha Fineman and Isabel Karpin. New York: Columbia University Press.

Rollins, Joe (2004) *AIDS and the Sexuality of Law: Ironic Jurisprudence*. New York: Palgrave Macmillan.

Saunders, Debra (2007) "Heavy Time for Drug Lightweights," *San Francisco Chronicle*, July 10, C11.

Say, Elizabeth A., and Mark R. Kowalewski (1998) *Gays, Lesbians and Family Values*. Cleveland: Pilgrim.

Schacter, Jane S. (1994) "The Gay Civil Rights Debate in the States: Decoding the Discourse of Equivalents," 29(2) *Harvard Civil Rights–Civil Liberties Law Review* 283.

Scheingold, Stuart (1974) *The Politics of Rights: Lawyers, Public Policy, and Political Change.* New Haven, CT: Yale University Press.

Scheingold, Stuart (1989) "Constitutional Rights and Social Change." In *Judging the Constitution.* Ed. Michael W. McCann and Gerald L. Houseman. Glenview, IL: Scott, Foresman/Little, Brown.

Sella, Carmen B. (1991) "When a Mother Is a Legal Stranger to Her Child: The Law's Challenge to the Lesbian Nonbiological Families," 1 *UCLA Women's Law Journal* 135.

Silverstein, Helena (1999) "The Proliferation of Rights of Rights: Moral Progress or Empty Rhetoric? (Review)," 93(4) *American Political Science Review* 965.

Silverstein, Helena (2001) "In the Matter of Anonymous, A Minor: Fetal Representation in Hearings to Waive Parental Consent for Abortion," 11 *Cornell Journal of Law and Public Policy* 69.

Simmons, Peter (1956) "The Use and Abuse of Dissenting Opinions," 16 *Louisiana Law Review* 497.

Simon, David R. (1999) *Elite Deviance.* Boston: Allyn and Bacon.

Stacey, Judith (1996) *In the Name of the Family: Rethinking Family Values in the Postmodern Age.* Boston: Beacon.

Stacey, Judith (1998) *Brave New Families: Stories of Domestic Upheaval in Late-Twentieth-Century America.* New York: Basic Books.

Stacey, Judith, and Timothy J. Biblarz (2001) "(How) Does the Sexual Orientation of Parents Matter?" 66(2) *American Sociological Review* 159.

Stack, Carol B. (1974) *All Our Kin: Strategies for Survival in a Black Community.* New York: Harper & Row.

Stein, Arlene (1997) *Sex and Sensibility: Stories of a Lesbian Generation.* Berkeley: University of California Press.

Sullivan, Maureen (1996) "Rozzie and Harriet? Gender and Family Patterns of Lesbian Coparents," 10 *Gender & Society* 747.

Sunstein, Cass R. (2007) "Ginsburg's Dissent May Yet Prevail," *Los Angeles Times,* April 20, A31.

Swidler, Ann (1986) "Culture in Action: Symbols and Strategies," 51 *American Sociological Review* 273.

Tribe, Lawrence H. (1998) *American Constitutional Law,* 2nd ed. Mineola, NY: Foundation Press.

Tully, James (1995) *Strange Multiplicity: Constitutionalism in an Age of Diversity.* New York: Cambridge University Press.

Tushnet, Mark (1984) "An Essay on Rights," 62(8) *Texas Law Review* 1363.

Tushnet, Mark (1996) "Defending the Indeterminacy Thesis," 16 *Quinnipiac Law Review* 339.

Voss, Edward C. (1992) "Dissent: Sign of a Healthy Court," 24(2) *Arizona State Law Journal* 643.

Wald, Michael (2006) "Adults' Sexual Orientation and State Determinations Regarding Placement of Children," 40 *Family Law Quarterly* 381.

Weeks, Jeffrey (1995) *Invented Moralities: Sexual Values in an Age of Uncertainty*. Cambridge, UK: Polity.

Westen, Peter (1986) "The Rueful Rhetoric of Rights," 33 *UCLA Law Review* 977.

Weston, Kath (1991) *Families We Choose: Lesbians, Gays, Kinship*. New York: Columbia University Press.

Woodhouse, Barbara Bennett (1993) "Hatching the Egg: A Child-Centered Perspective on Children's Rights," 14 *Cardozo Law Review* 1747.

Yngvesson, Barbara (1997) "Negotiating Motherhood: Identity and Difference in 'Open' Adoptions," 31(1) *Law & Society Review* 31.

Yoshino, Kenji (2000) "The Epistemic Contract of Bisexual Erasure," 52(2) *Stanford Law Review* 353.

ZoBell, Karl M. (1959) "Division of Opinion in the Supreme Court: A History of Judicial Disintegration," 44 *Cornell Law Quarterly* 186.

Index

"abuse of discretion" standard, 32
adoption: absence of legal marriage, 62; adoptive families, 57–58; barriers to, removal of, 36; biological fatherhood, 36–37; changes in judicial opinion, 129; children's right to, 107; disputes over (*see* adoption disputes); eligibility requirements for adoptive parents, 36; Europe, 175–176; fundamental rights to parenthood, 90–91, 93; by gay men (*see* adoption by gay men); goal of, 35–36, 78; homosexuality and, 43; by lesbians (*see* adoption by lesbians); by nonbiological parent, 93; parental rights, 216n20; by same-sex couples (*see* adoption by same-sex couples); second-parent adoption (*see* second-parent adoption); stepparents, 35, 37, 62, 71, 226n18; surviving mother in a lesbian couple, 59; unilateral statutory rejection of gay and lesbian adoptions, 153; "unmarried cohabitants," 36; unmarried partners, 43
adoption by gay men: Arizona, 156, 215n138, 223n44; Chinese government, 116; Florida, 1, 2, 36, 78, 101, 140–141, 202n31, 206n55, 227n28; Indiana, 1–2; LGBT planned families headed

by gay males, 20; Mississippi, 36; Ohio, 128, 142, 156; prohibitions against, striking down of, 2
adoption by lesbians: Arizona, 156, 215n138, 223n44; Chinese government, 116; Florida, 1, 2, 36, 78, 101, 140–141, 202n31, 206n55, 227n28; Mississippi, 36; Ohio, 128, 142, 156; prohibitions against, striking down of, 2
adoption by same-sex couples: Florida, 206n55; Mississippi, 206n55; New Hampshire, 77; parent not biologically related to the child, 36–37; Pennsylvania, 2; validity of LGBT adoptions performed in a different state, 211n78
adoption disputes: *Adoption of Tammy,* 135–136, 146; *Adoption of T.J.K.,* 106; *In re Adoption of Baby Z.* (see *In re Adoption of Baby Z.*); *In re Adoption of Luke,* 142, 149; *In re Adoption of R.B.F. and R.C.F.* (see *In re Adoption of R.B.F. and R.C.F.*); *In the Matter of Adoption of Charles B.* (see *In the Matter of Adoption of Charles B.*); *Lofton v Kearney,* 78, 107, 140; *Matter of Adoption of Camilla,* 43; Arizona, 77; "best interest of the child" standard, 34–35; bisexual man, 77; Chinese government, 116;

50, 205n37; *conditional* legal
support for, 80, 166; constitutional rights, 84, 96, 97, 217n39;
contempt charge for telling son
he's gay, 95; due process, 117;
equal protection, 117; fathers, 165;
"good" LGBT parents, 170; as
"legal strangers," 46, 58–59, 165;
mothers (*see* lesbian mothers); privacy rights, 117; public discourse
about, 154–155; right to parent-
child bond, 107–109, 115, 166;
suppression of gay identity, 165; as
"third parties," 46, 91; third party
challenges to gay/lesbian parents,
87; *Troxel v Granville*, 90
gay rights activism: *J.L.P.(H.) v D.J.P.*,
111; *Marlow v Marlow*, 74–75;
custody disputes, 74–75; family
law, 22; Hawaii, 216n27; identity,
74–75; Indiana, 74–75; Kendell
on, Kate, 111; legal assistance
from activists, 111, 216n27; LGBT
families, 20; Missouri, 111; New
Jersey, 74; privacy rights, 87–88;
sodomy laws, 23, 87–88. *See also*
lesbian activism
gayby boom: impact on courts, 9,
16; opposition to, 26–31; period
defined as, 16; planned LGBT
families, 20; visibility of LGBT
families, 2
"generist" perspective, 37
Georgia: *Bowers v Hardwick*, 23, 24,
85, 218n62; *In re R.E.W.*, 15, 124;
sodomy laws, 15, 23, 221n9; visitation disputes, 15, 124
Germany, 175
Ginsburg, Ruth Bader, 127, 132
Glendon, Mary Ann, 103
Goffman, Erving, 214n128, 214n129
Goldberg-Hiller, Jonathan, 91, 216n27

Goodrich, Peter, 178
*Goodridge v Massachusetts Depart-
ment of Public Health*, 24, 167,
171, 176
Grattet, Ryken, 151, 173
Great Britain, 176
Griswold v Connecticut, 23, 85, 99
Guinan v Guinan, 52

Hall v Hall, 76
Halley, Janet, 73
Hartog, Heinrich, 51
Hassenstab v Hassenstab, 146
hate crime, 173
Hawaii: *Baehr v Lewin*, 26; gay rights
activism, 216n27; rights-based
claims, 216n27; same-sex domestic
partnerships, 211n69; same-sex
marriage, 26; second-parent adoption, 206n51
Heche, Anne, 44
Henry v Henry, 55
Hertzler, Pamela, 48
Hertzler v Hertzler, 48, 125
Hogue v Hogue, 94–95, 102, 107,
213n119
Holmes, Oliver Wendell, 131
Holtzman, Sandra, 59
homosexuality: acceptance of, 40,
55–56; acts distinguished from
identity, 41, 73; adoption and, 43;
Arkansas, 52; bisexuality equated
to, 40, 209n32; "coming out"
process, 73–74; as a contagion,
50, 69–70; "conversion" model of,
48–49; as "crime against nature,"
99; decriminalization of, 52; as
deviance, 53–56, 209n37; effects
on children, 53, 74; family life, 88;
"family values," 203n24; fitness as
parents, 53; "flaunting" of, 72, 75,
163, 170; immutability, 47;

About the Author

KIMBERLY D. RICHMAN is an assistant professor of sociology and legal studies at the University of San Francisco.